The Practical Pilot

The PRACTICAL PILOT

Coastal Navigation
by Eye, Intuition, and
Common Sense

Leonard Eyges

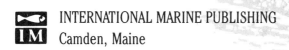
INTERNATIONAL MARINE PUBLISHING
Camden, Maine

Published by International Marine Publishing

10 9 8 7 6 5 4 3

Library of Congress Cataloging-in-Publication Data

Eyges, Leonard, 1920–
   The practical pilot : coastal navigation by eye, intuition, and common sense / Leonard Eyges.
      p. cm.
   Includes index.
   ISBN 0-87742-969-3
   1. Coastwise navigation. I. Title.
VK559.E94 1989   88-31338
623.89'22—dc19   CIP

TAB BOOKS offers software for sale. For information and a catalog, please contact TAB Software Department, Blue Ridge Summit, PA 17294-0850.

Questions regarding the content of this book should be addressed to:

International Marine Publishing
P.O. Box 220
Camden, ME 04843

Typeset by Graphic Composition, Athens, Georgia

Printed and bound by Hamilton Printing, Castleton-on-Hudson, NY

Design by Patrice M. Rossi

Illustrated by Lisa Scott

Edited by Jonathan Eaton, Felicity Myers, and David Oppenheim

Contents

For David, Jennifer and Eric.

Acknowledgments

A large part of almost any writer's book is derived from the work of others; for this part a good memory and filing system are more important than a rich, creative imagination. Many of these "others" are anonymous; if their names were ever known they are soon forgotten. For this book they are, in part, the authors of magazine articles with some salient point or interesting remark, students whose fresh viewpoints opened up a new avenue of thought, sailing companions who have taught by word or example, even the speaker in the club lounge whose conversation was overheard. To these anonymous preceptors, my gratitude.

But beyond these nameless tutors, and certainly of no less importance, are people, very much not anonymous, who made unambiguous and valued contributions that can be spelled out in detail. It is a pleasure to thank them wholeheartedly. These are some of them.

My editor at International Marine, Jonathan Eaton, supported this project from the beginning, and his insight and suggestions for the work in progress improved it in many ways. He deserved better of me than my always overoptimistic estimates of the time the next chapter would be done, but he met the consequent delays with unfailing courtesy. It was a pleasure to work with him.

Doris Eyges, wife, crew and critic was usually right when she stood up to the captain in disputed questions of style—and was rewarded by having to retype.

The drawings were done by Lisa Scott, who always grasped quickly the aim of my rough sketches and always found some way of getting that aim artistically on target.

The openmindedness to suggestion and unflappable professionalism of Molly Mulhern, production director at International Marine, have greased the skids admirably for this book's launching.

Richard Barc, Cynthia Nyary and Nick Yannoni saw this book project in an early amorphous form, but discerned enough shape in it to encourage me to continue. Later, Nick read some chapters and improved them with his suggestions.

David Eyges gave Telefix the big initial push that eventually led to the use of it for small angle navigation, and so to Chapter 22.

Reed Cournoyer and PAM Spierings have listened and read, and given me their sound judgments on various matters; they have been especially helpful as onboard companions during the experiments on currents that ultimately led to Chapter 26, *Current Affairs.*

Burton Sherman, president of E. S. Ritchie and Sons, listened, supplied pictures, and read and commented on the chapters on the compass.

Robert Eldridge White, publisher of the *Eldridge Tide and Pilot Book,* kindly read all the chapters on the compass, made many valuable technical suggestions, and didn't hesitate to characterize (politely) the original manuscript as verbose. He was right and I am grateful for the remark, but I emphasize that in the now condensed version all the statements and opinions are mine and he is in no way responsible for any errors in this final product.

Once again, and to all, my thanks.

Introduction

What This Book is About

This book is about coastal navigation (or piloting), the art and half-science of navigating a vessel along a coast, a few yards to a few miles offshore. Coastal navigation is done on a great variety of vessels, from sea kayaks to supertankers, although the techniques of the sea kayaker may be quite different from those of the tanker captain. Somewhere between sea kayak and supertanker is the small cruising boat, sail or power, perhaps 20, 30, or even 40 feet long, making its way on daysailing, weekend, or month-long trips off the shores of Maine, through Chesapeake Bay, near the Florida or California coasts—or wherever. This book seeks to outline practical and tested methods for making the navigation on such trips simple, enjoyable, and efficient.

At times I may seem to be talking exclusively about sailboats, since I write, for example, about "sailing past the lighthouse," but this wording is for economy only. It saves thickening the writing with parentheses, as in "sailing (or perhaps motoring) past the lighthouse." In fact, the subject matter is equally applicable to powerboaters.

It is probably easier to navigate a powerboat along the coast; there is almost certainly less leeway than the sailor has to contend with, and at 10 or 20 knots any current is relatively less important than for the 5- or 6-knot sloop. The powerboater can go in any direction he wants, doesn't heel over at 30 degrees when he does so, and can find a haven much more quickly than the sailor, should the weather make up. For simplicity then, I write in terms of sailors and sailboats, but everything here is applicable to powerboats as well, and is perhaps even a little easier in its application to them.

Some of the origins of this book lie in a course on navigation that I taught for several years for the Coast Guard Auxiliary. I had the company of devoted and competent fellow teachers and we taught the usual subjects: the compass, bearings, fixes, variation, deviation, and the rest. In short, we covered the same topics one tends to find in textbooks on coastal navigation, as well as in the course offered by the U.S. Power Squadron—what I will call the *standard course* or *standard syllabus*. Finally, after all this teaching—and this will not be a paradox to anyone who has ever taught—I learned the subject, or thought I did.

During those teaching years I had sailed on my own boat or on chartered boats up and down the New England coast, in the Chesapeake, in the Caribbean and elsewhere. I sailed also with friends who were competent skippers and who had taken, either with the Coast Guard Auxiliary or the U.S. Power Squadron, the kind of course I had taught. Gradually in this time I began to realize a striking fact. It slowly became clear to me that neither I nor my skipper friends regularly used the techniques we had learned in the standard courses. What we usually did was "eyeball it," as the phrase goes—run for the next buoy, take an educated guess, and sweat it out when the guess turned out to be less than educated. We made mistakes whose only redeeming virtue was to provide material for bar stories about how the depth finder suddenly read 5 feet and breaking waves were heard, or how the harbor entrance buoys didn't agree with the chart. Of course, it turned out later to be the wrong harbor.

Now, since I had spent many an evening hour in drafty high school auditoriums expounding the standard methods, it was disconcerting to realize that I rarely used them myself. In fact, for a while I became more serious and full of high resolve to navigate according to the book, but that phase passed.

After that phase, I began to think of why it passed. Why do skippers, myself included, tend not to use the "tried and true," the "standard" methods known so well in principle? I concluded that there were at least two reasons. The first, in its short form, is laziness. On a good day with the sun and wind on your face, the sound of the water slipping by, and all that good stuff, there is little incentive—if you think you can avoid it—to go below and sit hunched over a chart table making pencil marks on paper. In fact, you may have gone sailing just to get away from hunching over a desk making little marks on paper—tax form paper, bank balance paper, or whatever.

Laziness aside, my second conclusion was that many of the standard techniques require more time, space, or help than are available on your average 30-footer. And the reason for this, in turn, is that these techniques tend to derive from the practices of larger boats, navy or commercial vessels. If you examine, as I tend to do, every navigational publication you can lay your hands on—from the large treatises for commercial or naval vessels, to the slimmer ones for the yachtsman—you will find that the sections on coastal navigation are usually very similar. There are superficial differences to be sure; the illustrations in the tomes will be of 300-foot vessels doing 20 knots while the yachtsman's volume will show a 30-foot sloop doing five knots, but the techniques described are basically the same. In my opinion it is ultimately this fact that turns the small boat sailor away from the standard coastal navigation scheme, since what is not taken into account is the fact that conditions on small boats are very different from those on large ones. What can be done with relative ease on a frigate or freighter may be difficult or impossible on a small sloop. There is a variety of reasons.

First, the large boat is a relatively stable platform, and in taking bearings or measuring angles with compass or sextant stability is an enormous advantage. By comparison a 30-foot sloop is a bobbing cork. There is more space on the larger boat, with a navigation station and chart table which, perhaps unlike the smaller one, is not covered by a half dozen empty beverage cans and a fragment of tunafish sandwich. There is an enclosed bridge on a larger vessel, with a good view in all directions. Its speed can be held closely constant, independent of any fickle wind, and its very bulk and inertia means that a compass course can be held to a degree or two by the average helmsman, even in disturbed water that would make it difficult for a small boat skipper to hold a course to five degrees.

So there is a difference, even a profound difference, between navigational possibilities on large and small vessels; it is then not surprising that techniques suitable for the one may be quite out of place on the other.

An example of the unfortunate application of large boat practices to small boat coastal piloting is the insistence in the standard course on plotting bearings and course lines with respect to the direction of true north; they are then called *true bearings* and *true course lines.* An alternative possibility is to plot them with respect to magnetic north: *magnetic bearings* and *courses.*

It is magnetic bearings that are particularly useful to the small boat sailor. He is, say, sailing to Smuttynose Island. He draws on the chart the course line from his position to the destination, Can "2" off Smuttynose. He readily reads the course line's magnetic bearing of 162° from the magnetic compass rose on the chart. He then uses his magnetic compass on deck to try to keep to a course of 162° magnetic. It is magnetic, magnetic all the way. Nonetheless, in the standard syllabus he is required to *express* everything in true, even though he *uses* it in magnetic. This entails much adding and subtracting of the *variation,* the angular difference between the directions of true and magnetic north. If he wants as well to take into account the compass inaccuracy, the *deviation,* things can get quite messy. To sort this out a series of mnemonics have been invented which are supposed to help: Can Dead Men Vote Twice (for "**c**ompass plus or minus **d**eviation equals **m**agnetic plus or minus **v**ariation equals **t**rue"); True Virgins Make Dull Company (for working from degrees true back to degrees compass). I find them more trouble than they are worth. They have to be read backwards for some applications, and they don't help with crucial questions of plus or minus signs. I think they simply add new possibilities for error, and I can testify from my teaching experience that there are few things in coastal navigation more dispiriting than the true-to-magnetic conversion process and the "simplifying" mnemonics that have grown up around it.

Now all this extra entropy comes about for reasons that have no cogency for the coastal navigator, and that originated in the practices of large vessels. Large vessels when offshore use either celestial navigation or a gyrocompass to navigate. Both relate naturally to the direction of true north, so it is convenient to plot true courses and true bearings. But when such a vessel closes with the coast it becomes more natural to rely on the magnetic compass and magnetic bearings. There is good reason, then, according to the occasion, to plot either true bearings or magnetic bearings aboard such a ship. One could of course use both—true offshore and magnetic close to the coast—but such switching would be arbitrary and confusing. It is simpler to make one choice and stick to it. For various reasons, including perhaps the fact that most of the time large vessels are offshore, the choice is for true, and true bearings and courses are standard on large vessels.

But the coastal navigator does not use celestial navigation, does not have a gyrocompass, and is rarely far offshore. He steers in magnetic and plots in magnetic and there is no reason—no sound reason—to encourage him constantly to switch from true to magnetic and back again. The switching just adds extra arithmetic that increases the probability of error. Big boat practices are simply not relevant here.

With examples such as these in mind I gradually began to put to the test everything in the standard syllabus. Not the test of whether it was correct—it always was—or whether it was sensible for a large vessel— it always was—but the test of whether it was practical on my imagined 30-footer a mile or two offshore. So I sharpened up my mental image of the skipper for whom I was writing. I thought of him as singlehanded in fact, or singlehanded in effect by virtue of a green crew, sitting in the cockpit with tiller in one hand and the chart held on his knee with the other, and with perhaps a light drizzle soggying up both him and the chart. I asked what was practical for that skipper to do to get safely from one point to another along the coast. The answer to that question is to a large extent what this book is about.

Now the main instruments for such a sailor can only be his eye and his brain. And the main reference data comprise first the shape of the land itself, then the larger and more prominent landmarks, and finally buoys and other navigation aids (commonly known as "navaids"). He must navigate by visual observation of all these—by *visual navigation*. This is obviously not a new idea. Any boatman who has taken his boat from its mooring, sailed around the jetty, passing the gas tank on the other side, and returned by looking for the gas tank, rounding the jetty, and picking up his mooring, has used visual navigation.

What is new in this book is mainly the emphasis on the use of the shape of the land and its larger natural features, and on the distinguishing of one part from another so that the parts can be used as navigational references. It is an emphasis secondarily on the large landmarks that are sometimes not used because they may be well inshore, or are hard to identify, or are not on the chart. To state it inversely, what is new here is a downplaying of the use of buoys and navaids.

Don't misunderstand me. I think that modern buoyage systems and the Coast Guards who maintain them are admirable. There can be no question that many a vessel and many a life has been saved by the timely warnings that buoys and navaids provide. But like any good thing there can be too much of them. They can become addictive. We can come to depend so much on them that we are made weaker rather than stronger navigators. I am thinking particularly of the practice of "buoy hopping" that I have seen many a skipper use to move along the coast. In its extreme manifestation it is the technique of somehow picking up a first buoy, finding on the chart a possible next buoy, plotting a course to it, straining to see it until it finally appears; finding a next possible buoy on the chart, plotting, straining to see ... You end up getting slowly to your destination in a series of graceless doglegs. There is much tension. The crew is always peering in the distance for the little black or green or red speck that is the next buoy. There are worried looks. Then it is seen; there is elation; there are hurrahs; tenseness disappears from the faces.

At this point the speck may fly off with a fish in its mouth.

How much more satisfactory to orient oneself at large distances from the land by its shape itself. The land is there year after year; you don't have to look in *Notices to Mariners* to ensure that it has not been removed. It is not dragged under by currents; it doesn't break loose from its mooring chain. It does not disappear from chart to chart. Years, centuries ago, before Coast Guards and buoys, it was this kind of coastal navigation that was used. Many coastal charts had views of the land included on them. Fine steel engravings showed the view of the harbor on entering from seaward, or the spit of land and rocks to be avoided on the northern approach. Even today, in sailing guides to the Caribbean or the Bahamas, regions that are not heavily buoyed, there is an emphasis on pictures or drawings of the land's features as seen from the sea.

But there is more to visual navigation than simply an enhanced skill in identifying land features and other reference marks. What do you do with these marks after you have identified them? Now it may be that such a mark is your destination; you may want to sail to the island or point of land that you have learned to recognize at a distance. Fine. Check that there are no dangers on the way and set sail. More often, however, the reference marks are not your destination, but are merely observed along your way, perhaps abeam of the boat or even astern. Then they can be used as position-finding aids to help find or corroborate your whereabouts. Used in pairs they can provide a *line of position*.

Common to all kinds of navigation is this concept of a line of position—a line on the chart (possibly a curved line) somewhere along which the navigator knows he is situated. For example, the magnetic (compass) bearing of a charted shore object gives such a line of position.

The analog in visual navigation is the transit line of position, or simply the *transit line.* From the deck two reference marks on shore are seen to line up, one behind the other. On the chart this implies that the ship's position is on the straight line drawn through these two objects; this is the transit line. Such lines play an important role in visual navigation. They are very accurate and of course require no instrument except the eye.

The trouble with a transit line is that you have to wait for two objects to line up; you can't get one whenever you wish. By contrast you can take the magnetic bearing of a lighthouse at any time you wish so that the corresponding line of position is always available. If you are alert you can often find more transits than you might have thought, involving not only landmarks, but ends of islands, peaks or saddles in the land, etc., but ultimately you do have to wait for each one.

This difficulty is overcome in a generalization of transit lines that is a new feature of this book. Suppose Tower and Tank are behind one another on the coast, Tower near the shore and Tank farther inland. As you begin to sail past that part of the shore, Tank may initially appear to be to the *right* of Tower. As you continue to sail, however, the "visual gap" between them will diminish; Tank will appear to be closer to Tower and will finally be seen just behind it. The two landmarks are of course then *in transit.* As you continue to sail, Tank will appear to move to the *left* of Tower and the visual gap between them will begin to increase in size.

We can make more precise the meaning of the size of this visual gap: it is simply the magnitude of the small angle seen between Tower and Tank. That is, imagine the line of sight drawn from an observer on deck to Tower and a similar line of sight to Tank. There is an angle included between, or defined by, these two lines of sight, and this angle is called the *horizontal angle* between the landmarks. The size of this angle can be exploited to give valuable information about your position, in the form of a *small angle circle of position,* a generalization of the transit line.

To use these small angle circles one has to be able to do two things: first, measure the small angle between two landmarks; second, plot or somehow exploit this measurement on the chart. We will discuss simple means to effect both these ends. On deck, for example, one can use the knuckles of the outstretched hand as an angle measuring device, or an ancient Arabian instrument called the *kamal,* or a modern version of it that I have developed. There is also a variety of simple ways of exploiting the measurement on the chart, from crude hand sketches of the circle to computer plotting of its coordinates.

Although I have by now written at length about visual navigation, it is obvious that it has its limits and can't be the whole navigational story. One can't navigate visually in fog; one can't navigate visually in the dead of night. Also, the degree of success of visual navigation depends to some extent on how varied and rich the landscape is. Its potential off the coast of Maine, rich in islands, promontories, and steep cliffs, is quite different from off the relatively uniform and undistinguished (navigationally) coast of Florida.

There are, then, times when the coastal skipper must fall back on the other canonical methods of navigation. He must know how to do dead reckoning, take and plot compass bearings, use a depth sounder and possibly a radio direction finder, etc. Even in good visibility he may want to calculate time-speed-distance relationships and estimate his time of arrival. The latter part of this book describes such coastal navigational techniques. They are common to most navigational texts, but I have tried to scrutinize each with the small-boat owner's eye: Is this technique really suitable for small boats or is it a thoughtless transcription of large-boat practice?

A particular example of this kind is *compass adjustment.* I have read many techniques for checking compass accuracy and correcting or compensating it where it appears to be in error. Very often the techniques exhibit the large boat syndrome, requiring more time, space, and assistance than exist on the average small boat. The method presented here is suitable for small boats. It can scarcely be called new—there is very little novelty possible in this old subject—but it is a combination of the best features of several methods found in the literature. I have tested it on my own 30-foot sloop and on a variety of other boats. It works, and more important, it works on small boats.

A final example of small-boat versus big-boat techniques is the detection and measurement of current. A big-boat captain wants to go from marked point A to point B. He calculates the compass course and hands it to the helmsman with instructions to keep carefully to it and to keep the ship's speed constant. Knowing his speed he can easily calculate the trip duration, and at the end of that time he finds by a fix that he is not at point B, but somewhere else, at point C. He ascribes to current the difference between where he aimed and where he got. He can in fact calculate the magnitude of that current in terms of the (vector) difference between the locations of B and C. It is a simple example in vector addition, and is a standard textbook navigational technique.

An implicit requirement here is that the helmsman steer an accurate compass course and that the vessel's speed be known and constant. Now a large vessel, by virtue of its very inertia, can keep to a given compass course even in waves or a chop; with engines turning over at a steady 1,500 rotations per minute and a well-tested speed versus rpm chart, the speed is constant and known. The calculational method is then feasible. Even so the method is a little fussy and it is almost certainly not worked out by the helmsman himself but by a navigator, with adequate navigational tools and the time and space to use them in his comfortable navigational station.

The small boat is, however, another matter. Aside from the comfort and convenience of the navigator, the basic predicates of the solution are not satisfied. The current deviation effect may amount to several degrees, but in any kind of sea the skipper can't keep to a prescribed compass course to better than a few degrees. This amount is perhaps almost as large as the current deviation effect he is looking for. In any but unusually uniform conditions the wind strength and hence his speed varies from minute to minute. Even with a purportedly good knotmeter—and I have checked out quite a few—he may not know his speed at any instant to better than 10 percent. With cruder, noninstrumental methods he may be farther off. All these errors, possibly cumulative, add up to the fact that the technique that is possible for a large ship is just not in the cards for his smaller vessel.

Size makes a difference. In heavy weather, in collision avoidance, in docking and close quarters in general, big boats require different techniques from small ones. It is not surprising that techniques of coastal navigation should be different as well. What is surprising is that this fact has been so little recognized or acted on. I hope this book will do something to redress that imbalance.

SECTION I

Book Learning,
Chart Learning

1

Charts: A Primer

charts and maps

You have in all likelihood seen a nautical chart. If by some chance you haven't, Figure 1–1 shows a portion of the U.S. Government chart of San Francisco Bay. If you haven't seen a chart you have undoubtedly seen a road map, and a chart is like a map in that it is a miniaturized representation of the earth's landmasses and of certain features on them—an aerial photograph formalized into a drawing with certain conventions. A chart has a different emphasis from the map; instead of depicting the land and the roads on it, it focuses on the water: where the water is, where there are dangers in it, where it isn't. Charts and maps also differ in that distance on charts is usually expressed in *nautical miles* (abbreviated n.m.). One nautical mile equals 6076.1 feet, but accurately enough for coastal piloting we can take:

One nautical mile (n.m.) = 6080 feet.

The nautical mile is then larger than the statute mile of 5280 feet by the ratio 6080/5280 = 1.15. In marine tradition charts are always referred to as *charts* and not *maps,* so if you want a reputation for salty sophistication leave the word "map" ashore.

scale

The *scale* of a chart is the ratio of a dimension on the chart, say the length of a breakwater, to the actual length. Suppose the breakwater were 400 feet long and that its length on the chart was ¼ inch. Then, since 1 inch = ¹⁄₁₂ foot, its length on the chart is ¹⁄₄₈ feet so that the scale is:

12

$$\text{Scale} = \frac{\frac{1}{48}}{400} = \frac{1}{19,200} \text{ or } 1{:}19,200$$

One can also express the scale by noting how many miles (nautical miles, kilometers, etc.) are represented by one inch (centimeter, etc.) on the chart. In the present case this *numerical scale,* as it is sometimes called is: One inch = 1600 feet.

In coastal piloting the chart scales usually range from 1:80,000 to 1:15,000. Standard terminology here can be confusing. The *larger* the number in the denominator (downstairs) in the scale fraction the *smaller* is the fraction itself. Thus, 1:50,000 is a *smaller* fraction than is 1:10,000. So it is said that the 1:50,000 chart is to smaller scale than the 1:10,000 chart. This may be clear now but, in my experience, the fact that the bigger number downstairs means the smaller chart scale is often forgotten and takes one by surprise. As a mnemonic I translate "scale" into "detail" to remember that for much detail, a large scale chart is called for.

"large" and "small" scale

Large scale = Large (abundant) detail
Small scale = Small (skimpy) detail

In addition to the relatively large scale coastal and harbor charts there are smaller scale charts for longer voyages that require more global planning. Among these are *sailing charts* with scales as small as 1:1,200,000 (One inch = 20 miles), and *general charts* with scales in the neighborhood of 1:200,000. The harbor chart in Figure 1–1 is rendered to a scale of 1:20,000.

The chartmaker faces one insuperable problem. The earth is round (spherical) and the chart is flat; ideally he would like to transfer the shapes and boundaries of the spherical earth to the flat chart without distorting them. In fact there is no solution; it can't be done. You can see this (if it isn't already intuitively clear to you) if you imagine a globe of the earth, with the continents imprinted on it, that is hollow and made of white rubber a few millimeters thick, like a child's ball. If you were to cut this rubber globe in half and put one of the hemispheres on a table, open side down, like an upside down soup bowl, you could with enough force press down and flatten the globe so that it became a plane surface. But the rubber would have to stretch to permit this, and in its stretching the figures and shapes that were on it would necessarily distort. There is no getting around it.

Since chartmakers cannot make an undistorted chart they do the next best thing. They make charts in which the distortion is controlled and known in advance. This is done by certain formulae called *projections,* which are basically mathematical rules for transferring or project-

projections

General Chart
Scale 1:210,688

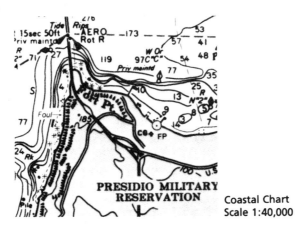

PRESIDIO MILITARY
RESERVATION

Coastal Chart
Scale 1:40,000

Harbor Chart
Scale 1:20,000

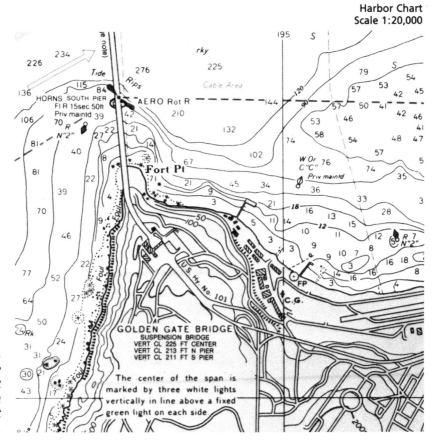

FIGURE 1-1.

Three chart views of the same area (Fort Point, at the south end of Golden Gate Bridge), to different scales.

ing a drawing on the sphere's surface to the chart. You may well have heard of them; they go by such names as *Mercator,* or *polyconic* or *gnomonic projection.*

In fact I mention these projections only to be complete. Happily, in coastal piloting the portion of the earth's surface that is dealt with is so small that it is essentially flat; to the practical accuracy required, projection formulae aren't needed. This point is illustrated in Figure 1–2, which shows a section of the earth's surface to a numerical scale in which one centimeter equals 50 miles. This corresponds to a scale factor of 1:8,050,000. You see that in the 1000-mile section of the earth that is drawn, even a section as large as 50 miles is relatively so small that it is to all intents and purposes flat. Now the typical chart used in coastal piloting spans much less than 50 miles, so there is no appreciable distortion in transferring the earth's boundary shapes to its flat surface. The kind of projection is irrelevant. But if you should go long distances offshore, say transatlantic or transpacific, the effect of distortion does become significant and you do have to take into account in your planning the kind of projection that has been used to make the chart.

On almost every nautical chart, there is a scale of numbers across the bottom and another up the side. The bottom, horizontal scale measures *longitude* and the vertical side scale measures *latitude.* You probably recall that these are the two numbers that locate a point on the earth's surface. In fact the coastal pilot doesn't often use latitude and longitude, but if he does the need-to-know may be critical, so I review them now.

latitude and longitude

First recall from Geography I that the earth spins on an axis that pierces the surface at the North and South poles. If the earth is cut by a plane that passes through this spin-axis, the edge of the cut defines a circle called a *meridian* (Figure 1–3). Similarly, if the earth is cut by a plane at right angles to the axis the cut edge is a horizontal circle, larger or smaller according to the plane's distance from the earth's center. The particular circle of this kind that passes through the center of the earth is the *equator.*

Given a point on the earth's surface, there is a meridian that passes through it. The length in degrees of the arc of the meridian between the point and the equator is the *latitude.* If the point is north of the equator the number of degrees is followed by N, if south, by S. Latitude then

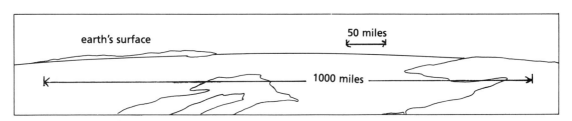

FIGURE 1-2. *Part of a cross section through the earth's surface to a scale of 1:8,050,000.*

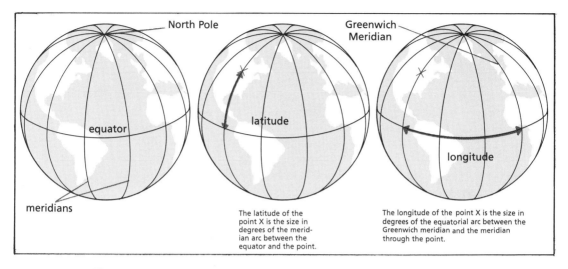

The latitude of the point X is the size in degrees of the meridian arc between the equator and the point.

The longitude of the point X is the size in degrees of the equatorial arc between the Greenwich meridian and the meridian through the point.

FIGURE 1-3.   *Meridians and the equator.*

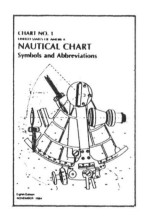

chart #1

ranges from 0° to 90° North and from 0° to 90° South. The latitude of the Statue of Liberty is 40.69° N in decimal notation or 40° 41′ 22″ in angular minutes and seconds.

Longitude is also defined in terms of an arc, but this time with respect to the standard *Greenwich meridian*—that meridian that passes through Greenwich, England. The longitude of a point is the length in degrees of the arc of the equator between the Greenwich meridian and the meridian through the point. Longitudes range over two 180-degree intervals. Points 180° or less east of Greenwich are followed by an E; points west of Greenwich by a W. The longitude of the Statue of Liberty is 74.09° W or 70° 02′ 44″ W.

This chapter was intended as a bare-bones introduction to charts. I have said nothing about the variety of numbers, symbols, abbreviations, color codings, and printing styles that you can find even in the fragment of the harbor chart in Figure 1–1, as well as in Figure 1–4. These chart markings describe features of the coast, natural features of the land, topography, buildings and structures, buoys and beacons, radio and radar stations, dangers, water depths, tides and currents, etc.

The list in the last sentence was not made up by me. It is part of the table of contents of the governmental publication *Chart #1*. This is in fact not a chart at all but an invaluable 25-page booklet entitled Nautical Chart Symbols and Abbreviations. A sampling from it is given in Chapter 4 on learning aids. It will repay handsomely any effort you make to get acquainted with it.

FIGURE 1-4 (OVERLEAF).   *A chart sample created by selecting out and reassembling portions of the NOAA chart of Muscongus Bay, Maine. Everything on the sample comes from the NOAA chart, but of course not everything on that chart is on the sample. In particular, the sample doesn't show the variety of colors and tints that convey such useful information on the NOAA chart.*

NATIONAL OCEAN SERVICE

UNITED STATES – EAST COAST

MAINE

MUSCONGUS BAY

Mercator Projection
Scale 1:40,000 at Lat. 43°55′
North American 1927 Datum

SOUNDINGS IN FEET
AT MEAN LOW WATER

Soundings may be expressed in fathoms on smaller scale charts—a fact to note carefully if small and large scale charts are used conjointly.

The heights of lights, rocks that uncover and often but not invariably, bridge clearances, are heights above Mean High Water.

TIDAL INFORMATION

Place	Height referred to datum of soundings (MLW)		
	Mean High Water	Mean Tide Level	Mean Low Water
	feet	feet	feet
New Harbor	8.8	4.4	0.0
Waldoboro	9.5	4.8	0.0
Thomaston	9.4	4.7	0.0
Tenants Harbor	9.3	4.6	0.0

(484)

For Symbols and Abbreviations see Chart No. 1

HEIGHTS
Heights in feet above Mean High Water.

CAUTION
Temporary changes or defects in aids to navigation are not indicated on this chart. See Notice to Mariners.
During some winter months or when endangered by ice, certain aids to navigation are replaced by other types or removed. For details see U.S. Coast Guard Light List.

CAUTION
Only marine radiobeacons have been calibrated for surface use. Limitations on the use of certain other radio signals as aids to marine navigation can be found in the U.S. Coast Guard Light Lists and Defense Mapping Agency Hydrographic/Topographic Center Publication 117 (A & B).
Radio direction-finder bearings to commercial broadcasting stations are subject to error and should be used with caution.
Station positions are shown thus:

⊙(Accurate location)   o(Approximate location)

WARNING
The prudent mariner will not rely solely on any single aid to navigation, particularly on floating aids. See U.S. Coast Guard Light List and U.S. Coast Pilot for details.

RADAR REFLECTORS
Radar reflectors have been placed on many floating aids to navigation. Individual radar reflector identification on these aids has been omitted from this chart.

One minute of latitude, equal to a nautical mile. One second of latitude is then very nearly 100 feet.

Note that all buoys are marked with the small circle that implies their location is approximate.

Longitude in degrees and minutes

Date of latest correction to chart. See note.

Chart number in NOAA Chart Catalog 1—U.S. Atlantic and Gulf Coasts

17th Ed., Oct. 27/84 ■

13301

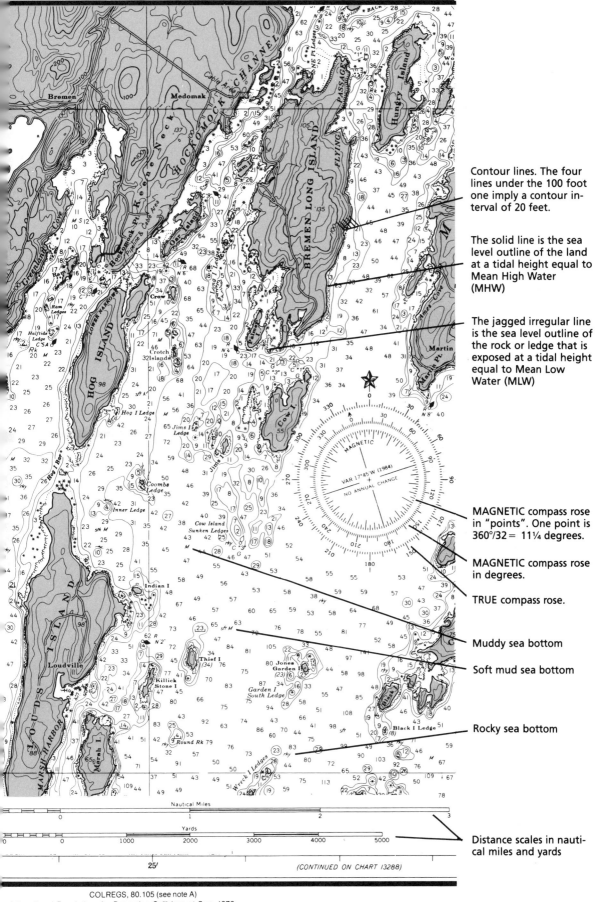

Contour lines. The four lines under the 100 foot one imply a contour interval of 20 feet.

The solid line is the sea level outline of the land at a tidal height equal to Mean High Water (MHW)

The jagged irregular line is the sea level outline of the rock or ledge that is exposed at a tidal height equal to Mean Low Water (MLW)

MAGNETIC compass rose in "points". One point is 360°/32 = 11¼ degrees.

MAGNETIC compass rose in degrees.

TRUE compass rose.

Muddy sea bottom

Soft mud sea bottom

Rocky sea bottom

Distance scales in nautical miles and yards

Nautical Miles

Yards

25'

(CONTINUED ON CHART 13288)

COLREGS, 80.105 (see note A)
International Regulations for Preventing Collisions at Sea, 1972.
The entire area of this chart falls seaward of the COLREGS Demarcation Line.

2

The U.S. Coast Pilots

The modern nautical chart compresses an amazing amount of information into a relatively small space. But remarkable as it is, the chart has limitations, and doesn't tell all. Many other publications take up where it leaves off. An example is the series of nine U.S. Coast Pilots. The introduction to any of the volumes describes it as well as I could. "The National Ocean Service Coast Pilots are a series of nine nautical books that cover a wide variety of information important to navigators of U.S. coastal waters, and waters of the Great Lakes. Most of this book information cannot be shown graphically on the standard charts and is not readily available elsewhere. Coast Pilot subjects include navigation regulations, outstanding landmarks, channel and anchorage peculiarities, dangers, weather, ice, freshets, routes, pilotage, and port facilities." Five of the volumes cover the Atlantic coast from Maine to the Gulf of Mexico, including Puerto Rico and the Virgin Islands. A sixth is for the Great Lakes, and the remaining three cover the Pacific coast, Alaska, and Hawaii.

nine volume series

I think the Coast Pilots are not used as often by cruising skippers as they should be. The reason may be that they appear to be directed mainly toward commercial shipping. If such a skipper glanced at the Pilot for Boston Harbor, noted the references to customs, immigration, piloting, and towage, and the fact that the Pittston petroleum wharf has storage tanks with a 630,000-barrel capacity, he might well wonder at the relevance of the volume for navigating his 30-foot sloop. There is, however, much that *is* relevant. Here are some examples.

prominent features

First, for many locales there is a section called Prominent Features, perhaps only a few sentences long but often uniquely useful. It is a listing of those landmarks that are *especially* visible or *especially* useful—the kind of information that the chart simply does not give. On the chart, all the landmarks—towers, spires, cupolas, tanks—have the same size print and the same size little circle and central dot. On the chart all landmarks are equal, but in reality, to paraphrase George Orwell, some landmarks are more equal than others. What makes a landmark more equal is that it is especially conspicuous from a variety of locales, and that it is un-ambiguous, not easily mistaken for another landmark. In our own waters we soon get to know which are the more equal landmarks. In approaching a new harbor or piece of coast, it would certainly be very helpful to have such information in advance. You can often acquire such "instant local knowledge" from the Coast Pilot. For example, here is part of the entry for Boston Harbor. "Conspicuous to a vessel approaching Boston Harbor from seaward is the tall red, white, and blue standpipe on Winthrop Head. From eastward, the most prominent island in the entrance is Great Brewster. On the south side of the entrance, a turreted tower is conspicuous on Point Allerton; also prominent are the tank and standpipe on Strawberry Hill." There is more, but that excerpt will give you the flavor. It should be obvious how useful such information can be, and in approaching a new harbor or anchorage, I try to make it a practice to first identify, in actuality and on the chart, the "prominent features" listed in the Coast Pilot.

Lighthouses provide a second example of the usefulness of a Coast Pilot. In principle, of course, these can be identified by their light characteristics and/or by their height, both of which are given on the chart. Sometimes however, there may be two (or more) lighthouses of similar heights in the same vicinity, and in the daytime, when they are unlit, it may be hard to tell them apart. Here the Coast Pilot can be invaluable. For example in the southern approaches to Baltimore Harbor there are four lighthouses within a few miles of one another: Sandy Point Light; Baltimore Light two miles to its north; Sevenfoot Knoll Light about five miles still farther north; and Love Point Light about five miles to the east. You can't tell these navigational players apart without a scorecard, and the scorecard is given by Coast Pilot #3, to wit:

description of light structures

> "Sandy Point Shoal Lt . . . red brick house with white roof on a brown cylindrical pier.
> Baltimore Lt. . . .white octagonal house.
> Sevenfoot Knoll Lt . . . red cylindrical pile structure.
> Love Point Lt. . . .skeleton tower with a red and white checkered daymark."

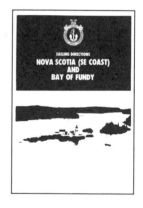

In fairness to other government publications this descriptive information is also found in the Light List (see Chapter 3). But it is *not* on the chart.

Here are some other examples, all taken from the Chesapeake Bay section of Coast Pilot #3, of what the Coast Pilot can do for the small boat skipper.

The Canadian counterpart: Sailing Directions, published by the Canadian Hydrographic Service in several volumes covering the Pacific and Atlantic coasts and the Great Lakes.

examples of small boat information

• Keep him from getting shot: "A naval rifle range is on the west side of the entrance to the creek (Carr Creek). Mariners are warned to keep out of the creek when the red flag is flying from Carr Point or the next point southward."

• Help him find an anchorage: "A special small vessel anchorage area is in the cove on the west side of Blackhole Creek two miles above the entrance."

• Locate repair facilities and marine supplies: "A boatyard just inside the north prong (Gray's Creek) has gasoline, water, berths and some marine supplies. Hull and engine repairs can be made; marine railway, 40 feet; lift, 3 tons."

In addition, Coast Pilot #3 has full-page pictures of the approaches to some of the busier ports, such as Annapolis and Baltimore; these can be very helpful on a first visit. It lists bridges, their clearances and, when pertinent, their times of opening and closing. It has statistical tables of meteorological data throughout the year, giving mean temperatures, average wind strength and direction, etc., so that if you visit the area covered by the guide you can plan your sail wardrobe as well as your personal one.

general information

The kind of information mentioned above is specific to the area covered by each Coast Pilot. But in addition there is information of universal application in Chapter 1, General Information, of every Coast Pilot. Much here is not only useful but is not easily available elsewhere. For example, there is a section called Distress Signals and Communication Procedures and another called Distress Assistance and Coordination Procedures. Briefly, the first section explains how to call for help when you need it, and the second describes what to do when help gets to you. These should be read once by every skipper. Having done that he should keep them available on board for rereading in case of emergency and indeed for rereading from time to time just to keep the memory fresh. Nobody wants to be evacuated by helicopter or to be helped in an emergency by the Coast Guard, but should it be necessary, a stressful emergency is not the time to begin reading and absorbing the many practical factors that can make or mar a rescue. In the measured words of the Coast Pilot: "The cooperation of vessel operators with (the) Coast Guard may mean the difference between life and death for some seaman or aviator; such cooperation is greatly facilitated by the prior knowledge on the part of vessel operators of the operational requirements of Coast Guard equipment and personnel. . . ."

limitations

Although it is obvious that I think Coast Pilots are very useful for the small-boat skipper, I don't want to oversell them. Unlike commercial small boat cruising guides, they won't tell you where to get the best fried clams or whether the marina has showers and a laundromat. They are written in a flat, dull style — no anecdotes, no rich prose, no local color.

One can't argue that they are oriented toward large boats. For example, there is a table for estimating transit times, given the speed of the boat; the lowest speed entered in the table is 8 knots! And you might begin to question my recommendation if you happened to open first to Chapter 2, Navigation Regulations, to find many pages devoted to a detailed description of big boat anchoring areas, rules on discharging dangerous cargoes, the use of radiotelephones on dredges, and quarantine and customs regulations.

Despite all this, however, I would estimate that a good 70 percent of the contents of a Coast Pilot are applicable to small boat piloting. And I think it is probably true that although it is reissued every year, it doesn't become outdated as quickly as does a chart or the Light List. The topography, large structures, and general navigational features it describes are usually more permanent than manmade navaids. There *is* some timely information, which should be checked before you use it, but on the whole even a Coast Pilot a few years old is a valuable volume to have aboard. And since its price is about that of a mediocre meal and bottle of wine, I think it is a good bargain well worth it for every small-boat navigator.

3

Learning from the Light Lists

The Light Lists are a seven-volume set of U.S. Coast Guard Publications, each for a different geographical area. For its specific area each Light List contains a listing of, in its own words,

Lights

Fog signals

Buoys

Daybeacons

Radiobeacons

Racons

Loran stations.

These are the aids to navigation – "navaids" for short – that implement the U.S. Aids to Navigation System. This is a huge advisory and warning system, a sprawling watery analog to the traffic lights and other signals that help control land traffic in our cities and towns. The seven volumes of the Light List cover the Atlantic, Gulf, and Pacific Coasts, the U.S. Caribbean and Pacific islands, the Mississippi and Ohio rivers, and finally the Great Lakes. All told they list some hundreds of thousands of navaids.

Most of the several hundred pages of any Light List are given to a catalog, navaid by navaid, location by location, of specific examples of the seven general kinds listed above. (A sample is printed below.) But in addition there is an important thirty-odd pages at the beginning of each volume that describe the Aids to Navigation System as a whole. In my opinion, it is the best description available; it is clear, it is thorough, and it is obviously authoritative! Its substance is restated and rewritten in any number of books, but I think none does it better. Indeed I am not convinced that I could do better in the space I have here, so I am not going to try to compete, especially not in thoroughness. But since the general framework of the navigation system is obviously important for the small-boat pilot, I'll summarize its essential features here and in Chapter 6 and hope you will decide to read about them in more detail in one of the seven Light Lists.

The navigation system is complicated not only because it covers such a large geographical area, but because it comprises three different subsystems. The first, or "coastal" system applies to the waters of the Atlantic, Gulf, and Pacific coasts, the U.S. Caribbean and Pacific islands, and the Great Lakes. The second applies to the Intracoastal Waterway and the third to Western rivers.

Now the first system, for "coastal" waters is almost certainly the one of interest to the majority of readers of this book. Since it is also the largest and most basic, I'll confine myself to a discussion of it and leave it to you to read about the others in a Light List or elsewhere. In fact the Intracoastal system is very similar to the coastal one. Mainly it adds yellow markings to identify navaids as Intracoastal ones, but if you understand the coastal system you will understand it as well. The Western rivers system differs rather more from the coastal one, but its basics are the same.

There are four fine color plates in the back of the Light Lists that elucidate these systems. If you have a good understanding of the coastal system you will be quickly able to see, just by turning the page, how the other U.S. systems differ from it. In addition to these federal systems there is a State Uniform Waterway Marking System administered by individual states for those waters completely within state borders, such as Lake George in New York. Still another color plate in the Light List displays its basics.

A central feature of the coastal system is obviously the seven kinds of navaids in the list of the first paragraph. The first four of these rely on the skipper's senses of sight, hearing, or both to make them work; the last three involve electromagnetic (radio) waves and so must be supplemented by electronic detecting devices aboard the boat. I'll discuss the four nonelectronic aids now and return later to the electronic ones.

Almost certainly you have some familiarity with the first four navaids: lights, fog signals, buoys, and daybeacons. But I know from experience in teaching that though these terms appear innocuous, they can have puzzling aspects. To clarify these I am going to classify all non-electronic aids in a systematic way that I hope will relieve any ambiguity.

the aids to navigation system

The Canadian counterpart, issued annually in English and French by the Canadian Coast Guard.

kinds of nonelectronic aids

All navaids are:

Floating	or	Fixed
Lighted	or	Unlighted
Emitters of sound signals	or	Non-emitters of sound signals.

These three category pairs are reasonably self-explanatory, but I'll expand on them briefly; more details are found in Chapter 6.

Floating/fixed
The floating navaids, usually called buoys, are of a great variety of shapes and sizes. They are constrained to a limited range of horizontal motion by chains that attach them to mooring anchors on the sea bottom. The fixed navaids are attached firmly to land—either land above water or the seabed—in any number of ways. The navaid may be merely a single pile driven into the shallows, a tripod of piles, an ironwork structure on land with legs set in cement bases, a lighthouse set on a granite foundation, etc.

Lighted/unlighted
Lighted navaids emit identifying light signals that vary greatly from one to the next. For example, they can emit a white or colored light that is steady, or one that flashes on periodically or that has a more complicated on-off pattern. Larger navaids may show differently colored lights when seen from different directions, etc.

Sound emitters/non-emitters
As with lights, there is a considerable variety, elaborated upon in Chapter 6, of sound signals—bells, gongs, whistles, horns, etc.

buoys   Let's look again at the four kinds of navaids in the list that began this chapter. First, *buoys.* I've already discussed these briefly, but for later reference I want to add one seemingly obvious point. It can be seen from the entries in the body of the Light List that buoys with lights are called *lighted buoys* and buoys with sound emitters become *bell buoys, whistle buoys,* etc. For example, in the sample below of a Light List page you will find Perkins Cove Bell Buoy and Cape Porpoise Lighted Whistle Buoy.

daybeacons   Next, *daybeacon.* This is defined in the Glossary of the Light List as: "An unlighted fixed structure which is equipped with a daymark for identification." This unlighted, fixed navaid is the obvious analog of an unlighted buoy. But although putting a light on an unlighted buoy leads it to be called a lighted buoy, putting a light on a daymark does *not* lead it to be called a lighted daybeacon. A lighted daybeacon is simply called a *light.*

"Light" is the third term, and an important one in the list above, so let's look more closely at it. The first point to clarify is that it is used with three different meanings. We find this in the Light List Glossary. "Light: (1) The signal emitted by an illuminated aid to navigation; (2) a piece of illuminating apparatus; (3) a lighted aid to navigation on a fixed structure." Thus if at night we were to see the signal from a fixed navaid, but couldn't see the navaid itself, we would be seeing the light in the first sense above. In the daytime we might inspect more closely the mechanism for sending out this signal—the "light bulb," its glass cover, the power supply, etc.—and all these would comprise light in its second meaning as a piece of illuminating apparatus. Finally if we think of the navaid as a whole, including its light-producing apparatus *and* its physical structure, we have the third meaning of light—a lighted fixed navaid.

It is this last meaning that is intended in the list above, so let's look at lights in this sense. Such lights can be large or small, size being, of course, a relative matter. By large, I mean not only large physically, but with a powerful beam that can be seen from relatively great distances. The largest lights are popularly called "lighthouses," but this is not an official term in the Coast Guard lexicon. What the layman calls a lighthouse is called a *seacoast light* in the Light List and is marked by a special boldface type; it may also be called a *primary light.*

In addition to seacoast lights there are *secondary lights,* which are not quite so large. Seacoast and secondary lights are usually found on the coast or some distance off it. They are intended for guidance from large distances, in contrast to the minor lights found in harbors, bays, and rivers for close-in navigation. A typical example of a minor light might be the daybeacon mentioned above, perhaps a single piling in shallow water topped with a daymark and a relatively weak light. There are, however, relatively large minor lights and relatively small secondary ones, so the nomenclature in this borderline region may be somewhat arbitrary.

One term in the Light List Glossary—*beacon*—appears to indicate a light but doesn't necessarily do so. The glossary tells us that a beacon is a "Lighted or unlighted aid to navigation attached to the earth's surface. (Lights and daybeacons both constitute beacons.)" In short, a beacon is any fixed navaid. This definition of beacon as a possibly unlighted aid is somewhat counterintuitive, since our intuitive everyday idea of a beacon is of something that shines brightly in the distance. But you can't argue with an official definition.

The final item in the navaid list of the first paragraph is *fog signals,* which are of course the sound signals I have mentioned above. They can be placed on either fixed or floating navaids, and are described in some detail in Chapter 6.

So much for navaids in general. The properties of individual navaids are found in the body of the Light List; following is a portion of a page.

lights

beacons

fog signals

(1) No.	(2) Name and location	(3) Position	(4) Characteristic	(5) Height	(6) Range	(7) Structure	(8) Remarks
				SEACOAST (Maine) – First District			
	BAY OF FUNDY TO CAPE COD	N/W (Chart 13260)					
80	*Old Anthony Lighted Whistle Buoy 22* Southwest Old Anthony Rock.	43 32.2 70 11.2	**Fl R** 4ˢ		6	Red	
85	Watts Ledge Bell Buoy 1	43 32.3 70 12.6				Green.	
90	*Wood Island Approach Lighted Whistle Buoy WI*	43 27.7 70 17.4	**Mo (A) W**		6	Red and white stripes with red spherical topmark.	
95	**Wood Island Light**	43 27.4 70 19.8	**Al W G** 10ˢ	71	W 16 G 14	White conical tower connected to dwelling.	HORN: 2 blasts ev 30ˢ (2ˢ bl-2ˢ si-2ˢ bl-24ˢ si). Emergency light of reduced intensity when main light is extinguished.
100	Hussey Rock Buoy 1HR					Green can.	
105 7955	**Goat Island Light**	43 21.5 70 25.5	**Fl W** 6ˢ	38	12	White cylindrical tower.	HORN: 1 blast ev 15ˢ (2ˢ bl).
115	*Cape Porpoise Lighted Whistle Buoy 2CP*	43 20.3 70 23.6	**Fl R** 4ˢ		4	Red.	
120	Bibb Rock Buoy	43 16.6 70 33.1				Red and green bands; nun.	
125	Perkins Cove Bell Buoy PC					Red and white stripes with red spherical topmark.	
130	**Cape Neddick Light**	43 09.9 70 35.5	**Iso R** 6ˢ	88	13	White conical tower, covered way to dwelling: 41	HORN: 1 blast ev 10ˢ (1ˢ bl).

As you can see, a navaid is defined by the eight categories that are numbered across the top of the page: Number, name and location, position, etc. The detailed meaning of these categories is given in the Light List and in Chapter 6 of this book, but let's see at least roughly what they are by looking at an example in the list above, the Cape Neddick Light.

1. No.—Navaids in the Light List are arranged in a numbered sequence and 130 is the number of the Cape Neddick Light.

2. Name and location—In this case the name and the location are identical: Cape Neddick. Note the boldface type that indicates a seacoast or primary light—a "lighthouse."

3. Position—The light is located at Latitude 43° 09.9′ N, Longitude 70° 35.5′ W.

4. Characteristic—Iso R 6s stands for an isophase light, red, with a period of 6 seconds. Isophase means the light is

on and off for equal time intervals; here it must be 3 seconds on and 3 seconds off to make up the 6-second period.

5. Height—Eighty-eight feet is the height above mean high water of the light beam.

6. Range—This is the distance in nautical miles that the light can be seen on a normally clear day, from a height sufficient to ensure that it is not hidden below the horizon.

7. Structure—The number 41 is the height in feet of the *structure* above the ground, which is of course different from the height of the *light beam* above the water.

8. Remarks—The navaid has a horn that produces a one-second blast every 10 seconds.

It goes without saying that navaids are an important part of the Aids to Navigation System, but equally important are the rules of the system itself. What do the various navaids tell you to do—or not to do? You see a red buoy with a flashing red light: What is its message? Let's look at these questions now.

It will help to answer them if we first recognize that there are two classes of navaids, which give two different messages. I'll begin by simply enumerating some of the first class: anchorage buoys, which define an approved area for anchoring; fish trap buoys, which tell you to stay clear of them; quarantine buoys, which tell you where to anchor while awaiting the customs officer. The common feature of these navaids is that the waters on one side of them are not meant to be differentiated from the waters on the other side. If you are waiting near the quarantine buoy you can equally well anchor to the north, south, east, or west of it. If you are entering the anchorage area you can pass the buoy that defines a corner of it on either the port or starboard side; it doesn't make any difference. In short these navaids do not discriminate in favor of left or right, port or starboard. To use a word soon to be important, they have no *lateral* significance; they are merely markers of position, or place.

navaids without lateral significance

The second class of navaids comprises those *with* lateral significance; it is a much larger class, to the extent that the Aids to Navigation System as a whole is called a *lateral system*. An important function of many of the navaids in this class is to warn the mariner that some danger exists and tell him how to avoid it. I'll illustrate that point with an example.

navaids with lateral significance

Suppose that in some waterway there is a subsurface rock, not very large, but clearly a potential taker-off of ships' keels. We want to mark it to protect the mariner from it. To do that we could put a buoy next to it, or perhaps even a daymark on it, to guide him in passing the rock to one side or the other. In fact such navaids exist in the Aids to Navigation

System; they are called *preferred channel* navaids. The reason for the name is not clear from the present context; it arises from the fact that such navaids are also used to mark a channel that divides into two different channels, with one of the two being preferred over the other. This is how the Light List describes their function: *"Preferred channel buoys mark junctions or bifurcations in the channel, or wrecks or obstructions which may be passed on either side."*

Now suppose that the rock was not isolated but, rather, was the terminus of a series of rocks and ledges that, if we passed the rock going in a certain well-defined direction, stretched out to its right. The rock now can't be passed on either side; the safe water is only to the left of it. How can we indicate this? It is obviously not practical to dot the whole series of rocks and ledges with buoys. One might imagine a buoy or daymark at the rock with SAFE painted on the safe side and DANGER on the side toward the rocks and ledges, but it's not worth imagining very long, since it is obviously not very practical. What *is* practical and what is done is to **red or green** use a convention and a set of instructions. The navaids that warn of this kind of extended danger are colored red or green; if you encounter a red buoy when you are going in a certain direction its message is that danger begins at that navaid and extends to the right of it, to the starboard side; if you pass a green navaid going in that same, specified direction the dangers begin at it and extend farther to the left.

These conventions can also be phrased in terms of *channels* as the Light Lists do; for *channel* read *safe water.* "Red buoys mark the starboard side of channels, or the location of wrecks or obstructions which must be passed by keeping the buoy on the right hand. Green buoys mark the port side of channels or the location of wrecks or obstructions which must be passed by keeping the buoy on the left hand." In view of this definition of the use of this kind of colored buoy I will refer to them as **channel buoys** *channel buoys* (or more generally, channel navaids) although these are not terms used by the Light Lists.

This then is the general rationale for channel navaids, but for a complete understanding of them there are obviously many details that must be filled in. For example, buoys and daymarks are defined not only by color, but by their shape and numbering; this redundancy is a hedge against error, or it may enable you to identify a mark at a distance by its shape, even if you can't determine the color. So we will have to look at the various channel navaids and the physical characteristics that identify them. This is a fairly big job and is left for Chapter 6.

But now let's look at the equally important problem of clarifying the convention for the direction of travel in terms of which left and right, port and starboard are to be construed. The convention is that the channel navaids are placed to display their messages for boats "proceeding from **returning from** seaward." A boat is proceeding from seaward (or returning from seaward) **seaward** when, roughly speaking, it is going from the open ocean to a harbor, or at least to a more enclosed body of water. This convention is, in part, the origin of the famous mnemonic that you may have heard: "Red, right, returning."

The convention can, however, be ambiguous. If you are sailing into San Diego, California and are passing Point Loma, you will see the waters ahead constrict into a narrow channel between Point Loma and North Island. There is then no question that the large Pacific Ocean is behind you and the relatively small San Diego harbor is before you (around a bend), and you are proceeding from seaward. The red navaids should then be kept to your right, and indeed you will find a long entrance channel with red navaids 6, 8, 10, 12, etc. to starboard and a similar chain of green ones to port. But it's not always that simple. If you are in Massachusetts waters in Woods Hole Passage, which is a channel between the southern tip of Woods Hole and the northern tip of Naushon Island, you are in fact between one large body of water, Vineyard Sound, and another, Buzzards Bay. The criteria above of going from ocean to harbor, or large body of water to small body, don't apply.

The Light List recognizes the possibility of such ambiguities, and it provides a statement that is meant to help. It essentially says that if there is a question as to the direction of "returning from seaward," that direction is as given by the arrows on the accompanying map—that is, clockwise around the Atlantic, Gulf, and Pacific coasts, and northerly and westerly in the Great Lakes, except southerly in Lake Michigan. This is fine as far as it goes, but often it doesn't go far enough.

In the present case, the passage between Buzzards Bay and Vineyard Sound is not a coastal passage, but is a passage in a complex scene of islands, promontories, and the mainland. There are many similar cases elsewhere, for example in Chesapeake Bay, where bays, river mouths, and narrows connect with one another and the coastal passage rule above is hard to apply. In these cases if there is any question in your mind the sensible thing is to forget all the rules and simply look at the buoys on the chart. You can almost always read the dangers on the chart that the buoys are supposed to mark and simply use common sense to stay in safe waters.

All the discussion thus far of navaids has been on the four nonelectronic ones listed at the beginning of this chapter, since they are the most important for this book's intended audience. For completeness, however, I add a paragraph on each of the three electronic aids that are also listed: radiobeacons, racons, and Loran stations.

Radiobeacons emit a coded radio-identifying signal that can be detected at various distances depending on the strength of the transmitter, atmospheric conditions, and the sensitivity of the receiver. For a ship to exploit a radiobeacon effectively it must have aboard a direction-finding radio receiver, commonly known as an RDF (radio direction finder). As the name implies, this receiver can indicate the direction from which the signal is coming, by means of a directional antenna. The received signal varies in relative strength as the antenna points more or less toward the

"Returning from seaward" is arbitrarily defined in ambiguous cases according to the arrows in this map.

radiobeacons

transmitter. If the navigator finds the direction from which the signal is coming, he can draw a line on the chart in that direction through the radiobeacon. For example, if he is sailing up the West Coast and finds that a radiobeacon on the coast is due east of him, he draws an east-west line on the chart through the transmitter position. He has then what is called a *line of position* (more detail on this in Chapter 20) somewhere along which his boat must lie. This is obviously an important navigational datum since it can be combined with a second line of position, perhaps from another radiobeacon, perhaps from some other source, to provide a fix where the lines cross (Chapter 23). Although the basic idea is simple, there are many practical questions of technique, optimum equipment, and accuracy that I will leave to specialized books.

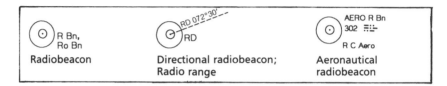

Radiobeacon	Directional radiobeacon; Radio range	Aeronautical radiobeacon

racons

Radar responder beacon

The second electronic aid in the Light List is the *racon,* which is in fact only of interest to those few small-boat pilots who have a radar aboard. A racon is a radar *transponder,* a device that responds to a received radar signal by emitting a signal of its own. As you probably know, a radar set is basically a short-wave radio transmitter that sends out a directional signal; if there is any kind of obstruction in the path of that signal—a ship, an island, a building—some of the energy in the signal is reflected back to the radar set where it is detected by a sensitive receiver. This "radar return" is the radar operator's clue, even at night or in the fog, that there is something out there in front of him. Radar return signals are not always easy to interpret. In a harbor entrance for example, there may be many *different* sources of return—anchored or moving boats, harbor islands, dredges, etc.—that are hard for the radar operator to sort out. The racon cuts through all this by responding with a unique identifying code when triggered by a radar signal; the operator can then unambiguously detect the racon and so locate his vessel with respect to its position.

loran–c

Loran tower (name)

Loran–C, an acronym for Long Range Navigation System, is a radio position-finding system based on coastal chains of *pairs* of radio transmitting stations. Schematically, it works like this. Each transmitter in such a pair emits a signal whose time of emission is precisely synchronized with the emission of the signal of the other member of the pair. The Loran–C receiver on shipboard then measures, to the required accuracy of millionths of seconds, the difference in the time of reception of the two signals. This *time difference* gives an indication of where the receiver is with respect to the stations. Thus if the two stations are called A and B, and the signal from A is received first, the receiver is closer to A than to B; if from B first, the receiver is closer to B; if from A and B simultaneously, the receiver is on a line equidistant from A and B. This concept can be extended mathematically to show that if the *time difference* between the two receptions is known exactly, the ship is on a certain *hyperbolic curve-of-position*. If now a second hyperbolic curve can be obtained from another pair in the Loran "chain," their intersection gives a position fix.

That is all I'll say in this book about electronic aids. It's not that I think they are unimportant—I use them myself. Rather it is the thought that if you are reading this book you are presumably not satisfied with your coastal piloting skills. Electronic aids, and loran in particular, are good servants but bad masters, and you should not have to accept their pronouncements with blind faith. It is statistically likely that some malfunction will make them unreliable one day, and they will tell a lie. Paradoxically, if it is a gross lie it will not be serious. If your loran claims you are off the Great Barrier Reef when you are sailing in Chesapeake Bay, you will not be fooled. But if it puts you a couple of miles from your actual location in the Bay it may be disastrous. There should be some way on these occasions of looking your loran squarely in its microprocessing eye and saying "You lie." One way to do this is to have a good knowledge of coastal piloting and the checks and cross-checks it can provide, and a sound and frequently updated sense of the boat's position.

4

Other Learning Aids

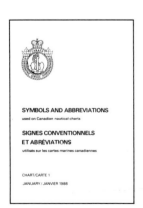

chart #1

SYMBOLS AND ABBREVIATIONS
used on Canadian nautical charts

SIGNES CONVENTIONNELS
ET ABRÉVIATIONS
utilisés sur les cartes marines canadiennes

CHART/CARTE 1
JANUARY / JANVIER 1988

The Canadian counterpart.

Important as they are, the Light Lists and Coast Pilots of the last two chapters are not the only sources of printed enlightenment. There is a variety of other useful government and private publications and in this chapter I point out and comment on some of these.

Probably the most important is a NOAA (National Oceanic and Atmospheric Administration) publication called Chart #1—even though it is not a chart at all. Its table of contents and a sample page are reproduced below. From these you will see that Chart #1 is a catalog of the symbols and abbreviations that appear on a modern nautical chart. There are 21 categories of information, from The Coastline through The Compass, and these include some 800 separate entries, many of them pictorial. Section O, on Dangers, reproduced here, gives an idea of the completeness and fine line of detail that prevails.

Not all the entries are equally important or used equally as often. The average coastal pilot will profit frequently from the knowledge, found in Section O, that a dotted line enclosing an entry signifies a danger to navigation. He will profit less frequently from being able to recognize the symbol (in Section I on Buildings and Structures) for a Moslem Shrine or a Buddhist Temple. Nonetheless I find even the more exotic entries interesting; they give Chart #1 a special cachet. I have always found it instructive to browse, and although I have been doing this for years I am often surprised to discover some fresh insight or piece of information that had previously escaped me.

There is not much I can say to enhance Chart #1 for you. Try it and you will see that it speaks for itself. Don't overlook the four-page Introduction, which is helpful in exploiting the booklet to maximum advantage.

If you talk to even an experienced sailor about the next publication I mention, and call it by its official title, *The American Practical Navigator,* he probably won't recognize it. But call it "Bowditch" and he probably will, so that's what I will call it.

Bowditch is one of the longest running hits in the U.S. government publishing repertory. It has gone through some 70 editions since first being published in 1802 by a true American original—Nathaniel Bowditch, shipmaster, navigator, mathematician, genius. It has now grown to include almost 2000 pages in the 1984 edition. In my earlier, single-

Bowditch

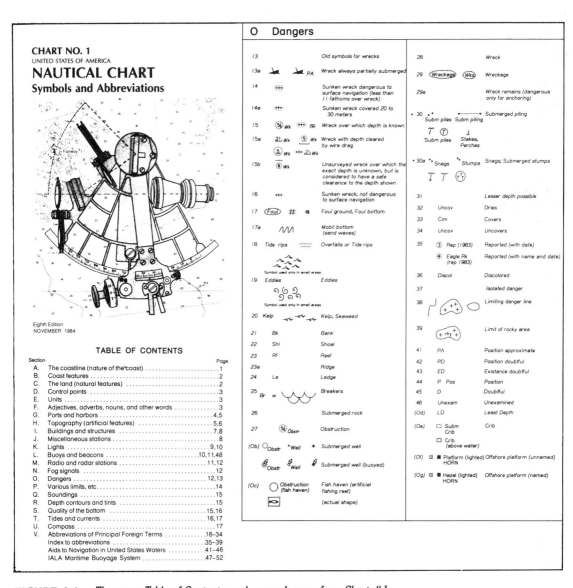

FIGURE 4-1. *The cover, Table of Contents, and a sample page from Chart #1.*

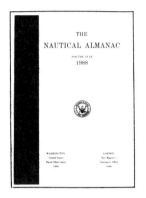

volume 1958 edition there were a total of 1524 pages, of which about 300 were mathematical and physical tables, and a glossary. The 1984 edition is in two volumes; the first is text, expanded even over the 1958 edition, and the tables and glossary now appear in the second volume.

Numbers of pages aside, what is this paragon of navigational information? It is in eight parts. Three of them comprise about 120 pages on coastal piloting and dead reckoning, and long parts on celestial and electronic navigation. The coastal piloting is of course oriented toward big-boat practice as opposed to the small-boat procedures I advocate in this book. Nonetheless, big-boat and small-boat are not so precisely defined and not so completely mutually exclusive but that there are points in Bowditch worthy of consideration by the small-boat skipper.

Aside from the part on coastal navigation there is a section called Lifeboat Navigation that is worth reading and is in the spirit of the book you are holding. This section is intended for sailors and merchant mariners whose ship has been wrecked and are cast adrift in a lifeboat, but it is of interest in less dire circumstances and to a wider audience. Basically, lifeboat navigation is a way of piloting and doing crude celestial navigation with the simplest kinds of instruments, such as might be crudely fashioned even on a lifeboat. In fact some of these, such as the crosstaff, are presented in this book.

The sections mentioned above, on celestial and electronic navigation, are each of book length and are accurate and authoritative; if nothing else they make Bowditch a bargain. At current book prices I would guess that either section could be sold at the price of Bowditch as a whole. In addition there are a couple of hundred pages on oceanography and meteorology, a fine section on charts that has information and insights not found elsewhere, and much else as well. All told, Bowditch is well worth considering for the ship's library.

Almanacs supply information specific to a given year. This may be astronomical data, or information on the state of the tides (which is of course basically astronomical). Quintessential is *The Nautical Almanac,* devoted largely to a listing day by day (in fact, second by second) of the positions, or astronomical coordinates, of the sun, moon, stars, and planets. This information is essential to celestial navigation, but may or may not be useful—at least in the detail provided—to the coastal pilot. Other almanacs, such as *Reed's Nautical Almanac and Coast Pilot,* contain this material but with day-to-day data on tides and currents as well. In addition it has sections on the weather and on buoys, lights, and piloting tips and techniques. In still other almanacs, such as *Eldridge's Tide and Pilot Book for the East Coast,* the bulk of the information is on tides and currents but there are valuable sections on lights and fog signals, radio-navigational aids, the weather, and other topics.

In sailing along the coast the practical skipper is concerned with more than mere navigation. Will there be diesel fuel at the next destination? Is there a little cove or bay on the way for a lunch stop? The answer to these kinds of questions are given in cruising guides, which come in large variety. Some are leisurely and anecdotal, and can be read almost like a narrative; others are terse and business-like with many-entried tables and chartlets that list or show where facilities and services can be found. Since there is such a variety there is not much that can be said in general. In a current nautical book list I find 90 cruising guides listed for areas that start in the Caribbean and end in Pacific islands.

Obviously any choice among them can't be made from where I sit. Whatever your locale, it probably would be beneficial, and interesting as well, to spend some time at a bookstore browsing among cruising guides to find those that suit not only your cruising grounds but your taste and temperament.

Beyond the books above there is a variety of publications too diverse to label neatly. If you live near a Coast Guard office, as I do, you may find useful brochures of one kind or another there, perhaps on Rules of the Road, or Visual Distress Signals or Safety Requirements. Sometimes these publications are available at meetings or in the classes of the Coast Guard Auxiliary or U.S. Power Squadron. There are also useful waterproof plastic cards at most marine supply stores, with tips and techniques for the coastal pilot printed on them.

Beyond this, there is a vast literature on other people's cruises and experience that is not primarily concerned with coastal piloting but that can, in a book chapter or section or even in the occasional interspersed remark, be enlightening. In a sense, these comprise the most important part of the literature in that they help to keep us going during the long winter months, or during the interminable spring days when the work list never seems to get shorter. I'll not mention any specific titles; so much is a matter of taste, and the literature is so large I can't pretend to have read it all. But it is out there waiting for you.

SECTION II

Chart Learning and the View on Deck
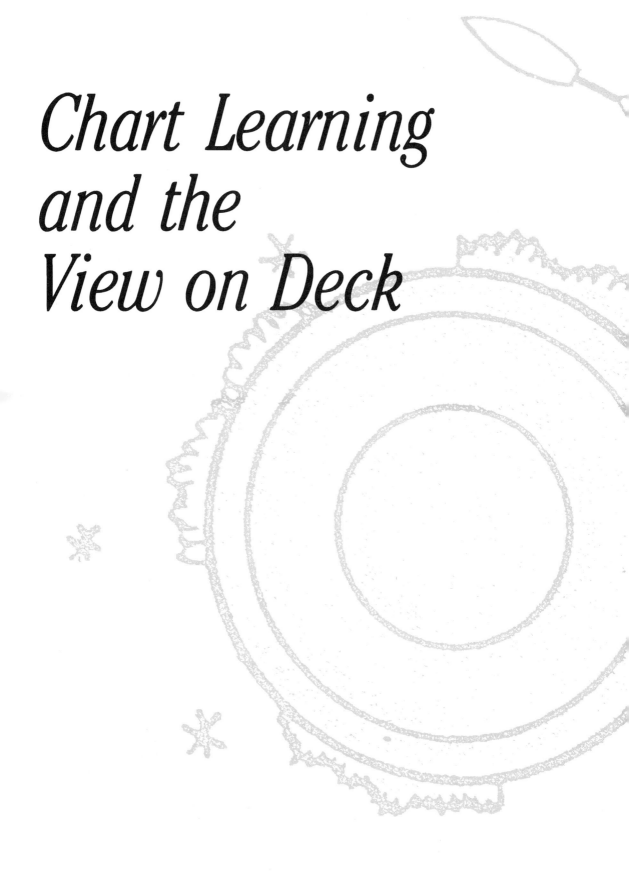

5

Landmarks

The coastal pilot can't always navigate from clues given by the shape of the land. The land may not have much shape! Along the low, indistinctive coasts of Florida or outer Cape Cod there can be mile after mile of shoreline every mile of which looks like every other one. If then nature is not on his side in helping him find his way the navigator must look to man's works—to *landmarks* and *navaids*. Functionally the two are similar; they are things, objects, visible from the water and (usually) marked on the chart. Although "landmark" is often taken to mean a manmade feature, it can also be a natural one—a distinctive mountain peak, a stretch of steep cliffs, etc. A standpipe on a hill, towers, water tanks, radio masts, bridges, and tall buildings are examples of manmade landmarks. These haven't in general been made with an aim to improving navigation; navaids have. They are the buoys, lighthouses, beacons etc. that have been specificaly put into place to help the sailor. They are always listed on the chart. Most of them—cans, nuns, bells, gongs, etc., are smaller than the average landmark. I discuss landmarks in this chapter, navaids in the next.

Many landmarks are private to the skipper, and are not listed on the chart. Anyone who regularly sails in and out of the same waters has his personal identifying marks—a pier, a cottage, a cluster of moored boats—to guide him. Not much can be said about these in general, so it is landmarks listed on the chart that I will discuss. But even these are so numerous and varied that I can't hope to characterize them completely; what follows then is not a definitive Treatise on the Nature of Landmarks, but some more or less random observations drawn from my own experience.

As always, the problem is to correlate what is printed on the chart with what is seen on the landscape. From the deck we see a church with a structure above it. On the chart is it this listing of SPIRE or that listing of CUPOLA? Or, looking at the chart, we see MONUMENT. On deck, is that the tall skinny cylinder off the starboard bow?

Ordinarily there is no great difficulty in identifying what you see on land. Landmarks usually differ enough from one another that there is no danger of confusion. If there is a problem the solution can sometimes be found in Bowditch, which has brief definitions of some of the chart notations. For example if you are not clear about the difference between SPIRE and CUPOLA you will find that a spire is a "slender pointed structure extending above a building" and that a cupola is a "small dome-shaped tower or turret rising from a building." If you see what seems to be a chimney on land, and don't see CHIMNEY on the chart but do see STACK, you might turn to Bowditch to find, in brief, that a chimney is relatively small and a stack relatively large. This is spelled out in the definition from Bowditch next to the picture below. From that definition, these stacks are clearly STACKS, not CHIMNEYS.

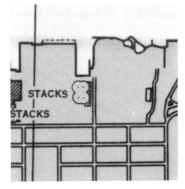

FIGURE 5-1.
Bowditch: "A stack is a tall smokestack or chimney. The term is used when the stack is more prominent than the accompanying buildings."

The picture below shows a conspicuous landmark in Boston Harbor, a large crane. My interest is not in the crane itself but in the "PA" printed beside CRANE on the chart. This stands for "Position Approximate" which is indeed appropriate since this is a traveling crane, which can be anywhere on a track that is hundreds of feet long. Note the very small circle that gives the crane's position; it is different from the usual small circle-with-central-dot that often marks position, as for example in MON to the lower right of CRANE. The entries I_n and I_o in Chart #1 clarify this. The common small circle-*cum*-dot marks a landmark whose position is accurate; the *very* small circle seen next to CRANE marks one whose position is approximate. We have then been told in two different ways that the position is approximate, and this is an example of the very useful redundancy one often finds on charts. Information is given in two or more ways so that if you miss the first way you have an independent chance to latch on to a second—obviously a good hedge against errors.

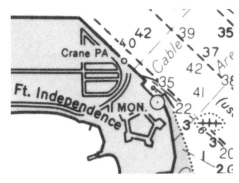

FIGURE 5-2.

Both the notation "PA" and the fact that the crane's position is marked by ∘ and not by ⊙ indicate Position Approximate.

Usually TANK refers to a water tank elevated on a metal framework. You see one below silhouetted against the sky. There are also tanks that hold gas or oil. Bowditch states that "Gas Tank or Oil Tank is used for the distinctive structures described by these words." The dictum is not observed for the two well-known gas tanks shown below in Dorchester Bay; they are marked only as Tanks on the chart. I don't mention this as a nitpicker anxious to show how clever he is in finding a small error in the chart—if it is an error. I have nothing but admiration for the remarkable accuracy and completeness of the modern nautical chart. Nonetheless, charts are made by fallible humans and sometimes one must resolve for himself what may appear to be an inconsistency on the chart. The redun-

FIGURE 5-3.
Water tank.

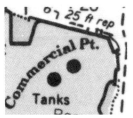

FIGURE 5-4.
Oil tanks.

dancy I mentioned earlier is of help here. Although the tanks are not listed as Gas Tanks on the chart they do have next to them the small solid circle that entry 71 in Section I of Chart #1 tells us indicates a Gas Tank.

Not only tanks hold water; standpipes do as well. A STANDPIPE is a "tall cylindrical structure whose height is several times its diameter." Tanks and standpipes are often excellent landmarks, since they are usually located as high as possible to ensure enough gravity pressure to supply the houses and buildings below them. The picture below is of a well-known standpipe on Winthrop Head in Massachusetts Bay.

FIGURE 5-5.
Standpipe.

This standpipe is typical in its shape but it is atypical in being especially prominent and particularly useful as a landmark. As I mentioned in Chapter 2, one of the first things the beginning coastal pilot learns is that not all landmarks are created equal, even though on the chart they are all marked by the same size circle and dot and the same size lettering. I quoted from Coast Pilot #2. "Conspicuous to a vessel approaching Boston harbor from northeastward is the tall red, white and blue standpipe on Winthrop Head." The standpipe mentioned here is the one in the picture above. It is indeed especially useful. Its unique red, white, and blue stripes make it instantly recognizable, not only from many miles distant in the northeast, but from the east and southeast as well. Once you have spotted it early on you can use it continuously to orient yourself, measure its bow angle, take its beam bearing, watch it come into transit with other landmarks. Altogether a much more satisfactory procedure than squinting in the distance to identify the tiny speck you hope will be a buoy—and will probably turn out not to be.

Q. What happened to the lighthouse when the light went out?
A. It became a TOWER.

I'll explain. When a lighthouse is taken off duty as a navaid—is *abandoned*—it is listed as a TOWER. Sometimes a parenthesis is added

(Aband. Lt. Ho.), sometimes not. I found this out the hard way after considerable mental travail one day on the Maine coast looking for a TOWER listed on the chart, and could only see, in what I thought was its place, a lighthouse. Clearly a lighthouse—tall white cylinder, iron balcony, glass light gallery on top, the whole bit. I didn't see any light flashing but since it was daytime was not surprised. In fact I didn't resolve the dilemma that day; it was only much later that I discovered that the "lighthouse" was really my sought-after TOWER.

The two pictures below illustrate this. Two lighthouses, both abandoned, but one is called TOWER and one is called TOWER (Aband. L H).

FIGURE 5-6.

Beyond abandoned lighthouses, what the cartographer chooses to call TOWER can vary greatly. To no great cosmic purpose the accompanying photographs provide some examples.

FIGURE 5-7. *If the criterion of a good landmark is that it is not easily confused with others, then this must get high marks. It is 353 feet high, and is important enough to be listed as one of the Coast Pilot's "prominent landmarks."*

FIGURE 5-8. *This is the extreme tower—the 700-foot John Hancock building in Boston. It alone is listed on the 1987 chart, but is in fact now one of many skyscrapers in downtown Boston. The skyline they create is an unmistakable navaid from many miles away.*

FIGURE 5-9. *This 40-foot tower is of no great navigational interest since it is hard to see from seaward, where it is hidden against the land background. This picture was taken from behind the tower, i.e. between it and the land, so it stands out against the sea surface. Although the tower is not interesting navigationally it is not without human interest. When taking its picture I learned, among other things, from inscriptions on its base, that Kevin Loves Kathleen (at least as of June 4, 1983) and that the Roxbury Raiders Are The Greatest.*

FIGURE 5-10. *This tower is only about 40' high but is on the highest point of a peninsula and so is never lost to sight in land behind it. An excellent landmark.*

FIGURE 5-11.   *For absolute certainty in identification always arrange to have your towers next to domes.*

6

Navaids

In Chapter 3, I discussed the rather dry and abstract Aids to Navigation System for coastal waters, with its dry and abstract classification of navaids as fixed or floating; light emitters or non-emitters; sound emitters or non-emitters; and with lateral significance or without lateral significance. Now it is time to make the abstractions concrete and look at real-life examples of navaids. There is an enormous variety. They can be buoys of all kinds, painted signboards on pilings, towers with wooden frameworks, towers with iron frameworks, cement lighthouses, granite block lighthouses. . . . They range from the smallest can buoy on a remote coast to the kind of aid epitomized by Ambrose Light in the busy entrance to New York Harbor, with its four steel legs sunk hundreds of feet into the harbor bottom supporting an 80- by 80-foot platform complete with helicopter landing pad, lights, and sound and electronic signaling apparatuses.

Fixed and floating navaids (buoys) can differ in many ways, but they have two common denominators. Either kind can emit sound signals; either kind can emit light signals. The kinds of sound and light signals on buoys are not altogether the same as those on fixed navaids, but there is enough common ground to make it logical to first discuss these signals in general and only later specialize.

First, sound signals. Six kinds are given in the Light List, and I will divide them into three classes, according to the mechanism of their sound production: (1) bells and gongs; (2) whistles; and (3) horns, sirens, and diaphones.

A bell on a navaid is the same in principle as any other kind of bell—cowbell, dinner bell, church bell: A hammer or clapper strikes a concave metal casting, and a sound is produced. A gong is basically the same; the

FIGURE 6-1.
A bell buoy always produces a sound with a single pitch from such a bell as is seen in the picture. The sound is produced by means of a hammer actuated by hand, a descending weight, compressed gas, or electricity.

45

bells and gongs

whistles

sirens, horns, diaphones

FIGURE 6-2.
A gong buoy produces sounds with different pitches from two or more gongs stacked one above the other, four in the above picture. The sound is made by clappers striking the gongs, activated by the natural motion of the buoy in the waves.

dictionary defines it to be a shallow bell. A gong *buoy* is however different from a bell *buoy* in that the bell buoy has a single bell producing a single tone, whereas the gong buoy has two or more gongs producing tones of two or more different pitches. Bells are found on buoys *and* on fixed navaids. Gongs are found *only* on buoys and they are often activated by the motion of the buoy itself, so that they may be more or less reliable depending on how calm the waters are.

A whistle produces its sound when a blast of compressed air passes through a slot in a resonant chamber. The small boy who puts two fingers in his mouth and blows a blast produces sound by the same mechanism. It is hard to say in words what a whistle sounds like; it is easier to say what it doesn't sound like. It doesn't sound like a policeman's whistle or a referee's whistle or a two-fingers-in-the-mouth whistle. The navaid whistle is deeper and more mournful than these. If you have ever heard the lugubrious tooot-toooot of a tugboat you may well have heard a whistle of the navaid kind. The compressed air that drives the whistle is generated by a mechanism that depends on the rise and fall of the buoy in the sea, so that the duration of the whistle sound is not fixed but depends on the sea state.

Sirens, horns, and diaphones have in common that their sound is produced by a moving mechanical element. In the siren, a rotor spins; the horn (also called a diaphragm horn) has a diaphragm that vibrates; in the diaphone there is a slotted reciprocating piston. Either compressed air or electricity may move these elements. The horn sound is usually higher in pitch than is the whistle, and the blasts are of fixed duration and repeated periodically.

Sirens are scarcer in my experience; I don't think I have ever heard one. When I called the local Coast Guard office to ask about them, the veteran navaids officer said that *he* had never heard one and thought they were very scarce indeed, so perhaps that is all that needs be said about sirens. A diaphone often emits a two-tone signal, with the first tone low and the second still lower—baritone, then bass.

The second common denominator of floating and fixed navaids is that both can have lights. There is a greater variation in complexity among light signals on small and large navaids than there is for sound signals. But whatever the complexity, all light systems have three features in common: *color, light characteristics,* and *sectors.*

Color needs no explanation, but light *characteristics* do. Some lights are steady: they are switched on, by photocells or by hand, and glow steadily for hours, days, or months. These lights are called *fixed*—a word usage not to be confused with lights on fixed structures. Other lights are on and off in a periodic pattern, one that repeats in time. For example, a light might be on for one second, off for nine; on for one second, off for nine; on for one second. . . . This kind of on-off pattern is called the light's characteristic (or its *rhythmics*); there are, of course, an infinity of other characteristics besides this simple illustrative example. The time needed to run through the pattern, together with the interval between pattern repetitions, is called the *period.*

There are four basic light characteristics; they are illustrated in Figure 6-3.

A light may be "on" more than once during a period and still be called a flashing light if the *total* time it is on is less than the *total* time it is off. Example: Two flashes per period consisting of one second on, one second off, one second on, seven seconds off, makes for a ten-second period, with only two seconds of light to eight seconds off. Lights such as these with multiple flashes are called *group flashing.* The light illustrated in Figure 6-3 is *simple flashing.*

Similarly, the occulting light in Figure 6-3 is not the most general; it is called *simple occulting.* A light is occulting in general if, being on and off for intervals during its period, its total "on" time is greater than its total "off" time.

The standard abbreviations for light characteristics are listed completely in Chart #1, Section K, and partially on many charts. They include: F = Fixed, Fl = Flashing, Iso = Isophase or equal intervals, Gr Fl = Group flashing. The color of the light is also abbreviated: R = Red, G = Green, W = White, etc. On the chart the characteristic, color, and period are given in that order. Thus "Fl G 10s" means a flashing green light with a 10-second period.

light characteristics

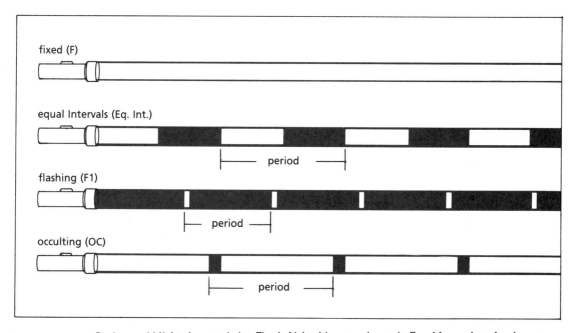

FIGURE 6-3. *Basic navaid light characteristics.* Fixed: *Light shines continuously.* Equal Intervals *or* Isophase: *Light is on for as long as it is off.* Flashing: *Light is on for less time than it is off.* Occulting: *Light is on for more time than it is off.*

A complete listing of the 16 different light characteristics in use on navaids is found in any Light List; here I'll simply cite two more examples. The first is a group flashing light. In its abbreviation the number of flashes is put in parentheses, followed by the color (if it is not white), then the period. For example, "GrFl (2) G 15 s" is a green light that flashes twice in 15 seconds.

In a flashing light, the duration of the individual flashes need not be equal; some can be longer than others. In one important example the first flash is short and the second long, much like a dot and dash in Morse code. In fact, this short-long flash is abbreviated Mo(A) since short-long (dot-dash) is the symbol for the letter "A" in Morse code.

sectors   A final feature of lights is that they may shine in *sectors.* A sector is, in everyday terms, the shape of a piece of pie. Mathematically it is the shape contained between two radii of a circle; it is measured by the angle between the radii. Cut a piece of pie into six equal pieces and you will have produced six 60-degree sectors. If you now imagine a light at the center of a large abstract pie, the light can have different colors, characteristics, or both in different sectors. Thus it might shine red in the 45-degree sector between north and northeast and green between northeast and east—one example from an infinity of possibilities. As a general rule, if you are in the sector where the light is seen as red, you are in a danger zone. Sectors can be of any angular width—a few degrees wide is not uncommon.

Ordinarily only the larger lights, the seacoast or secondary lights, have sectors. On the chart they are shown in plan view with the pie-shaped pieces clearly marked. The sectors are also shown less pictorially in the Light List, where they are defined in terms of the angular bearing of the light *as seen from the two edges of the sector,* not in terms of the bearings of the edges as seen from the light. This can be confusing until you realize what is going on. More details on this are given in Chapter 10.

So much for sound and light signals in general. It is now time to get physical and look at the actual navaids that display these signals, and

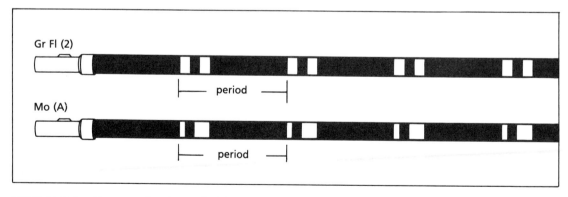

FIGURE 6-4. *Two examples of group flashing lights.*

other navaids as well. I pointed out in Chapter 3 that every navaid is one of two kinds: with lateral significance or without lateral significance. Typically the first kind informs the skipper—imagined as "returning from seaward"—that the waters are safe on one side of the navaid and unsafe on the other. Or they may tell the skipper that the waters are, for one reason or another, preferred on one side. In short, these navaids are not neutral; they take sides. They advise the navigator on how to move laterally with respect to them, hence their name. Navaids without lateral significance are, of course, ones for which there is no lateral connotation. For example: A buoy marked Cable Crossing to tell what lies on the seabed beneath it, and a buoy marked Speed Limit, 5 Knots, are both *without* lateral significance.

First, navaids *with* lateral significance. There are four kinds: unlighted buoys, lighted buoys, daybeacons, and minor lights. Instead of trying to discuss all these simultaneously, I'll focus on unlighted buoys, partly because there are probably more of them in the system and partly because the conventions of color, shape, and numbering that apply to them are in large part applicable to other kinds of navaids. The rules that govern them are valid for daymarks as well, and, with small modification, to lighted buoys and minor lights.

There are three kinds of unlighted buoys with lateral significance: *channel buoys, preferred channel buoys,* and *midchannel* (or safe-water) buoys. The name "channel buoys" is mine; it is not an official designation in the Light List. But it is a convenient and obvious one since I use it for the buoys that mark the port or starboard side of channels. These are described thus in the Light List: "Green buoys mark the port side of channels or the location of wrecks or obstructions which must be passed by keeping the buoys on the left hand." There is of course a similar statement with "red" in place of "green" and "starboard" in place of "port." (Remember always that left and right are to be construed as "when returning from seaward.")

Channel buoys are identified not only by their color but by their shape and numbering as well. All green buoys are can buoys and have odd numbers; all red buoys are nun buoys and have even numbers. This redundancy of means of identification is obviously a Good Thing. For example, you can often identify buoys by their shape at a distance long before you can see the number and even before you can be sure about the color. And if you see a red buoy with a "3" on it, and remember that red implies even numbers, you may be inspired to look more closely, perhaps to find that the "3" is an "8" with the left part worn away or covered with bird droppings.

Daybeacons, described briefly in Chapter 3, are fixed, unlighted structures with painted signs, or daymarks, on them. As I remarked above, the logic of the daymark's identification is essentially the same as for unlighted buoys. They are green or red, and the colors have the same meaning as for channel buoys. The green daymarks are square, since the flat top of a square recalls the flat top of a can buoy seen in silhouette; the

unlighted channel buoys

channel daybeacons

red daymarks are triangular to recall the pointy top of a nun buoy. Green daymarks are odd numbered; red daymarks, even numbered.

lighted channel buoys

Lighted channel buoys are governed by the same conventions as unlighted buoys and channel daymarks except that their shape has no navigational meaning—it may be anything. But their solid green or red color and their odd-even numbering are the same as for the other channel navaids above. The color of the light is the same as that of the buoy itself. There are a half-dozen possible light characteristics, fixed, flashing, etc.; they are shown in the next diagram.

minor channel lights

Finally, minor channel lights—small, fixed, lighted structures that mark channels—have the same conventions of light colors and numbers as do lighted channel buoys. But neither the shape *nor* the color of the structure itself has any navigational meaning.

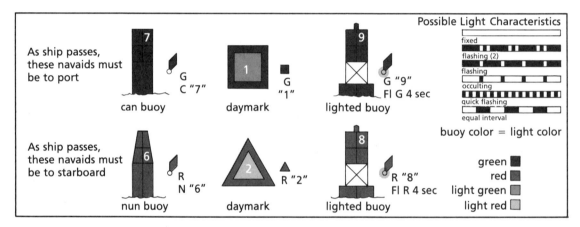

FIGURE 6-5. *CHANNEL NAVAIDS: For "returning from seaward" on all navigable U.S. waters except Western rivers and the Intracoastal Waterway.*

In the illustration above I note that the navaids must, depending on their kind, be left to port or starboard. This derives from the Light List, which uses "must" in the same way, if in slightly different phrasing. But the "must" should be interpreted with common sense. What the supertanker drawing 30 feet requires is not the same as for a sea kayaker. The "must" then is not an absolute prohibition to be heeded at all times and by all craft. Think of it rather as a warning, a suggestion that you interpret what the navaid is alerting you to. Then recall the state of the tide and decide whether the navaid's message applies to your craft. If you don't make this kind of informed decision about every channel navaid then sooner or later one will catch you out and you will be sorry.

Here are two examples, as seen from the deck and on the chart, of the workhorses of the unlighted channel buoys—cans and nuns.

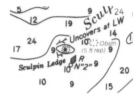

FIGURE 6-6. *This is the standard nun buoy, whose name derives from its resemblance to the pointy headgear worn by nuns. It comes in a variety of sizes. Sometimes its top is made of flat intersecting plates that act as a radar reflector but still maintain its pointy silhouette.*

FIGURE 6-7. *On the day that I took these pictures I noticed seagulls sitting on each of the many green buoys in the bay, but none on the equally numerous red ones. My quick intelligence immediately concluded that their particular hue of "buoy red" was a repellent for seagulls, and I imagined the fortune I would make by manufacturing paint of this hue and selling it to cover areas of boats, docks, etc. that are troubled by these pesky creatures and their droppings. Unfortunately I mentioned this to a pragmatic friend with a less quick intelligence and he opined that the reason the gulls avoid the red buoys might be that their pointy tops make a less secure perch than do the flat tops of the cans. . . .*

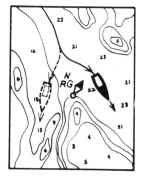

Preferred channel navaids comprise the second class of buoys with lateral significance. The Light List states: "Preferred channel buoys (navaids) mark junctions or bifurcations in the channel, or wrecks or obstructions which may be passed on either side." But one side may be preferred over the other for a variety of reasons. An example is shown here. Of the two possible passing channels shown, the one at the left will eventually peter out to 3- and 4-foot depths, whereas the channel on the right will remain relatively deep all the way. Or one side may be preferred because it helps separate traffic into lanes.

There are three kinds of preferred channel navaids: unlighted buoys, daybeacons, and lighted buoys. The conventions are similar to those for channel navaids; the main difference is that preferred channel aids are painted in *two* bands of different colors, with the top band defining the preferred channel. Top band red, preferred channel to port; top band green, preferred channel to starboard. The navaids are not numbered but they may be lettered. The lighted buoy has a light the color of the top band, and the characteristic is *composite group flashing* (2 + 1, or two flashes, a short interval, a third flash, and then a longer interval before the group repeats), as shown in Figure 6-8.

Midchannel or *safe-water* navaids comprise a third category with lateral significance. There are three kinds: a spherical unlighted buoy with vertical red and white stripes; an octagonal daymark with a vertical red and white stripe and a white reflective border; and a lighted buoy also with vertical red and white stripes, possibly with sound signals, and showing a white light with the characteristic of Morse "A," abbreviated Mo (A). (See page 48 for an explanation of this characteristic.)

These navaids do not mark dangers but are rather meant to tell you where you are. As their name implies they can be passed as closely as you wish. They are sometimes called *harbor buoys* because they are often found at favorable positions for entering a harbor or in the channel

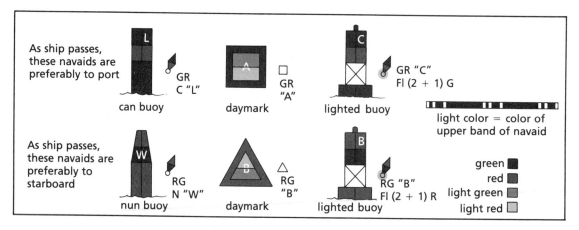

FIGURE 6-8. *PREFERRED CHANNEL NAVAIDS: For "returning from seaward" on all navigable U.S. waters except Western rivers and the Intracoastal Waterway.*

leading to a harbor. In such cases they may be marked by one or two letters intended to be descriptive. For example, at the entrance to Boston Harbor's North Channel you will find RW "NC" Mo(A) GONG, with "NC" standing, of course, for North Channel. And in Monterey Bay, California, the "SC" on the red and white vertically striped buoy tells you that Santa Cruz Harbor is in front of you.

harbor buoys

Another navaid with lateral significance, but of a different kind than we have just discussed, is one called the *range*. This consists, in fact, of a *pair* of structures that act mutually to define it. The navaids discussed previously instruct you on how to move laterally with respect to them; the range instructs you not to move laterally at all with respect to it—and if you do move laterally by inadvertence, to move back again immediately. I'll explain.

The range is based on the concept of the *transit*. When two objects are seen to be lined up, one behind the other, they are said to be *in transit*. The two objects together then constitute the range. If the objects are also found on the chart, the skipper who sees them line up on deck knows that his position on the chart is somewhere along the (extended) line drawn between them. This line is called the *transit line* or *transit line of position* and is highly accurate, since the eye can detect very small misalignments corresponding to very small lateral deviations from the transit.

This line of position is in fact so accurate that artificial ranges are set up as part of the Aids to Navigation system. For example, two marks may be placed to define an accurate mid-channel line in a difficult channel through hazardous waters. These *range daymarks* are standardized and consist of a large painted rectangle with a central stripe, standing on end on a supporting structure. The color of the rectangle is chosen to contrast with the background, and the color of the stripe is chosen to stand out against the rectangle. The colors used for either rectangle or stripe are green, red, white, or black. In a two-letter code in which the first letter stands for the background color, and the second for the stripe, the twelve color combinations are: GW, WG, WB, BW, WR, RW, RB, BR, GB, BG, GR, and RG.

Two range daymarks not quite in transit.

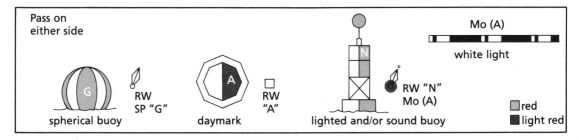

FIGURE 6-9. *MIDCHANNEL or SAFE-WATER NAVAIDS: For navigable U.S. waters except Western rivers and the Intracoastal Waterway.*

From the Light List: Black, white band midway of height; octagonal pyramid on granite base.

Navaids *without* lateral significance include beacons, lighted and un-lighted buoys and minor lights. As I mentioned in Chapter 3, a beacon is *any* fixed aid to navigation, usually of distinctive enough shape or structure that it can't be confused with anything else, especially if you have its detailed description from the Light List. Daybeacons and minor lights are then also beacons. In fact, in scanning through a Light List one sees relatively few beacons listed, compared with the profusion of other aids. The reason is partly semantic. If what otherwise might be listed as a beacon has a daymark or light put on it, it is then entered under the listing of daybeacon or minor light.

But a few beacons do exist in their own right. In the margin you see an example of one of them, the black and white beacon called Nixes Mate that warns of a shoal passage in Boston Harbor.

Now a look at buoys without lateral significance. The Light List divides these buoys into two categories: information and regulatory buoys, and special-purpose buoys. Information and regulatory buoys are colored white and orange, and the List quotes some of their typical uses as warnings of danger, of restricted operations, or of exclusion areas. Special-purpose buoys are colored yellow; they may be used, among many other possibilities, to designate anchorage areas or dredging or survey sites.

These examples of the uses of buoys without lateral significance don't begin to cover the large variety of uses that actually exists. In fact, the boundaries of the categories sometimes overlap and (it seems to me) a buoy could be put in one category as well as in another. Given this I think it best not to try to define the categories with strict logic and razor sharp definitions, but simply to list some samples of either kind of category and let you make your own inferences. Here then are five examples of each category, culled from the 1987 edition of Light List #1. The number that precedes each item is the number under which it is found in the Light List.

Information and regulatory

10735	New England Aquarium Intake Buoy	Orange and white bands.
20370	Eaton's Neck Rock Buoy	White can with orange near top and waterline, worded DANGER ROCK in orange diamond.
28195	Patchogue Bay Channel Regulatory Buoy	White and orange bands worded 5 MPH NO WAKE.
36171	Troy Dam East Danger Buoy	Orange and white bands with orange diamond; can. Marks turbulent area below dam.

38860	Reedy Island Dike Special Warning Buoy A	White can with orange band near top and waterline. Marks a submerged jetty.

Special-purpose buoys

935	Sewell Point Buoy A	Yellow can marks firing range. "Mariners are cautioned to keep outside buoy and give the area a wide berth."
18300	Test Buoy	Yellow
20392	Hay Island Lighted Mooring Buoy	Yellow spherical buoy.
20785	New London Dumping Ground Lighted Buoy NL	Yellow buoy flashing yellow light, 2.5 sec.
24825	Setauket Harbor Anchorage Buoy A	Yellow nun.

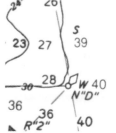

Anchorage buoy.

The first entry above, the Sewell Point buoy that marks the edge of a firing range, is an example of the ambiguity of classification that I mentioned above. It clearly marks a danger and one might think it belongs in the first, information and regulatory, category that warns of danger in other cases. But the Light List thinks otherwise and it is perhaps ours not to wonder why—or to be too pedantic. Ours to keep away from firing ranges, whether they are marked by orange and white *or* yellow buoys.

Minor lights are lighted, fixed (referring to the structure, not the light frequency), relatively small navaids. They can serve as channel navaids, in which case their lights and numbering are based on the conventions for channel buoys, or they can be without lateral significance, with their lights and daymarks modeled on buoys of that class. Minor lights can also be identified at a distance, at least tentatively, by their structure. This can be invaluable if you are trying to sort out some navigational dilemma and the only marks are distant ones. The information on structure is not given on the chart but *is* given in the Light List in such descriptions as: skeleton tower, single pile, cylindrical cement tower, etc. The Light List goes beyond the chart in other ways as well. For example, it gives the characteristic—that is, the on-off pattern—of any sound signal on the navaid.

Minor lights vary greatly in structure and size, and there is no typical one, but the accompanying pictures show two not uncommon types.

Minor lights have weak lights on small structures, but weak and small are relative and, as I noted in Chapter 3, increasingly powerful lights and larger structures begin at some point to be called secondary lights, then

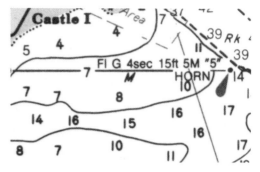

FIGURE 6-10.

Beyond the condensed chart description the Light List adds that the structure is pilings, the daymark is SG (square green), and, in addition to the light characteristics, the horn gives 2 blasts every 30 seconds, as follows: 2 sec blast; 2 sec silence; 2 sec blast; and 24 sec silence.

FIGURE 6-11.

The Light List describes the structure as a gray skeleton tower and adds that the bell sounds 1 stroke every 10 seconds.

primary lights (popularly, "lighthouses"). An example is given in that chapter of the tabulation in the Light List of the important features of Cape Neddick Light—range of the light, characteristics, description of the physical structure, etc. Now I want to take another lighthouse as example and show how the *chart markings* inform us about it—less completely than does the Light List but with crucial information nonetheless.

The light is the Highland Light in Truro, Massachusetts, on the dunes of Cape Cod, and a picture of it appears in Figure 6-12 along with a portion of the chart that describes it in an abbreviated manner. This is what the notation means. Fl 5 sec says that the light flashes once every five seconds; since no color is explicitly stated the light must be white. 183 ft is the height, not of the structure but of the light itself, above mean high water. (The height of the structure is given in the Light List as 66 feet, so the land on which the lighthouse is located is 183 − 66 = 117 feet above MHW.) The notation 23 M signifies that the nominal range of the light, its range on a meteorologically "clear day," is 23 nautical miles. "HORN" of course indicates that a horn is sounded; its sound characteristic is not given but it can be found in the Light List. 286 RBn signifies a radio beacon that operates on a frequency of 286 kHz. The notation •••• •• is the Morse code for HI, the *identifying signal* of the lighthouse. The marking &⸺ means that a continuous *homing signal* is also emitted.

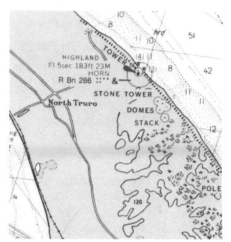

FIGURE 6-12.

7

The Shape of the Land

By now we have looked at a variety of manmade objects that are useful to the coastal navigator in his task: navaids that are specially designed for his use, and landmarks that are equally useful even though they were built for other ends. There are still other aids, although not manmade ones, that are invaluable to the skilled coastal navigator. These are the clues nature herself provides in the shape of the land and its distinctive features—its hummocks and hills, saddles, promontories, cliffs, heights. This chapter is on deciphering these clues.

The clues are well worth deciphering; they have several advantages over manmade ones. They change less rapidly over the years than do navaids or landmarks so that you don't have to find the very latest Light List or chart to have confidence in using them. More important, they are *large.* You can exploit them at distances from which you couldn't possibly see a buoy or even a tower. You can then navigate continuously, always being reasonably certain of where you are, instead of waiting for this or that mark to come into sight and confirm a conjectured position.

The coastal pilot should, then, learn to "read" the features of the land—to translate the markings on the chart to a mental picture of the shape of the land as seen from the deck. The chart shows the view of the hawk: From on high he sees clearly the overall outline of the land, but its hills and hummocks, slopes and cliffs are poorly defined. The sailor on deck close to the water has the view of the duck—and not only because he is so often wet. He can see at one time only a small portion of the land but can clearly see its elevations and contours. The trick is to go from hawk to duck quickly, to reconstruct with confidence and accuracy the sailor's view from the chart markings.

A key to reconstructing the sailor's view lies in the *contour lines* to be found on most large scale charts. (Remember: large scale = large or abundant detail; small scale = small or sparse detail.) Many readers will have some familiarity with contour lines, but I'll review them for those readers who don't.

Consider the very small island, really not much more than a large rock, in the picture below. I call it Egg Rock. It is not far offshore, and someone has conveniently provided next to it a scale in feet so that at any state of the tide the water height can be read. Land elevations are measured in feet above mean high water (MHW). Mean high water is defined as the height of the *average* high tide over the years. Day by day, of course, some high tides will be higher, and some lower, than this average.

FIGURE 7-1.
Egg Rock.

On the scale next to Egg Rock, "0" is marked at the MHW line. We wait for the day of a particularly high tide, and observe as the water comes in and more and more of the rock above zero level is submerged. When the scale reading is 2 feet, the water will have wetted a lower part of the rock, and with my waterproof grease pen I trace out this waterline on the rock. The line I have marked is called a 2-foot contour line, since every point on it is 2 feet above the zero level. When the tide has risen to 4 feet I do the same, then again at 6 feet, etc. I end up with a grease-marked rock that looks like this:

contour lines

FIGURE 7-2.
Contour lines drawn on Egg Rock.

If now we were to photograph Egg Rock from directly above, the network of contour lines, just as they might appear on the chart, would look like this:

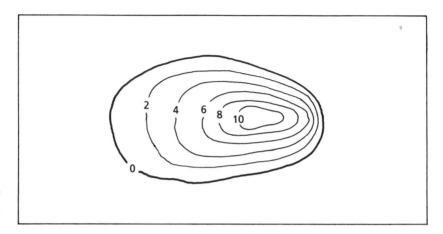

FIGURE 7-3.
Contour lines of Egg Rock, on the chart.

Notice: Where the actual Egg Rock is steep, to the right in its sketch, the chart's contour lines are close together. For the more gradually sloping left-hand side, the chart's contour lines are farther apart. Thus by simply looking at the relative closeness of contour lines on the chart you can tell where the island is steep, and where shallow. You can tell more; you can estimate the island's height. There is a 10-foot contour line shown on the chart, so the island is at least 10 feet high, but there is no 12-foot contour, so it is less than 12 feet high. Given the smallness of the 10-foot contour a guess of 10½ to 11 feet is probably not too far off. You can even say something about the island's shape. The 10-foot contour encloses the highest point, and a glance at Figure 7-3 shows that this highest point is about a quarter of an island-width away from the right-hand side of the island.

the contour interval The difference in height corresponding to any two adjacent contour lines is called the *contour interval.* The contour interval for Egg Rock above is two feet. Because Egg Rock is a made-up example this interval is rather smaller than those encountered on real charts, where typical intervals might be 20, 25, 50, 100 feet. A knowledge of the contour interval is very useful to the navigator; unfortunately it is not stated explicitly on present-day U.S. NOAA charts, although it is stated on the charts of many other countries as well as on U.S. Geological Survey maps. An important point to remember is that the contour interval is the same (even though you may not know it) *everywhere* on a given chart. *All* adjacent contour lines, wherever they are on the chart, represent the same height difference. This fact frequently enables us to deduce the contour interval; I'll give examples later.

As an illustration of these ideas let's look at four imaginary places shown below: Tunacan Island, Dome Island, Duncecap Rock, Circle Ledge. They are all roughly circular and about 100 feet in diameter at their bases; for convenience I will refer to them all as islands. Now these islands would be depicted differently on small and large scale charts. A small scale chart might well not include contour lines so that with one exception, the islands would appear as in the first drawing below, merely as small circles all of the same size. The exception is Circle Ledge. The fact that it is not shown on the first drawing is not a typographical error. As we see, Circle Ledge is so minor, visible only at low water, that it might well not be depicted at all on a small scale chart.

On the other hand, on a chart of large enough scale to include contour lines, the islands might look as in the second series of drawings below. Let's see what we can deduce about the shape of the islands from these drawings.

First, Duncecap Rock, since it gives the clue to the contour interval. Note that the central dot marks the highest point as being 92 feet high, and that there are four contour lines shown. It doesn't take much cleverness to guess that the contour interval is 20 feet, since then the four contour lines correspond to 20, 40, 60, and 80 feet. The fact that there is no fifth line shows the highest point must be at less than 100 feet; this checks nicely with the 92 feet listed. As to the shape, the contour lines are fairly evenly spaced so the steepness of the island is constant throughout its height. These simple criteria lead rather clearly to the

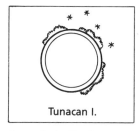 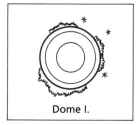 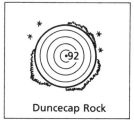 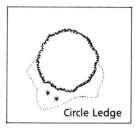

Small Scale Chart

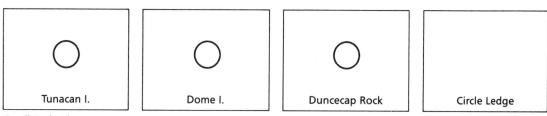

Large Scale Chart

FIGURE 7-4. *Four islands, as they might appear on a small scale chart and on a large scale chart.*

shape I have drawn. Next, let's look at Dome Island. Here two, but not three, contours are shown, so the height is between 40 and 60 feet, or roughly half the diameter as scaled from the chart. Moreover, since the first or 20-foot contour line is close to the line outlining the shape (the zero-foot contour) the rock is steep at its edges, and by the same token is rather shallow toward the middle. That's a pretty good description of Dome Island. Tunacan is slightly more ambiguous. The single contour close to the edge indicates that it is at least 20 feet high but less than 40 feet. From this evidence it might be humped in the middle, up to a 39-foot height, or might be flat as drawn. But even with this small ambiguity, the contour lines clearly distinguish its shape as different from Duncecap Rock or Dome Island.

Circle Ledge, as I have remarked, is a special case. There are no contour lines on it, not even the single, solid zero-height contour that would mark its outline at mean high water. No outline on the chart means no outline on the water—Circle Ledge is not visible near the time of high tide. The irregular, jaggedly indented outline the ledge *does* have, as you can confirm from Chart #1, is the shape of this rock at the "depth of soundings datum," which we can take to mean at a time close to low tide. The dotted line shows the extent of the land around it—sand, mud, or whatever—at that time. In contrast then to the other three islands, which are always above water and whose shape is shown at close to high tide, Circle Ledge appears and disappears in the course of a tidal cycle.

These examples are fairly simple—not every real island has a circular cross section which makes it look the same from all viewing directions. Some can change their shape quite markedly as the viewing direction changes. As an example, consider Saddle Island, shown in the next drawing as it might appear on the chart.

The drawing tells us that there are two high points on Saddle Island. From the number of contour lines surrounding the 172-foot point to the east we deduce that the contour interval is 25 feet, so the high point to the west is between 100 and 125 feet. It is probably closer to 100 feet, given the small area enclosed by the 100-foot contour line. With this information and the chart sketch one can, in a half hour or so at the draw-

Tunacan I.

Dome I.

Duncecap Rock

Circle Ledge — at a time near low tide

FIGURE 7-5. *The four islands.*

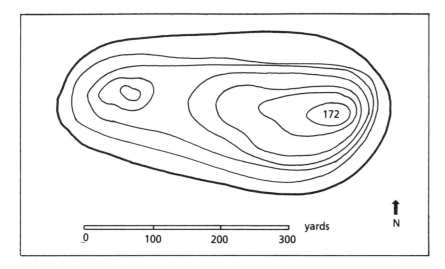

FIGURE 7-6.
Saddle Island, on the chart.

ing board, reconstruct a reasonable facsimile of Saddle Island from any viewing point. One first selects the viewing point—for example, a position one mile due south of the island center. A line is drawn from the viewing point to the center of the island (line of sight). Somewhere between the viewing point and the island a second line is drawn that cuts the line of sight perpendicularly. This line is the position of the *picture plane*—the plane perpendicular to the line of sight on which one can imagine the picture of the island is drawn. Now from the viewing point a line (or ray) is drawn to the left-hand side of the island, a second ray to the leftmost part of the 25-foot contour, a third ray to the leftmost part of the 50-foot contour, etc. Where these rays pierce the picture plane a dot is made (at appropriate scale) to represent sea level for the first ray, 25 feet for the second ray, 50 feet for the third ray, etc. One ends up with a series of dots on the picture plane like the connect-the-dot games in the Sunday comics. If you do connect the dots you get a more or less crude outline of the island.

I have applied this procedure to Saddle Island from two viewpoints; a mile due south and a mile due east. In fact, I have gone beyond the bare connect-the-dots outline, smoothing it out and adding some imaginary detail that doesn't change the basic shape of the island. The results are given below.

from one mile south

from one mile east

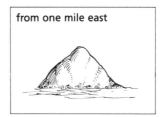

FIGURE 7-7.
Two views of Saddle Island.

It is important to note how quickly one can go, in real-life sailing, from the southern to the eastern viewing points of Saddle Island. I elaborate on this point in Chapter 8, Sailing Among Islands, but for the moment consider this. Saddle Island is only about 1500 feet long so that at four or five knots it takes only a few minutes to get from one end of it to the other, and perhaps only ten or fifteen minutes to go from the southern viewing point shown above to the eastern one, with its radically different shape. If you aren't familiar with this phenomenon and leave the helm to someone else to go below for those minutes, to return to what seems a different island, you may accuse the helmsman of malfeasance or think you are drunk or in a time warp. To avoid these unpleasant possibilities be aware of how quickly an island scene can change and defuse the change by studying the contours in advance so you can anticipate what will happen.

Contour lines aren't the only ways of representing slopes or degrees of steepness on charts. Also used are *hachures,* which are bold, wedge-shaped dashes that are supposed to look like the cross section of an ax blade, hence the name: in French, *hachure* = ax. Hachures, or *hatch marks* as they have come to be called in English, are always at right angles to the local contour lines, and are longest and heaviest where the slope is steepest. The accompanying excerpt from Chart #1 shows the same topography as depicted by contour lines and by hachures.

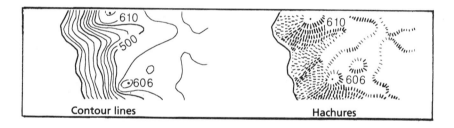

Contour lines   Hachures

Hatch marks are also used to indicate where a coastline is steep, and to give some idea of its height, in cases where contour lines would be so closely spaced as to be impractical. Relatively long hatch marks indicate a high coast and short marks a low one, as you can see in the illustration.

For practice in using contour lines for identification, here are the contour lines of six islands and, in different order, the view of each of them as seen from the south. Which picture goes with what contour?

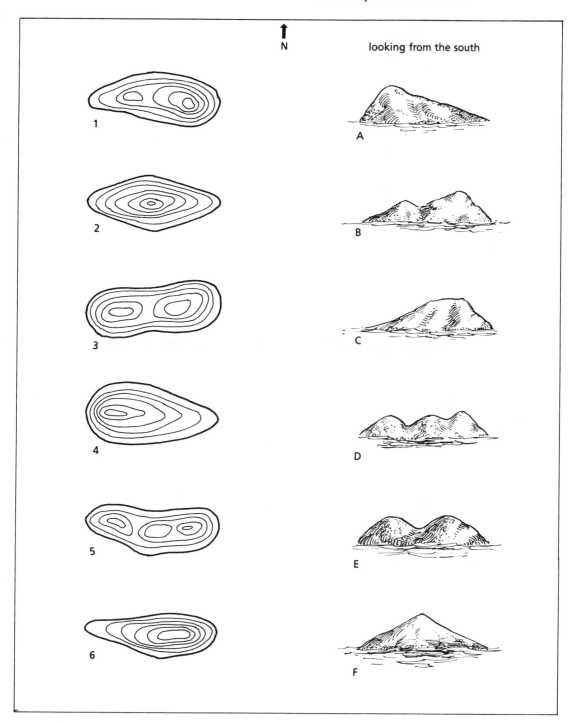

N

looking from the south

FIGURE 7-8.   *For practice, match each set of contour lines to a picture. Does 1 go with A,B,C,D,E, or F? Answers: 1 = B; 2 = F; 3 = E; 4 = A; 5 = D; 6 = C.*

8

Sailing Among Islands

This chapter is about the piloting problems that arise in sailing among islands. I don't mean large islands many miles long, but clusters of islands of medium size—a few hundred feet to a few miles—so that in the course of the day's sailing you pass by at least a few of them. Examples might be the Thousand Islands of the St. Lawrence, the Thimble Islands of Connecticut, the San Juans in Washington, the islands of Maine. . . .

In sailing among islands, as in sailing along a long coast, you want to correlate the chart with the view from the deck—you want to read the shape of the land. But there is one difference; in island sailing you have to be a fast reader. Appearances can change quickly. Recall the dramatic change of shape of Saddle Island in Chapter 7 in the relatively few minutes it takes to go from the south to the east of it. When there are many islands the difficulties compound quickly and there are many ways to be confused. Two islands can merge into one as the first obstructs the view of the second. Spires, chimneys, even lighthouses that are visible from one viewpoint can be completely hidden from another. An island with several hills or hummocks on it can appear, especially from a distance, as two or three islands. The low, sprawling island that was so visible at low tide may shrink dramatically when the tide rolls in.

The maxim about one picture and ten thousand words is especially relevant here, so the accompanying drawing shows the changing appearance of three small islands in the hour or so that it takes for a boat to pass them.

In sailing among islands it is common, even inevitable, that on occasion a closer island will partially hide an island behind it, leaving only part of the further island visible. Sometimes the two islands so blend visually that it is not clear where the one ends and the other begins. On the other hand, the islands may be distinguishable from one another, usually for one of two reasons. First, their silhouettes may be so different that there is an obvious discontinuity at the end of the closer island, where the silhouettes join. Or if the observer is near enough to the closer island, its details of topography, foliage, etc. will be seen as darker and

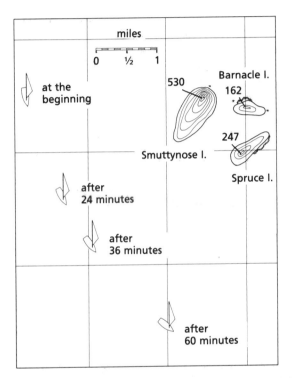

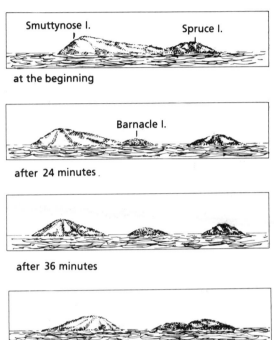

FIGURE 8-1. *In the hawk's-eye view you see the good ship* Lyria *running southeasterly in view of Smuttynose, Barnacle, and Spruce islands. In the other drawings you see the pictures they present at various times within the hour. The drawings are not figments of the artist's imagination; they are carefully constructed from the chart scale and contour heights in the hawk's-eye view.*

At the beginning, Barnacle I. is hidden, and part of Spruce appears beyond Smuttynose. It is unlikely, however, that you could distinguish where Smuttynose ends and Spruce begins, especially if their surface textures and vegetation were similar.

● After 24 minutes Spruce is well separated visually from Smuttynose, and Barnacle begins to emerge. If the latter has a different texture you might be able to distinguish it from Smuttynose; otherwise you would see only two landmasses separated by water.

● After 36 minutes, however, the three islands would definitely be distinct, with water gaps between them. (You can verify this with a straightedge applied to the drawing.)

● After 60 minutes Barnacle moves behind Spruce and there appear to be two landmasses again.

The picture has not been drawn above, but after only another 40 minutes Barnacle would be completely behind Spruce, and the water gap between Spruce and Smuttynose would disappear so that there would again appear to be only one island—but of a much different shape than at the beginning!

sharper than those of the further island, so there will be no question as to which is which.

One can't make a consistent rule for when two island silhouettes will or will not merge; it all depends on the particular islands. But I have observed a general, if rough, rule for predicting crudely when visual details will blend. Here it is, for what it is worth. If on a reasonably clear day the observer's *distance to* the front island is about the same as the *distance between* front and back islands, the front one will be darker and with sharper detail and so be distinguishable from the back island. If the *distance to* is moderately larger, say two or possibly even three times as large as the *distance between,* there may still be a detectable difference between the appearances of the front and back islands. But if the *distance to* is much larger than the *distance between,* say more than four or five times larger, the two islands will blend visually.

Obviously this rough-and-ready "rule" is meant to apply on a reasonably clear day. If it is so foggy that you can't see the back island, then all bets are off.

These remarks are illustrated by the pictures below of Spectacle Island as seen behind Thompson's. Shown first are the islands as seen on the chart. Notice that the distance to the left end of Thompson's is a little more than twice the distance between the islands, so that from the "rule" above you might expect a detectable but not striking difference in the appearance of the islands. In fact, in the picture below, you will see that the closer island is noticeably darker. If, however, the viewing point were more distant, say twice the distance of the above case, the darkness and detail would be so similar that it might be hard to tell where one island ends and the other begins. Sometimes looking through binoculars helps in such cases, sometimes not; much depends on the clarity of the atmosphere. Note incidentally that the silhouettes of the two islands merge so smoothly that, by that criterion alone, they give no clue to the fact that there are indeed two of them.

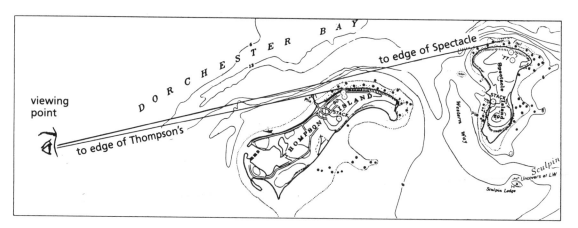

FIGURE 8-2. *Part of Spectacle Island can be seen beyond the edge of Thompson's I.*

edge of Spectacle I.

edge of Thompson's I.

FIGURE 8-3.
The silhouettes of Thompson's and Spectacle islands merge smoothly, but the closer island appears darker and sharper.

Here is a portion of a chart to a scale of 1:94,000. Below it is a photograph looking toward Peddock's Island from the viewing point marked on the chart portion. One sees three islands—A, B, and C. Which one is Peddock's?

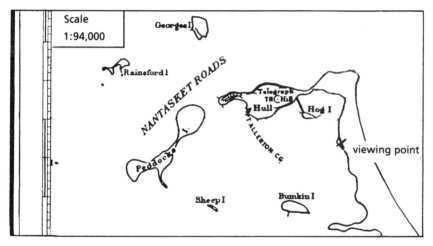

Scale
1:94,000

Georges I

Rainsford I

NANTASKET ROADS

Telegraph
TR Hill
Hull
Hog I

ALLERTON C.

viewing point

Peddock's I.

Sheep I

Bumkin I

FIGURE 8-4.
Peddock's Island on the chart.

A   B   C

FIGURE 8-5.
Peddock's Island seen from "viewing point."

The answer is: They all are. How can that be? First, let me say it in words. It is easily possible, by virtue of "accidents" of topography, that one island can appear as two or more. The word "accidents" is in quotes because this phenomenon is not really unusual or accidental; it has misled me many a time.

To see how one island can become three in the present case let's look at the clarifying contours on Peddock's Island as seen on a large scale (1:30,000) chart. Here it is, along with the solution to the mystery. On the northern part of the island the pair of hills marked as 123 and 100 feet high on the chart are seen as a unit as "Island" C. The island becomes less than 20 feet high (and from the observer's vantage point, invisible) on the narrow neck south of these hills before rising again to a hummock, which joins visually with the 90-foot height of West Head behind it to produce "Island" B. As the eye sweeps still farther south it sees, or rather doesn't see, the narrow strip, less than 20 feet high, connecting Prince's Head with the rest of the island. But then it *does* see Prince's Head— "Island" A.

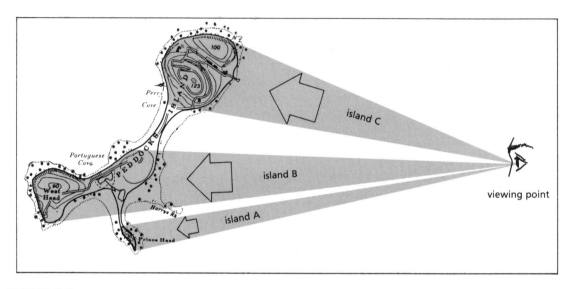

FIGURE 8-6.
Solution to the "mystery of three islands."

So the paradox is resolved. You have to get used to unconventional arithmetic in island sailing. One can easily equal three and three often is equivalent to one.

The puzzling aspects of which island in a cluster is what can sometimes be sorted out with this old trick. Hold the folded chart with your ship's position near the edge and your eye just above that position, then scan across the chart in the direction of the islands. In this way you get closer to the duck's-eye view (instead of the hawk's view) of the chart to compare with the duck's-eye view you get on deck, and this comparison can often resolve a dilemma.

In identifying an individual island it is often useful to know its height, which can then be related to some horizontal dimension read from the chart scale. And in distinguishing one island from a neighbor it is often useful to know their relative heights; two islands may have undistinctive silhouettes, but if the chart tells you that one is three times the height of the other you don't have to look much farther to tell which is which.

Heights can be inferred approximately from contour lines, or they may be explicitly stated on the chart as in the example above of Peddock's Island. But there are two complications in using these heights—tidal range and vegetation. On the chart, the height of an island is given as height above mean high water. At lower states of the tide its height above sea water level will be greater. With an island a few hundred feet high, say, and a tidal range of a few feet you can neglect this correction for practical purposes. But with smaller islands and larger ranges you may want to include it. What I often do is add half the tidal range to the listed height. For a 10-foot range I add 5 feet and know I'll be right on the nose at mid-tide and not more than 5 feet off at mean high or mean low tides.

Vegetation is trickier. The listed heights are of the land itself, not the vegetation. A heavily wooded island will then appear higher, by the average tree height, than the chart indicates. Whether or not you have to worry about this obviously depends on the islands where you are sailing. In the Virgins or off Southern California the islands may be hundreds of feet high and the vegetation sparse, so you can forget about it. In Maine on the other hand the spruce or fir that often covers an island is usually about 40 to 60 feet tall, so that if you add 50 feet as an average you are not too far off. Wherever you sail you can get some idea of the average vegetation height and add it to the chart height. The result may not be perfectly accurate, but it is useful.

The necessity of adding vegetation height to the charted height of an island to get the observed height may be obvious, but I found it out the hard way. Sailing in Maine one day I saw two neighboring islands, of which the first, I inferred from the chart, was about 20 feet high and the other somewhat more than 50. This factor of almost three in their heights should have been strikingly obvious from on deck, but it wasn't—although the one did appear to be somewhat higher than the other. After puzzling for a while I found the answer in simple arithmetic. Both were spruce-covered, and a 20-foot charted island with 50-foot spruces is a 70-foot island. A 50-foot island with 50-foot spruces merely becomes a 100-foot one—not all that different from its 70-foot neighbor.

SECTION III

Knowing All
the Angles

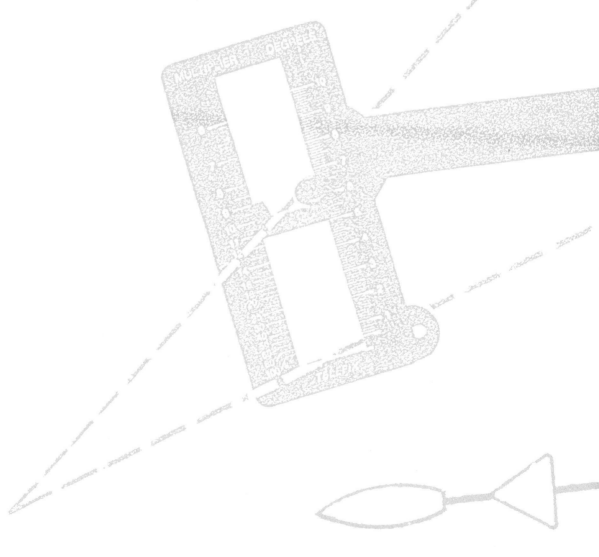

9

Angles and the Rule of Sixty

Later in this book we will have much to do with angles of one kind or another, including vertical angles defined by the heights of lighthouses or hills, horizontal angles between two navaids or landmarks, and the angle (called the magnetic heading) between the boat's direction and the direction of magnetic north. The main aim of this chapter is to introduce some simple formulae that will facilitate the use of such angles. An important one of these is called the Rule of Sixty; it is prominently displayed below. The next few paragraphs are devoted to deriving the Rule of Sixty, and I have tried to keep this derivation simple. But if even the few equations of these paragraphs are not clear or are intimidating, feel free to bypass them and go directly to the Rule of Sixty itself. (But if you do, *please* use the saved time usefully—for example, in studying Chart #1.)

Angles are so common, so everyday, that I will not attempt a fancy mathematical definition but simply direct your attention to the angle in the right-hand side of Figure 9-1. Two lines meet at a point; the angle is what is in between. But there is an alternative and equivalent concept of angle. An angle is also defined by an arc, a portion of the circumference of a circle. In fact this definition is the more basic one. The equivalence of angle-as-arc and angle-as-intersecting-lines is illustrated in Figure 9-1. Given an arc of a circle, we draw the radii from its two ends to generate the two intersecting lines that we ordinarily think of as an *angle*.

Angle-as-arc is basic since the unit of angle measurement is based on it. We always measure in terms of some unit: length in units of meters or feet, etc.; weight in units of pounds or kilos, etc. The unit of measurement of the angle is, as you know, called the *degree*. It is defined by dividing the circumference of a circle into 360 equal parts, 360 tiny arcs. The angle associated with each of these parts is taken to be the unit angle—the degree.

Why the number 360 and not another? It sounds arbitrary; it *is* arbitrary. Any other number could have been chosen. In fact there are proponents of a redefinition of the degree by a 100-part division, and they are right in saying that this would be more rational and convenient in many ways. But the 360-part division is so firmly entrenched in both our lives and our instruments that it is unlikely it will be changed soon. We can blame the Babylonians or some other ancient race for whatever inconvenience 360 degrees entails, for it was in antiquity that the number was chosen. The choice is connected with the fact that the earth takes about 360 days to complete its approximately circular orbit around the sun.

Given the 360-degree convention we can measure the number of degrees in any angle by considering it an angle-as-arc. If the total circumference of the circle contains 360°, then an arc that is half as long, the arc of a semicircle, contains 180°; the arc of a quarter circle contains 90°; an arc that is 0.62 times as long as the circumference contains $0.62 \times 360° = 223.2°$. In general then, the magnitude of any angle A is determined by dividing its arc length by the circumference of the circle of which the arc is part.

$$A° = 360 \times \frac{\text{Arc length}}{\text{Circumference}}$$

As another way of writing this, suppose the radius of the circle is R. The circumference is then $2\pi R$, and the exact formula for angle A is:

$$A° = \frac{360}{2\pi} \times \frac{\text{Arc length}}{\text{Radius}}$$

exact formula

The relationship is depicted graphically in Figure 9–2.

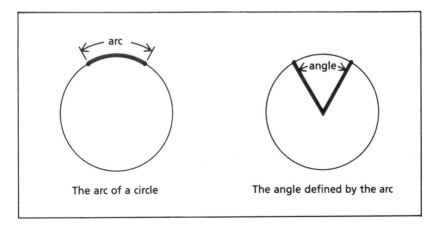

The arc of a circle   The angle defined by the arc

FIGURE 9-1.
Angle-as-arc and angle-as-intersecting-lines.

The angle of 223.2° just mentioned is an example of a *decimal degree,* since it is the whole number 223 plus the decimal fraction 0.2. As you probably know, fractions of a degree are also expressed in *angular minutes* (no connection with minutes of time) with sixty such minutes to one degree:

$$\text{One degree} = 60 \text{ minutes}$$

Then 0.2° corresponds to 0.2° × 60 = 12 minutes (12′), so that 223.2° can also be written as 223° 12′. When angles are measured very precisely, as in celestial navigation, there is a further division of the angular minute into sixty angular seconds, but that won't concern us here.

Now for the Rule of Sixty. In coastal piloting a long, thin triangle often shows up in one context or another. The triangle may be isosceles (two sides of equal length) or it may be a right triangle, which is a triangle that contains one right, or 90°, angle (Figure 9–3).

Frequently one wants to find the angle A when the lengths of L and S are known. One might first think of drawing the triangle to scale and measuring A with a protractor, but for small angles (a few degrees) this is inaccurate as well as clumsy. Happily there are easy approximate formulas, of which the Rule of Sixty is one, for finding A. To get at them let's first think in terms of the isosceles triangle in Figure 9–3, comparing it with the drawing in Figure 9–2. The two drawings resemble each other closely, with two differences: First, "radius" in Figure 9–2 becomes L in Figure 9–3; second, Figure 9–2 refers to the "arc length," whereas the straight side of length S is referred to above. It is clear, however, for small angles that arc length is so close to S, or in other words the arc is so close to a straight line, that one can approximate arc length by S. If then,

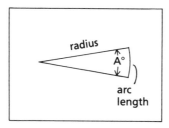

FIGURE 9–2.

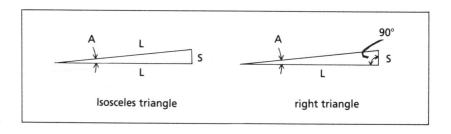

Isosceles triangle   right triangle

FIGURE 9-3.

we substitute L for radius and S for arc length in the Exact Formula above, and further use the time-honored approximation of 3.14 for π and set $360/2\pi$ equal to 57.3, we have:

$$A° = 57.3 \frac{S}{L}$$

Strictly speaking the equals sign is inappropriate in this formula since the left-hand side doesn't precisely equal the right-hand side, but with this understanding I leave it in place.

   This formula has been derived for the isosceles triangle, but it is clear that even for the right triangle the arc length is reasonably approximated by the side S. In short, we can consider the Approximate Formula applies to *both* isosceles and right triangles. As an indication of its accuracy let's apply it to a right triangle for which L = 10, using the three cases S = 1, 2, and 3. The exact results for A can be found by some simple trigonometry; the approximate ones are calculated from the formula above. Here is the comparison.

	Exact	**Approximate Formula**
S = 1	5.72	5.73
S = 2	11.3	11.5
S = 3	16.7	17.2

   Finally, the Rule of Sixty. This is derived simply by approximating the number 57.3 in the Approximate Formula as 60, because the number 60 is easier to remember and easier to multiply. Remember again that despite the equals sign this is not an equality but an approximation.

$$A° = 60 \frac{S}{L}$$

The Rule of Sixty is never as accurate as the first Approximate Formula above, since it always gives results that at best are too large by the factor $60/57.3 = 1.045$, but it is convenient and adequate for many purposes. There will be many examples of its use later in this book. It can also prove useful in the alternative forms $L = 60S/A°$ and $S = LA°/60$.

   In various articles and books I have seen the *sixty* in the Rule of Sixty "explained" by a somewhat woolly reference to the fact that there are sixty minutes to a degree or sixty seconds to a minute. This is incorrect. As we have just seen, the *sixty* in the formula enters only as a convenient approximation to 57.3.

10

Bearings

The word "bearing" is used with two somewhat different senses. Sometimes it may simply mean a rough sense of direction. We may have been sailing down the coast with you at the helm; the land and its features are familiar to you. You go below for a half hour or so, and when you return you are confused about the relation of chart to shoreline. You say "I seem to have lost my bearings." "That's easy" I say, and I point. "There's Ferguson's Bluff and that's Smuttynose and there is the lighthouse on Egg Rock." You say "Of course, thanks." You have got back your bearings, your sense of direction.

Beyond this loose meaning there is a more precise definition that we will be using: bearing as angle. An angle is simple; it is made by two lines that come together at a point. At the risk of being overfussy, let's look at each of these lines separately.

A bearing is always of some object—such as lighthouse, buoy, spire—as seen by a more or less distant observer. The first line of the bearing angle, the *sightline,* is drawn *from* the observer *to* the object. In Figure 10-1 this is the line between the observer on the boat and the tower.

The second line is some reference line—several different ones are possible—drawn from the observer's position. The bearing is the angle, measured clockwise from 0° to 360°, between the reference line and sightline. There are three important reference lines:

> 1. The direction of true north. On the chart the longitude lines run from true north to south.

78

2. The direction of magnetic north. At any point on the earth's surface, magnetic north is the direction in which a compass needle points. On the chart it is the direction from the center of a compass rose to the zero-degree mark on the inner, or magnetic, graduated circle.

3. The centerline of the ship.

The corresponding bearings from these reference lines are called *true bearings, magnetic bearings,* and *relative bearings,* and are illustrated in Figure 10-2.

Since they are all angles, different kinds of bearings can be added or subtracted and one kind of bearing can be expressed in terms of another, as is evident from Figure 10-3. As an example, since the angle between the directions of true and magnetic north is called the *variation,* then: True bearing = Magnetic bearing + Variation.

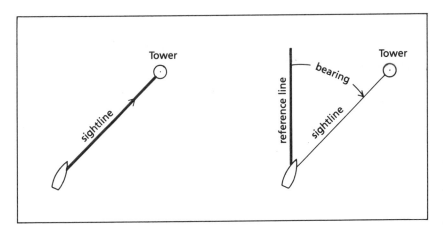

FIGURE 10-1.
The first line of the bearing angle is the sightline drawn from the observer to the object. The second line of the bearing angle is one of several possible reference lines.

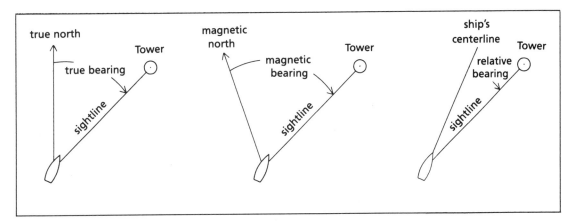

FIGURE 10-2. *True, magnetic, and relative bearings.*

I have been discussing the bearing of a lighthouse as seen *from* the ship. But there equally well might be an observer on the lighthouse who takes a bearing *of* the ship. This latter bearing is the *reciprocal bearing* of the first; numerically it always differs from the first by 180°. To see this let us construct the reciprocal bearing angle according to the recipe above when, say, the reference line is true north. In Figure 10-4 then, we first draw the sightline from lighthouse to ship; then the reference line starting at the lighthouse; finally, the angle running clockwise *from* the reference line *to* the sightline. From the drawing it is obvious that:

Reciprocal bearing = Bearing + 180°

Reciprocal bearings are used in Light Lists in a description of a light's sector. Consider the red sector of the light in Figure 10-5; it goes between east and southeast. You would understand me if I were to say that the sector sweeps from 90° to 135° on the chart. In effect, 90° is the bearing of some point on the upper edge of the sector as seen *from* the light-house, and similarly for the 135° that defines the lower edge. In a Light List, however, the sector would be described in terms of the 270° bearing of the lighthouse as seen *by* an observer on the top edge of the sector and the 315° bearing of the lighthouse as seen from the bottom edge. The Light List would simply have under "Remarks": "Shows red from 270° to 315°." The reason for this convention is that it is obviously more convenient for the mariner, who is in fact taking bearings *of* the lighthouse *from* his ship.

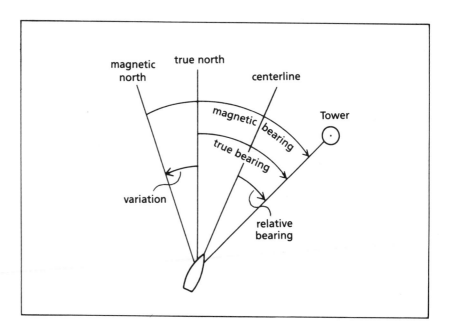

FIGURE 10-3.
Relations of the different kinds of bearings.

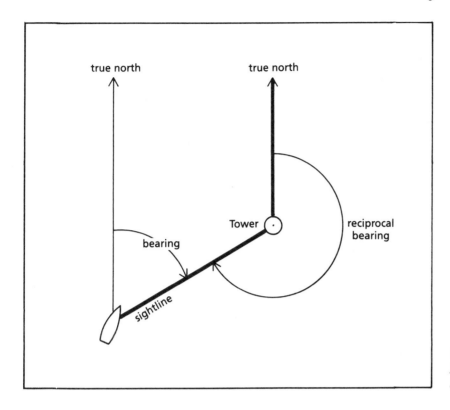

FIGURE 10-4.
Bearing and reciprocal bearing.

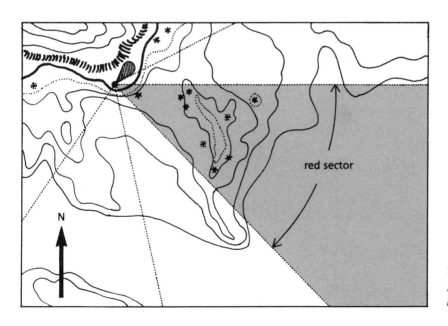

FIGURE 10-5.
Lighthouse with 45-degree red sector.

The relative bearing defined above is an angle that sweeps clockwise from 0° to 360°, starting at the ship's centerline. This conventional definition is fine for some purposes, but it is not very intuitive. If a helmsman on a magnetic course of 19° asks where the danger rock is and I say its relative bearing is 349°, he will probably just look pained and confused. But if instead I say it is 30° off the port bow (which is the same thing), he will understand me immediately. It is then much more convenient to measure relative bearings as going from 0° to 90° (occasionally to 180°) off the port or starboard bow. If I am facing forward and see an object on the starboard side I define its *starboard bow angle* or its *starboard bow bearing* as one measured clockwise from the centerline to the line of sight to the object. For an object seen on the port side the similar angles measured counterclockwise from the centerline are of course the *port bow angle* or *port bow bearing*. These angles will be important in Chapter 13 on the orientation program.

11

Measuring Angles on Deck

The cryptic phrase that is the title of this section of the book—Knowing All the Angles—is obviously meant to suggest that angles are important in coastal navigation. It also suggests three questions: What angles are useful? How do we measure them? How do we exploit the measurement results? I try to answer the first two questions in this chapter. The multiple answers to the last question will appear and reappear in the rest of the book.

For a pictorial synopsis of the subjects of this chapter look at its first three figures: *vertical angles, horizontal angles,* and *bow angles.* Let's look at the instruments and techniques for measuring them.

A vertical angle for the lighthouse of Figure 11-1 is formed by the sightlines of an observer to its light and base; there is an analogous angle for other kinds of vertical structures or landmarks — stacks, standpipes, cliffs, etc. These angles are useful in finding the distance from the vertical

vertical angles

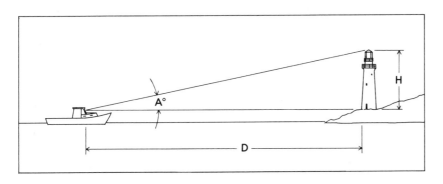

FIGURE 11-1.
Vertical angle.

object. If, from a chart listing or other means, the height H is known and the angle A can be measured, then the distance D can be found, for example, by the Rule of Sixty: D = 60 H/A°. Useful vertical angles are usually small. For example, a 100-foot lighthouse seen from one nautical mile away will have a vertical angle of only one degree. (Rule of Sixty: 1° = 60 × 100 feet / 6080.) Rarely are we interested in vertical angles of more than 10°.

horizontal angles

A *horizontal angle,* illustrated below, is simply the angle between the sightlines of an observer to two objects of about the same height. This angle is useful because it implies an *angular circle of position* (COP), somewhere on which the observer must be located. An angular COP is illustrated below. That an angle on deck implies a circle on the chart is not intuitively obvious; much more detail is given in later chapters. But it is a fact nonetheless, and "large angle" (greater than 30°) circles of position are used routinely, both in marine surveying and by the Coast Guard in setting its buoys accurately.

The angular circles of position for "small" angles, less than 10°, are also very useful but they have to be dealt with rather differently than do large-angle COPs. On the chart, for example, a large-angle COP can be drawn with a pencil compass, but for small angles, as it turns out, the circles get so large that an ordinary compass won't do, and other techniques are used.

bow angles

The final angle we consider is the *bow angle* of a shore object as seen from the deck: the angle between the object, seen either to port or starboard, and the ship's centerline (Figure 11-3). This angle is useful in sorting out and relating what is seen on the deck to what is shown on the chart, as I discuss in Chapter 13.

So much for the angles; now let's look at how to measure them. I will begin by discussing two instruments that do *not* solve the problem of measuring vertical or horizontal angles from the deck of a small boat. These are the *pelorus* and the *sextant.*

You will ask: why bother? Why take time to consider non-solutions to a problem? The answer is that the pelorus and sextant are often men-

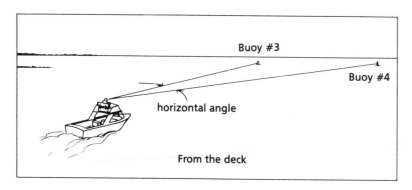

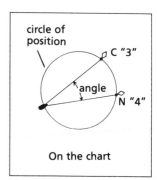

FIGURE 11-2. *A horizontal angle and the circle of position it implies on the chart.*

tioned, and even recommended, in books on piloting—usually big-boat piloting. I would like to put them in what is, in my opinion, their proper perspective.

First the pelorus. A basic one is shown in the margin; many minor variants are possible. It consists first of a circle marked on a flat base and graduated from 0° to 360°. Two vertical sights are held at opposite ends of a diameter by being fixed to a flat member that pivots around the center of the circle.

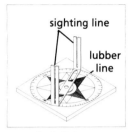

Basic Pelorus

The pelorus is similar in principle to other well-known land instruments. For example, the surveyor's theodolite or transit is basically the same: a graduated circle and a sighting telescope instead of sighting vanes. Pelorus or theodolite are eminently satisfactory for measuring horizontal or vertical angles—on land. You sight first an object in the telescope or sighting vanes and read the angular scale. You then rotate the telescope or vane until a second object is centered, and again read the angular scale. Subtract the two readings, and there is your angle. You can, of course, take as much time as you like between readings since the instrument is fixed and stable. Take the reading for object A; take a nap or have a beer; later take the reading for object B. Subtract the two readings.

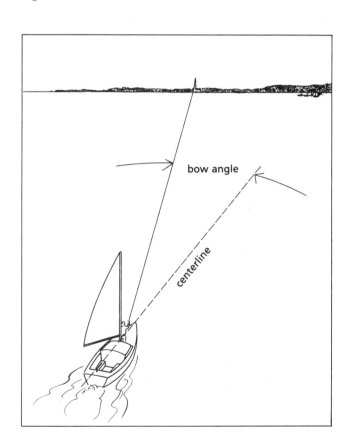

FIGURE 11-3.
Port bow angle.

*limitations of
the pelorus*

A small boat is different. What you *cannot* do on a small boat is wait between readings. Obviously, if the boat—the instrument platform—moves between readings, the measurement is invalidated, and it is thus meaningless to subtract one reading from the other. And on a small boat you can't guarantee that even in the few seconds between readings the boat won't move. You can't, therefore, use the pelorus to take two successive sights except on the calmest days.

There is one case where two sights are not needed to get a useful angle, and that is in measuring the bow angle of a shore object. To effect this, the pelorus is installed so its *lubberline*—the line through the center of the circle and the zero degree mark—is accurately parallel to the centerline of the boat.

If you sight on a shore object, the single angle reading you get will be the bow angle (or relative bearing, as it is also known). This relative bearing can be useful—on a big boat—in finding *distance off by two successive relative bearings.* But for a variety of reasons discussed in Chapter 23, this technique of finding distance off is not satisfactory for small boats.

The pelorus can also be used on a big boat to take a magnetic bearing of a shore object when other methods aren't satisfactory. The technique requires two crew members, one of whom reads the ship's compass while the other simultaneously (it is hoped) reads the pelorus. The method is not particularly satisfactory on large boats and is too complicated to be generally useful on a small boat. Moreover, in any of these uses of the pelorus, its lubberline must be carefully aligned with the centerline of the boat—not an easy task on a small craft. The pelorus should be sited so that it has an unobstructed view in all directions, which is also not easy to realize on your average 25- or 30-footer. Once again we see that a big boat's navigational techniques and instruments are not those of a small boat.

The sextant. This is a lovely instrument and nothing I write here should be construed as criticizing the sextant *per se.* I will just be discussing its suitability for measuring horizontal or vertical angles.

In its commonest use, in celestial navigation, the sextant measures the vertical angle between two objects. The first "object" is the horizon and the second some astronomical body—sun, moon, star, or planet. For brevity I will write in terms of the sun, by which in fact I mean its bottom edge (lower limb) since that is what is usually sighted. But the same ideas will apply to any astronomical body or object.

With the sextant, unlike the pelorus or theodolite, both objects are sighted simultaneously. The one object, the horizon, is seen directly through the clear half of a small glass rectangle, the *horizon glass.* The other half of the horizon glass is silvered to form a mirror, and an image of the sun is seen in it. This image appears by virtue of its having been reflected off another mirror, the *index mirror,* which can be made to rotate. In practice, the index mirror is rotated by an *index arm* until the horizon in the clear half of the horizon glass and the sun in the silvered half line up side by side. The angle through which the index mirror was rotated to effect this is measured, and from it is derived the angle between horizon and sun.

All this is fine in principle, but there can be problems in practice. Aside from atmospheric problems—haze, clouds, or heavy dusk,—sextant measurements are affected by boat motion. If you are taking a sun sight and the ship is bobbing up and down, the horizon as seen in the horizon glass will also bob up and down and may even bob up and out of the glass or bob down and out of it. The sun's image also moves in its silvered half, not only up and down but left and right, and on a really rough day it may be impossible to get the horizon and the sun to line up with each other.

From the brief theoretical description above it should be clear that the sextant can in principle measure *any* vertical angle, not only celestial ones, and that when it is turned on its side it can measure horizontal ones as well. But let's look now not at the theory but at the practice of measuring the angles of present interest—small vertical angles and large and small horizontal ones. I consider large horizontal angles first, since they are the most challenging.

Sad to relate, it is much harder to measure large horizontal angles than it is to measure the vertical angles of celestial navigation, which also are usually large. There is a variety of reasons. First, in the celestial case you are looking at two easily identifiable objects: the sun with nothing to camouflage it, and the horizon, which is not only easily identifiable but is large, usually extending far to the left and right. In measuring horizontal angles you *may* have easily identifiable objects—a lighthouse, or tank, or spire on top of a hill—but equally often you have two navaids or landmarks that are less conspicuous, and it is hard to keep the one in constant sight in the clear half of the horizon glass while you try to bring the other into view, then into coincidence, in the index glass. The problem is worse than in the celestial case, where the horizon can be lost to sight by moving up or down out of the horizon glass but can't be lost by moving left or right because there is almost always more horizon to be seen on either side. If instead of the horizon you must sight an object that is more nearly a point than a line, it can be lost through all sides of the clear horizon glass, as can the other object out of the index glass.

Also, if the objects aren't in the same horizontal plane, as is often the case—navaid by the water's edge and tank on a hill—you have to tilt the sextant from the horizontal, thus making life more difficult still. In short, if there is any motion in the boat it is very hard to measure large horizontal angles, much harder than measuring the vertical angles of celestial navigation, and these can be difficult enough.

If I appear to belabor the point that large horizontal angles are difficult on a small boat it is in reaction to certain statements in the literature that promote them thoughtlessly. Horizontal angles can be used in prin-

limitations of the sextant

ciple in a procedure called the *three-point fix,* which, given three objects A, B, and C, requires the measurement of the horizontal angle between A and B and that between B and C.

This three-point fix procedure, which, I repeat, necessitates the successive measurements of *two* horizontal angles, is sometimes touted as a useful navigational technique when other methods fail. One reads for example in Chapman's that "this procedure is useful on any boat, but it can be especially valuable in a sailboat in rough weather or when racing. Under such conditions the taking of accurate bearings across the steering compass, or with a handbearing compass, may be very difficult."

I heartily disagree with these remarks. I would very much like to learn from someone the secret of measuring horizontal angles in weather too rough to permit a bearing with a handbearing compass. Reed's Nautical Almanac has more candor and more common sense (1987 edition, p. 229). "It must be realized that the method requires smooth operating conditions. In a small vessel, even with moderate sea conditions, a reliable three-point fix becomes extremely difficult." Amen.

For *small* horizontal and vertical angles the sextant is much easier to use than for large, and is a quite feasible instrument. It is also true however that there are other satisfactory devices for measuring these angles. Although I do have a sextant aboard, and cherish it, I tend to use these others because they are simpler and hence more foolproof, adequately accurate, and most important, rugged enough for the knockabout atmosphere of a small boat's cockpit.

alternative methods of angle measurement

All of these methods are based on one ancient idea—the transverse calibrated scale—as shown in Figure 11-4. Essentially, a scale is held a definite distance D from the eye and is kept perpendicular to the observer's sightline to it (hence *transverse*). The scale is calibrated by horizontal lines whose spacing, as seen by the observer, corresponds to a degree or a convenient fraction of a degree of vertical angle. The scale is shown as floating in space, but in practice there is, of course, some means of holding it and of making constant the distance D. You use the scale to measure the vertical angle of Tank by moving it up or down until the base

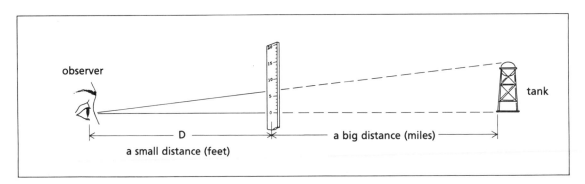

FIGURE 11-4. *Calibrated scale for measuring a vertical angle.*

of Tank is seen at the scale's zero; then you read the size of the angle at the point on the scale where the top of Tank is seen.

The calibration can be done in a variety of ways. For small angles, up to about 10°, you can use the Approximate Formula on page 77 to find:

$$\text{Spacing between one degree angle marks} = D/57.3$$

Thus if you took D to be a convenient 28.6 cm., the degree marks would be a half centimeter apart (28.6/57.3 = ½).

Obviously you can turn this scale on its side to measure horizontal angles. Moreover it does not have the defect of the pelorus. If the angle is not too large—if it is less than the 30- or 40-degree angle of your cone of vision—you can see both top and bottom at the same time, so there is no need to take two successive readings. And unlike the sextant, the image doesn't tend to disappear if hand or boat is unsteady and your attention is momentarily diverted. Also, the scale is more rugged than the sextant. (In fairness to the noble sextant, however, the transverse scale is not as accurate in those conditions of perfect tranquility that allow a sextant to be used.)

Since the principle of the transverse scale is so simple it is not surprising that over the centuries there have been many practical realizations of it. One of the oldest is called the *cross-staff.* You see it to the right being used by an Ancient Mariner to measure the angle between the horizon and a star. The principle here is a slight variant on that above. In the cross-staff, a transverse scale (or *traversal*) of *fixed* width is used but it delineates different angles as it is moved along the staff (the longitudinal member). Then the staff itself is calibrated in terms of the now *variable* distance D.

One disadvantage of the cross-staff is that it requires several different sizes of traversals to get a useful range of angles, because the traversal can't be closer to the eye than perhaps 12 to 15 inches and still permit the average eye to focus on it. And it can't conveniently be farther away than the length of the arm that moves it, a distance of perhaps twice 12 to 15 inches. Roughly then, the factor of two between closest and farthest positions of the traversal means a factor of two in the angle range of any single traversal. So, if you wanted to measure angles between 5° and 40°, you would require three traversals, one each for the ranges 5° to 10°, 10° to 20°, and 20° to 40°.

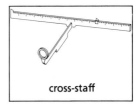

cross-staff

An even older realization of the principle of the transverse scale is the kamal or El-Kamal (meaning guiding line) of early Indian and Arabic navigators. Like the cross-staff, the kamal has a rectangular piece of wood, a *kamal traversal,* for sighting. Instead of a staff along which the traversal moves, the kamal traversal is held at various distances from the eye by a lanyard, imparting to it the advantage of compactness. The lanyard has a series of knots on it, and by touching one or another of the knots to the nose or cheekbone, the distance of the traversal from the eye is varied. The angle varies predictably with this distance. The kamal suffers the disadvantage of the cross-staff in requiring a series of different sizes of traversals if it is to cover an extensive range of angles.

To get around the need for multiple traversals a natural idea would be to use the calibrated transverse scale of Figure 11-4. This could be combined with a lanyard to fix the distance D to produce a compact, modern kamal. This would, in fact, be fine—on land. But on a boat, the old problem of motion messes things up. Let's see why.

FIGURE 11-5.
The kamal.

Suppose I am trying to measure the vertical angle of a lighthouse with a handheld scale in front of me. I must first move the scale up or down until the bottom of the lighthouse is on the scale's zero. I must then observe where on the upper part of the scale the top of the lighthouse is seen. Since it won't usually be seen exactly on a calibration line, I must quickly read the number of the nearest calibration line and interpolate mentally. This can be done in a second or two—or perhaps three—or four if the boat is rolling and pitching. But this reading and interpolation does take enough time that, having done it, I must check to see that the bottom of the lighthouse is still on the zero. With boat motion it probably won't be, so I must readjust it, and having done that look to the top of the lighthouse to check it, and then. . . . I have tried this, and in my experience the process often has not converged. In any kind of seaway, it may simply be impossible to get a reading. The hand, eye, and brain may have to work more quickly together to make the process effective than they are capable of doing.

This problem is much alleviated in a modern version of the kamal that I devised and manufacture. It is called Telefix, and is shown in Figure 11-6. It has a chain lanyard that fits around the neck and a calibrated vertical angle scale, but the scale is on the side of a rectangular viewing aperture within the frame of the instrument. A horizontal slide that moves up or down can, in effect, change the height of the aperture. In use the slide is moved up or down until the aperture is just the right height to frame the object visually. With this done the scale is brought closer to the eye to read it carefully and at leisure. This process of framing the image and *then* reading the scale is much more practicable than trying to do everything at once. In fact, as one reflects, it becomes clear that the reason the cross-staff and kamal are successful on moving boats is that they too separate the measurement process into two parts—basically a quick framing by moving the traversal backward or forward, and then a reading of the calibrated staff or knotted lanyard.

Telefix is available in various ship's chandleries, or information about it can be had from Nautigon Marine, Box 218, One Grove St., Wellesley, MA 02181.

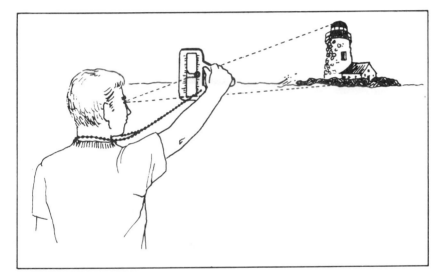

FIGURE 11-6.
Telefix, a modern kamal.

Telefix reads from one to ten degrees since that is about the range of interest for vertical angles. Also, keeping the range limited makes the instrument more compact. For horizontal angles, however, we will see later that large angles, say greater than 30 degrees, are useful. To measure these it is easy to fabricate a variant of the cross-staff, but with a single transverse scale. But for the reasons that I have discussed above it is imperative to have a slide on the scale so that the actions of framing and reading can be separated. An eyepiece is useful to help ensure that the distance D is constant from reading to reading. Altogether then, such a "modern cross-staff" looks something like the drawing below. I have put together a serviceable model of this kind with pieces of lath for the staff and crosspiece, a ring of bent solder for the eyepiece, and slides made from thin sheet aluminum—for which beer cans are a good source.

If in this cross-staff the distance D is taken as a foot or so, then a scale that reads up to about 70 degrees is about 18 inches long. This is not too cumbersome, especially if the scale can be detached or rotated to lie parallel with the staff for storage. To calibrate the scale some elementary trigonometry is needed, as shown in the formula in the margin, which gives the spacing of the degree marks L in terms of the trigonometric tangent function. From it one gets the distance L_1, L_2, L_3 ... from the center of the crosspiece for 1°, 2°, 3° .... For example, from trig tables I find L_1 = D tan 1° = 0.017D, L_2 = D tan 2° = 0.035D, etc. For D = 30 cm, say, this gives marks at L_1 = 0.52 cm, L_2 = 1.05 cm, L_3 = 1.56 cm, and so on. The spacing between any two such marks is just one degree. If you make, say, 25 such marks to the right of the center of the staff and, using the same formula, 25 to the left you will have 50 marks with the spacing between any two adjacent marks equal to one degree. Now label the leftmost mark at 0°, the next as 1°, the next as 2°, etc., and you will end up with a scale that, reading from left to right, goes from 0° to 50°, which is a useful range for most purposes.

Both Telefix and the modern cross-staff are convenient and reasonably accurate—usually to a few percent. Sometimes however, one wants more convenience, even at the expense of accuracy. Let's look in that direction, then, for the measurement of small horizontal angles, which will turn out later to be very useful.

A convenient way of holding something a fixed distance in front of the eye is at the end of an outstretched arm. And if you somehow make

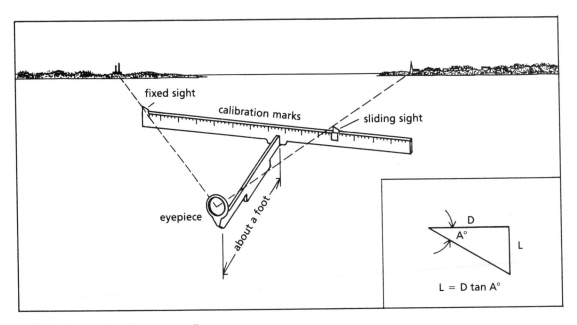

FIGURE 11-7. *A modern cross-staff.*

hand, fist, or fingers into a scale you have a simple, convenient, indestructible (lifetime guarantee) measuring device. Several are shown below, along with some typical calibration figures—but before you use the figures you should check them on your own hand. The clenched fist is particularly useful since the knuckles provide calibration points.

For most people the angle between first and fourth knuckles is about 9°, and the angle between pairs of knuckles is about 3°. There are many ways of checking this out on yourself. For example, from a yacht club porch or marina pier, look for two landmarks that are close together. Find these landmarks on a local chart and with a protractor measure (on the chart) the angle between them from your sighting point. Then from porch or pier "measure" the angle between them with your knuckles and you will have once and for all a truly portable angle measuring device that you can never absentmindedly leave at home. You can also calibrate your knuckles (and anything else you like) by measuring the distance between them, and the distance of the hand from the eye, and using the Rule of Sixty. If the distance between knuckles is 1 inch and the distance from knuckle to eye is 24 inches, then the angle between knuckles is $60 \times \frac{1}{24} = 2.5°$.

There are many other ways of roughly measuring small angles. Here are two:

With a telescope or binoculars one can estimate angles as a fraction of F°, the total angular field of view. This can be found from the common expression of the field of view as X feet per thousand yards. The formula is $F° = 0.019\ X$. For example, with X = 350 feet the angular field of view is $F° = 0.019 \times 350 = 6.7°$. Or the instrument can simply be calibrated against a known sextant or chart angle as suggested above.

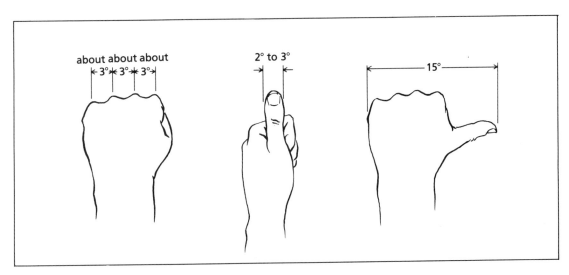

FIGURE 11-8.   *The outstretched arm and the hand provide a convenient small-angle estimator.*

The alternating-eye technique of estimating small angles depends on establishing a six- or seven-degree reference angle. Hold some vertical slender object, such as a pencil, in the hand of one outstretched arm and look at it with the right eye, closing the left eye. The pencil will appear in front of some point, call it Point 1, on whatever landscape or scene is before you. Without moving the arm and hand, shut the right eye and open the left, and the pencil will appear to jump across the scene and be at Point 2. The angle of the jump—that is, the horizontal angle between Points 1 and 2—is usually between 6° and 7°, and of course each user should calibrate himself. With the 6- to 7-degree benchmark established, he can estimate larger or smaller angles in terms of it.

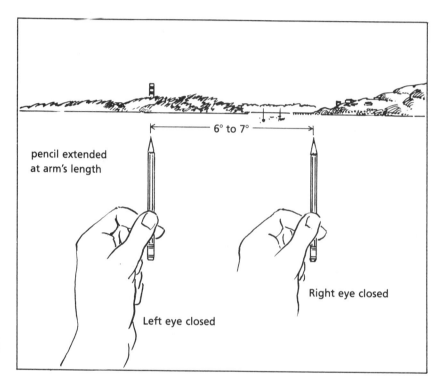

FIGURE 11-9.
Alternate-eye method of estimating angles.

The last angle that I consider is the bow angle, the angle between the centerline of the boat and the sightline to an object ashore, either to port or starboard. Let's look at a simple method of crudely measuring a bow angle. The method is a good example of the tradeoff between convenience and accuracy, because it is enormously convenient and not at all accurate. But we will see later that it is accurate enough, and that is all that counts.

The idea is simply to find a convenient place in the cockpit to stand —the sighting point—and in effect use the edges of the deck as the scale to be calibrated, and shrouds, stanchions, and identifying markers on the

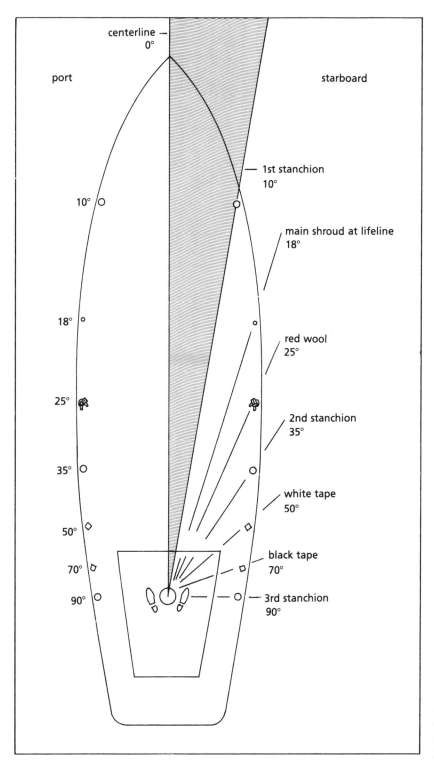

FIGURE 11-10.
The calibrated ship as a measurer of bow angles. Not a precision instrument, but a very practical one.

lifelines as calibrating marks. If then you have found the angle between centerline and first stanchion to be, say, 10°, and later see a shore object behind the first stanchion, the angle between centerline and shore object is obviously 10°.

To set up such an angle measurer you must do three things: decide on a suitable sighting point; select the reference marks; and calibrate them. Obviously, the details of doing all this will vary from boat to boat, so I will discuss them only generally, but with a few particular references to my own boat, an Alberg 30 sloop.

In the Alberg 30 there is a round inspection plate in the cockpit sole just forward of the tiller, and this is a convenient place to stand; in Figure 11-10 you see my feet straddling it. The reference marks are also shown in that figure, as are shrouds, stanchions, and markers of white tape, black tape, and red wool on the lifelines. Here are some ways of calibrating such a set of marks.

First, if you have an accurate plan drawing of the deck, from the manufacturer's literature perhaps, you can locate the reference marks on it by using a tape measure on deck to find their distance aft from the bow along the centerline. With these reference marks filled in on the plan it is simply a matter of putting a protractor to the paper and measuring the angles in question. If you have a good handbearing compass another possibility, and perhaps the easiest, is to stand at the sighting point, find the bearing of the centerline by sighting the mast center, and then take the bearings of each of the marks. Subtracting the mark bearing from the centerline bearing then gives you the angle between centerline and mark. But make sure the boat doesn't swing in the time it takes to measure the two bearings! If you have a Telefix you can measure angles of less than 10° with it and can measure larger angles in terms of as many 10-degree steps as is required. Or you can make a simple cross-staff such as that shown in Figure 11-7 to measure the larger angles directly. The best technique is of course to use two or more methods as cross checks on each other.

An important deck angle that is not discussed in this chapter is the *magnetic angle*. This is the angle between magnetic north and some line. If, for example, the line is the sightline to a shore object, the angle is the *magnetic bearing* of that object. The instrument for measuring magnetic angles is well known—it is a compass. But a complete treatment of the compass takes more space than this chapter affords, so you will see it discussed in several later chapters.

12

Angles on the Chart

Suppose that some fine afternoon you have been on deck using the techniques of the last chapter to measure a magnetic or horizontal or vertical angle. Or suppose even better that in your navigational zeal you have measured a magnetic angle *and* a horizontal angle *and* a vertical angle. What do you do next? How do you use them to ascertain your distance from Tower or to fix the boat's position? In short, how do you relate these angles to the chart; how do you measure them out on it and plot them? Read on.

I will begin with the problem of plotting a magnetic angle which is, as you may remember, the angle between a line on the chart and the direction of magnetic north. The subject is a can of worms that I am somewhat reluctant to open since it sometimes seems that there are as many ways of plotting magnetic angles as there are coastal pilots. Everyone seems to have a favorite way, based partly on his personal taste and partly on the space and layout of his boat. There is no consensus about the "best" and "worst" devices, and I won't make any pronouncements along those lines. I will simply list and classify the various kinds of plotting devices, state my opinion of their relative advantages and disadvantages, and let you take it from there. I will consider about 20 instruments that plot magnetic angles. The fact that they are all currently on the market makes it clear that none is universally superior to all the others—otherwise there would be one on the market and nineteen hanging in museums of nautical history.

Magnetic angles manifest themselves in two ways: when the magnetic direction of a course line is to be found, and when a magnetic bearing is plotted to give a line of position. Let's look first at the course line (Figure 12-1). Suppose that at the beginning of a trip you are at the point

plotting courses and bearings

marked Start and want to sail to Destination. On the chart you draw some sensible course line, avoiding obstacles and shallows, to Destination, and want to know what magnetic (hence, compass) reading you must steer to stay on that course line. You want, in short, to measure the angle between the course line and magnetic north. Now if one of the chart's compass roses *happened* to be exactly in the right place, with its center on the course line, you could measure the course angle straightaway. But it never is in exactly the right place (Murphy's Law); it is always some distance removed. How then to use a distant compass rose to measure the magnetic angle of the course line? One way to do this would be to draw a line parallel to the course line through the center of the distant compass rose; the angle of this parallel line with magnetic north would of course be the same as the angle of the original course line. Here then is the problem: to move a line across the chart while keeping it parallel to its original direction. I will call this the problem of *parallel transfer* of a line.

The second use of magnetic angles on the chart is in connection with a magnetic line of position. Suppose that on deck you have found with a

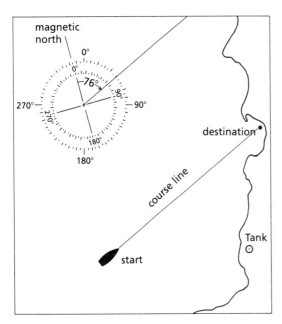

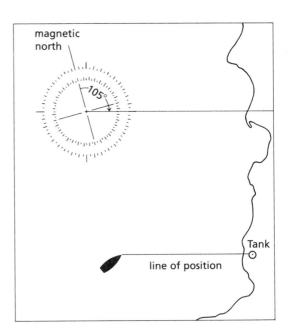

FIGURE 12-1. *A course line has been drawn between Start and Destination on the chart. The magnetic angle of the course line is measured as 76° after moving the course line parallel to itself to the center of the magnetic compass rose.*

FIGURE 12-2. *On deck the magnetic bearing of Tank has been measured as 105°. On the chart a line at that angle has been drawn through the center of the magnetic compass rose. If that 105° line can be moved parallel to itself to pass through Tank it becomes a line of position.*

handbearing compass that Tank has a magnetic bearing of 105° (Figure 12-2). You want then to draw a line on the chart that makes an angle of 105° with magnetic north *and* passes through Tank; this will be your line of position. You can, of course, draw a line through the center of the nearest compass rose at that 105° angle, but this line will *not* pass through Tank except by a very unlikely coincidence. What you must do in general is draw the 105° line at *some* compass rose and then move it, keeping it parallel to its original position, until it passes through Tank. Once again you are faced with the problem of parallel transfer of a line.

So *parallel transfer* is the magic phrase, and there is a whole series of less than magical devices with which to realize it. Four common ones are shown in Figure 12-3: *parallel rules,* a *courser,* a *rolling* ruler, and a pair of *drafting triangles.*

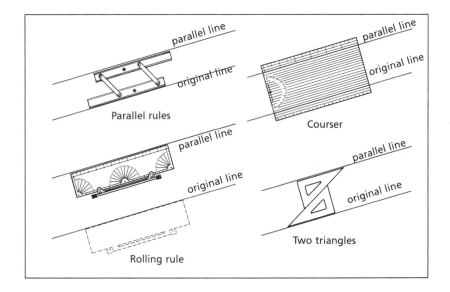

FIGURE 12-3.
Four devices for drawing a line parallel to an original line.

Parallel rules—two separate rulers joined by a linkage—are an ancient invention. One of the pair of rulers is held firmly against the original line while the second is extended to the desired position for drawing the parallel line. If this position is too far from the original one the rules may have to be walked across the chart in several successive steps in which the front rule is held fixed and the second moved, then the second is fixed while the first moves, etc.

In the pair of drafting triangles the top triangle slides along the hypotenuse of the triangle whose base is oriented on the original line. This technique works only over a limited range of separations of the original and parallel lines—neither too close nor too far.

The rolling ruler, or Paraline, rolls on two serrated wheels or cogs that are connected by an axle. With care the ruler remains parallel to its original position when rolled across the chart and, unlike the pair of triangles, there is no limitation on the distance between the original and parallel lines.

The courser is simply a series of parallel lines printed on a transparent, flexible vinyl sheet measuring perhaps a foot by a foot and a half. One of the printed lines is placed over the original line, at which point another, distant imprinted line is usually close enough to transiting the center of the compass rose that by a little eyeball interpolation and shifting of the courser a magnetic course line can be read off the rose. A disadvantage of the courser is that it can't easily be used for plotting bearings.

When they are used for drawing the magnetic angles of Figures 12-1 and 12-2, these four devices have the great virtue of dealing only with magnetic directions; they use only the inner, magnetic compass rose. You never have to refer to true directions or the outer compass rose, never have to add or subtract variation (and suddenly panic because you realize you have added it when you should have subtracted). You measure in magnetic degrees with a compass on deck and plot in the same magnetic degrees on the chart. But nothing is perfect, and these devices are no exception. To use any of them, the chart must obviously be folded open large enough to show a compass rose, and it must be flat and smooth, particularly for the three devices that move bodily across the chart. This is often not practical on a small boat, on which there is rarely an adequately large, dry, flat surface on which to spread a chart.

Let's try another tack. Instead of moving lines across the chart because the compass rose is never where it "should be," why not have a portable compass rose that you can plunk down wherever you need it? After all, a compass rose is simply a protractor on paper; why not use as the compass rose a transparent plastic protractor that you position for your own convenience? The problem with this idea is, of course, that if you want such a portable protractor to measure magnetic degrees you must orient its zero line to be parallel to the zero line on a magnetic compass rose on the chart. You are then back to the problem of having to transfer the direction of magnetic north on the distant rose parallel to itself across the chart, and so haven't gained anything.

But there is one way of using a local protractor without having to orient it with respect to a distant compass rose. You can instead orient it with respect to a meridian, one of the true north-south lines that appear on all charts. Let's think in terms of a course line. When drawn on the chart a course line will often, if it is of an ordinary length, cross a meridian, since meridians are usually spaced relatively closely together. If it doesn't cross the meridian it can be extended to intersect a meridian. If you then put the center of the protractor at the intersection of course line and meridian and orient its zero *along* the meridian, you can read the angle between course line and meridian. This will of course be in true degrees, and to convert this to a magnetic reading you have to add or subtract *variation*. This is just the process that I have earlier inveighed

Man's ingenuity has developed a variety of exotic devices, some of which are larger and more complicated and will help in constructing vector diagrams as well as in plotting courses and taking bearings. Some are shown in the margin illustrations in these pages.

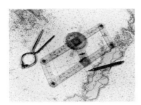

Para-Plotter

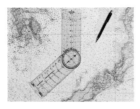

Wizard protractor

against, but I will hold my fire now since I promised in this chapter to be more descriptive than judgmental. In fact some skippers do use this technique, and if your arithmetic is good, and you are naturally careful about algebraic signs and never make a mistake with them, it may be for you. If it is, there is no lack of protractors that you can use; four are shown in Figure 12-4.

The common drafting protractor shown there needs no explanation. The square Douglas protractor has the advantage that its angle range is the whole 360°; its straight edges are also useful in drawing straight lines on the chart. The course plotter shown is often recommended in U.S. Power Squadron courses. The course protractor is the only device with a movable arm, and this can be convenient. Some course protractors, but not all, have on the moving arm part a circular *variation scale* of degrees that moves around next to the circular scale of degrees on the fixed part. If you mark the variation scale with a little dot or arrow corresponding to the particular value of the variation for the chart you are using, and read the arm of the protractor *against* that dot, you will be reading directly in magnetic degrees. This is a great advantage, and if you opt for a course protractor it is well worth seeking out one with this feature.

If you think these devices exhaust the ingenuity of clever gadgeteers, you are wrong. There are many others, but there is no point in my trying to describe every one that I have seen, so I have left further description to pictures and drawings in the margin. Among them you will see examples of another class of plotting devices—drafting machines on whose board you put the folded chart. On large boats plotting is almost always done with such machines, and if space is available they are very satisfactory. Some of those you see depicted in the margin claim they are small enough to be used in a small boat's cockpit, but you will have to decide for yourself whether these claims are valid for your boat.

Beyond, or perhaps before, the devices described above, there are even simpler possibilities. In transferring a line from one position to an-

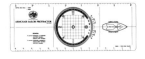

Armchair Sailor plotter

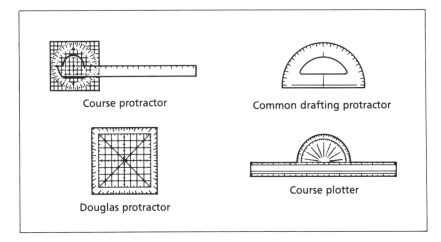

Course protractor

Common drafting protractor

Douglas protractor

Course plotter

FIGURE 12-4.
Four kinds of protractors for use with a meridian.

other, parallel position it is often accurate enough to judge parallelism by eye. If a straightedge defines the original line, you can usually judge to reasonable accuracy the parallelism of a second, distant straightedge. Whether reasonable accuracy is adequate accuracy must be assessed for every individual case; sometimes five-degree accuracy is acceptable; sometimes you want parallelism to a degree.

When judging by eye is not adequate I tend to use the course protractor mentioned above, with the variation scale that enables one to read it in magnetic degrees. On occasion, when there is plenty of space, say in the winter planning of a cruise, on a chart fully spread out on the kitchen table, I take pleasure in the elegant simplicity of parallel rules.

plotting horizontal angles

So much for magnetic angles. As I mentioned before, small horizontal angles—say, less than about 10°—can be very useful when measured on deck (Chapter 22). Let's look then at the problem of plotting them on the chart. We want to plot them to about the same accuracy with which they are found on deck, so there is no waste of precision. With Telefix, for instance, one can get an accuracy of about 0.2°, and with a sextant one can do even better, so I will aim at this somewhat arbitrary figure.

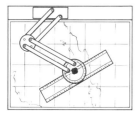

portable drafting board

A common half-round drafting protractor with 6-inch diameter can't provide accuracy of 0.2°. The spacing between degree marks on it is less than a sixteenth of an inch so you certainly can't interpolate to better than a half degree or so. To provide the required accuracy this kind of protractor must be several times larger. But a 15- or 20-inch half-round protractor is too cumbersome to be practical. What can be done, however, is to make a protractor that is in effect physically large for small angles and small for other angles. It sounds peculiar, but is easily done, as Figure 12-5 shows. The protractor shown there consists simply of a rectangular piece of transparent plastic, a millimeter or two thick and perhaps 10 to 15 inches long, with lines drawn at one-degree intervals. To draw the lines, marks can be made on the right-hand edge at a spacing appropriate to a degree. This spacing can be derived from the Approxi-

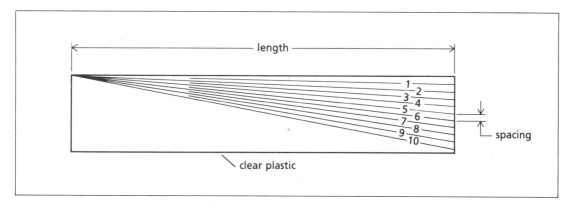

FIGURE 12-5. *Small-angle protractor.*

mate Formula of page 77, and is:

$$\text{Spacing} = \frac{\text{Length}}{57.3}$$

This formula is accurate enough up to 10° where, and this is where it is least accurate, it is off by a tolerable one-half percent. A particularly easy length to choose is 28.6 cm since the spacing between degree marks will then be a convenient one-half centimeter. In fact, I find that a protractor somewhat longer—say 35 to 40 centimeters or 14 to 16 inches—is still convenient and is somewhat more accurate.

If you would like to make such a protractor, here are some hints from my experience. It is preferable to draw the degree lines on the *bottom* of the protractor. If you draw them on the top they tend to cast shadows on the paper, which make them hard to read. When the lines are drawn on the top there is also the problem of parallax; you have to be sure you are looking straight down when you read them. The marks can be made with one of the fine-line plastic marking pens that are readily available. It is easier to read the protractor if two colors are used for the degree marks—black for the even ones and red for the odd, for example. With a protractor such as this, one can interpolate by eye to get accuracies of 0.2 to 0.3°.

Ritchie plotting board

Both the accuracy of this protractor and the ease of reading it can be improved by adding a movable arm with a line down its middle. Such a protractor is shown in Figure 12-6. This type of protractor is perhaps not so easy to fabricate at home as the one above, but it is commercially

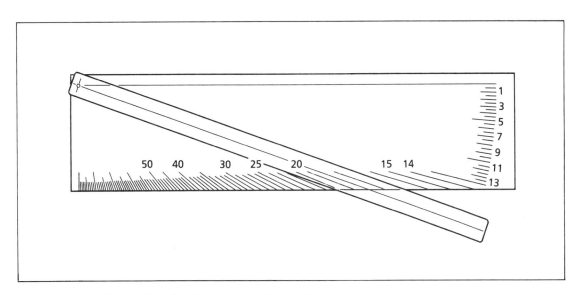

FIGURE 12-6. *Improved small angle protractor with movable arm.*

available. If your local marine supply source doesn't have it you can get information on it from Nautigon Marine, Box 218, One Grove St., Wellesley, MA 02181.

There are important uses for large angles, greater than around 30°, as well as small angles, in coastal navigation. In plotting them, however, you don't usually need the 0.2° accuracy we sought for small angles; a degree or so is adequate. Unfortunately one can't use an ordinary half-round drafting protractor, not because it lacks accuracy but because it is ordinarily not big enough. Usually the large angle arises in a situation such as this: There is a point on the chart that represents the possible position of the boat. There are two objects ashore—landmarks, nav-aids—whose horizontal angle has been measured from the deck. The objects are also found on the chart, and you want to plot the deck angle that has been measured. Now the objects can be any distance away; typically on a coastal piloting chart they will be from a few inches to a foot or more. On the average they are not close enough to the vessel's possible position for an ordinary protractor with, say, a 3-inch radius to be feasible. What is needed is a protractor with long arms on it, so that one arm can pass through the one object and the other arm through the other.

The protractor of Figure 12-6 has long arms and is calibrated to 90°, so it works well for large angles as well as for small. But if, when you have read later in this book about the uses of large angles, you want to try them for yourself, you won't have to invest in this protractor. An ordinary course protractor already has one long arm, and it is easy enough to improvise another of Bristol board or thin plastic and attach it as in Figure 12-7 to provide a serviceable two-arm large-angle protractor.

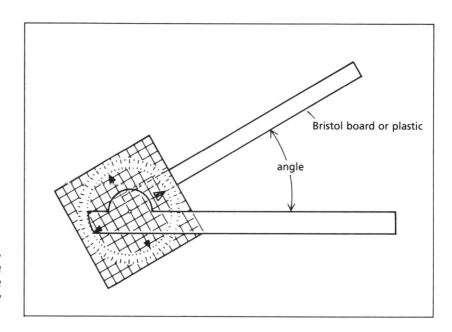

FIGURE 12-7.

A course protractor with an improvised added arm makes a good large-angle protractor.

The final angle that needs plotting on the chart is the bow angle, the angle between the centerline and the line of sight to a shore object. Here you need a quite different kind of protractor, one with large, bold markings, not necessarily very accurate—a couple of degrees is good enough. I call this a Big Bold Protractor. Logically its description belongs in this chapter, but in fact I will save it for Chapter 13, where its use is described. It will be much easier to see why it is what it is within the context of its functioning.

13

The Orientation Program

One of the aims of coastal piloting is to know where the boat is at all times. But you can know where it is and still have problems. You may have just rounded a point and a section of the coast that was previously hidden now becomes visible in all its possible complexity. You may know you are 50 feet from the entrance buoy to a large harbor, such as Baltimore or Charlotte Amalie, but still need to quickly sort out what is where farther into the harbor so you can find your way to a fuel dock. You may emerge from the shelter of one island and see a whole new cluster that must be identified and sailed around.

In these circumstances a compass may not be of much help. Plotting and using compass courses is a slow business; you may not have enough time, especially if the safe course has several bends in it, as it often does. And there may be currents that make an uncorrected compass course dangerous.

on being one's own pilot

What you really want instead of a compass is a guide who is able to navigate by the landmarks and navaids that can be seen on deck and on the chart. Ideally you would like a seasoned pilot who can look at Tower on the chart and then point to the land and tell you that Tower is that redbrick cylinder to the right of the gray building. Or who can look at the flashing green light off the port bow and instantly put his finger on the chart at Fl G 6 sec, 7 M. Obviously you won't usually have such a pilot aboard. You must then use the chart as pilot and do for yourself what a real pilot might have done for you, and do it as quickly and efficiently, with no dawdling or hesitation.

To get a clue as to how to do this, imagine a real pilot aboard. You are the skipper, steering from the cockpit, and he is conning the boat from the foredeck. Since he is not at your side it is not accurate enough for you simply to have him point at objects. He must inform you verbally where to look. How can he do this?

One quick and intuitive procedure is to use a *relative bearing,* (Chapter 10) or *bow angle* in which the object is located by the angle between its sightline and the ship's centerline. Thus, the pilot might call out that Tank is 37° off the starboard bow, and as you stood in the cockpit you could sight past stay or stanchion at that angle, using the ship as an angle measurer (Chapter 11). The use of relative bearings is in a great tradition. In whaling books, for example, the whale's position is usually given in terms of relative bearings—expressed in points rather than degrees. (One point equals 360°/32, or 11¼°.) "Whar blows she?" queries the captain. "Two points off the starboard bow," says the mate.

relative bearings or bow angles

Note, incidentally, how much more intuitive, as well as speedier, the bow angle is than the magnetic bearing. The mate could answer the captain's "Whar blows she?" by giving the magnetic bearing of the whale. But there is no record of any mate with a subsequent long life who answered "She blows at 279° magnetic, sir, and the variation is 11° westerly."

Bow angles are then Good Things for locating objects, but another quick and intuitive way of locating an object is in relation to some other one that has already been identified. If Lighthouse is clearly visible to both you and the pilot, but Tower is less conspicuous, the pilot can use his calibrated knuckles, say (Chapter 11), to find that Tower is 5° to the right of Lighthouse. He calls out that information to you and equally quickly you can use your knuckles to find where to look. It takes less time than you have taken here to read about it, and for this kind of identification the accuracy of knuckles, or Telefix, is more than adequate. I'll call this second kind of identifying angle—the angle of a second object relative to a first—a *relative angle.*

relative angles

The orientation program works then to provide "instant local knowledge" by comparing either bow angles or relative angles seen on deck to those measured on the chart. For example, as you begin down the coast you see from the deck a little vertical something—tower? stack? monument? You measure its bow angle by using the ship as an angle measurer (Chapter 11), and find that the angle is 28° on the starboard side. On the chart you use a protractor to see what sort of landmark can be raised at 28° to starboard of the ship's centerline. Or you can go from the chart to a deck view. If the chart claims there is a standpipe to be found at 44° off the port bow, you look at that angle on deck—perhaps with the naked eye, perhaps with binoculars.

You can equally well exploit relative angles. Once you have identified some landmark or navaid you can locate a second object by the angle it makes with respect to the first. If Lighthouse is clearly visible and unmistakable, identify Tower by the angle between it and Lighthouse as measured on deck with Telefix, knuckles, or the ship-as-pelorus. In the practice of correlating chart and deck views one often uses a mix of bow and

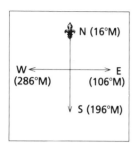

EXAMPLE:

For 16° westerly variation, the four magnetic courses that correspond to true N,E,S,W.

relative angles, according to the circumstances.

Relative angles are easy to deal with; you use them on deck or chart without any preliminaries. But to plot a bow angle on the chart you must of course know in what direction the centerline is pointing. When measuring a bow angle on deck, you should then point the boat in a known and convenient direction. Four particularly convenient directions are true North, East, South, and West, since, as will appear later, they make it easy to use a suitable protractor on the chart—one can align the protractor's edge against a meridian or a parallel of latitude. So the first step in measuring a bow angle is to put the boat momentarily on that true course closest to your general line of direction. That is, if the desired direction is more or less southerly, put the boat momentarily on an *exact* true southerly course. If your destination is toward the west, put the boat on an *exact* westerly course for some seconds. You put the boat on these true courses by using the ship's compass. Subtract the local variation with the proper sign from the four true courses of 0°, 90°, 180°, and 270° to get their magnetic counterparts according to the equation: Magnetic = True − Variation or M = T − V. For example, if the variation is 16° westerly (V = − 16), then M = T + 16°, and the four magnetic courses corresponding to true N, E, S, and W are 16°, 106°, 196°, and 286°. This business of putting the boat on a true course and measuring a deck angle is quite quick—ordinarily 10 or 15 seconds suffices—and the result is usually well worth the effort.

Suppose you have begun the orientation program by making an appropriate course change and measuring one or more bow angles. You want to plot these on the chart and so need a protractor—but not any protractor will do. For example the ordinary half-round drafting protractor a few inches in diameter is too small; it will generally not reach from the observation point to the objects of interest on the chart without drawing lines. Thus on the common coastal piloting chart to a scale of 1:40,000, one nautical mile is about 4.5 cm, so that a landmark five miles away is 22.5 cm distant, or about 9 inches. That distance becomes 14 inches on a chart to scale 1:25,000.

The standard course protractor (Figure 12-4) does have an arm between 12 and 15 inches long, so in one respect it is better than a drafting protractor. But it doesn't work well for the present use since it reads from 0 to 360° and so loses the helpful intuitive quality of bow angles in going from 0 to 90°. Moreover it is intended to be read for angles that increase in a clockwise direction, so it is good for starboard bow angles but confusing for port angles. The same observation applies to the Telefix protractor of Chapter 12. Moreover, both these protractors are *too* accurate—for which read, too fussy. You have to bend close over them to read them and make sure that in the course of operations their movable arms don't move. Suitable as they are on the chart table, they are not what is wanted in the cockpit pilotage we are discussing here. What *is* wanted is a big protractor with bold markings—a Big, Bold, Protractor—that is rugged and can be read easily to the couple of degrees' accuracy that is all

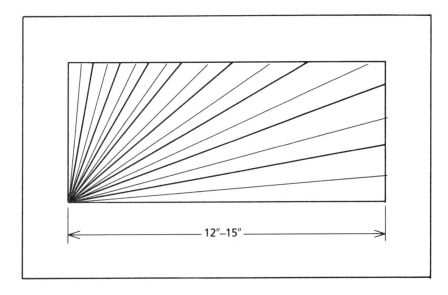

12"–15"

FIGURE 13-1.
Big, Bold Protractor.

that is required.

Such a protractor can be made in a few minutes from a piece of Plexiglas, usually available at hardware or art supply stores. It is perhaps 12 to 15 inches long and is marked heavily in 10-degree intervals with a bold marking pen of one color and more lightly in 5-degree intervals with another color. The bold markings allow you to read the protractor when looking down on it from a height. Thus if the chart is folded and lies on the cockpit seat you can simply put the protractor on it, stand at the tiller or wheel, and without even bending over measure angles to adequate accuracy. There are no numbers on the protractor; this is not the disadvantage it might appear to be. If the degrees are numbered to read starboard bow angles the numbers become confusingly reversed when the protractor is flipped to read port angles. But even with no numbers the bold markings make it easy to count up the 10-degree lines and get readings equally well to port or starboard. The protractor is best made of fairly heavy material, say at least a sixteenth of an inch thick. Thinner pieces of acetate or vinyl will tend to curl and not stay put in a windy cockpit. The heavier protractor can be dropped on an imperfectly folded, irregular chart surface, and will stay there.

Now we have the tools: techniques for measuring bow angles or relative angles on deck, and the Big, Bold Protractor to plot them on the chart. Let's look at the kind of problem they are supposed to solve.

Suppose that you have begun the day by leaving Port Halcyon and have now moved about a mile beyond Halcyon Point (Figure 13-2). You are about to turn more or less westerly and follow the coast. Your final destination is a harbor about 10 miles beyond Spruce Point, to get to which you must first safely round the Point. Before you lies a stretch of coast that is completely new to you. You can assure yourself of easy, relaxed piloting in the next few hours if you take a couple of minutes now to sort out what will be seen along the way. In fact, if you are in a sailboat, you may never have a better time than now, since if you have to tack offshore later your views of some shore features may never be as good again.

You may ask: Why fuss about the look of the coast on the way to Spruce Point? If all you want to do is get to Spruce Point, why not simply aim for it if you can see it, or work out the compass course if you can't? This can be a perfectly sensible procedure if yours is a fast powerboat that can move at 20 or 25 knots. The passage will take only 20 minutes or so. The boat is minimally affected by current and leeway, and the weather is not likely to worsen appreciably in 20 minutes, so push down on the throttle and take off. The only instance in which the skipper of a fast powerboat might want to identify coastal landmarks en route is if his engine breaks down and he needs a fix from shore objects, perhaps to relay to the Coast Guard. But even then a fix is not necessary if the skipper knows his boat speed and has been prudent enough to note his time of departure, since he can then easily calculate his position along the course line.

On the other hand, consider a sailboat embarked on the same passage. Even if the skipper knows the compass course or can see Spruce Point, the wind may not be right for him to sail in the required direction. It is not going to take 20 minutes but more like a couple of hours to get to Spruce Point, and there is a correspondingly larger chance for the weather to worsen—perhaps with the visibility decreasing, perhaps with a squall coming up. Even if the wind is right he has to hold his course in

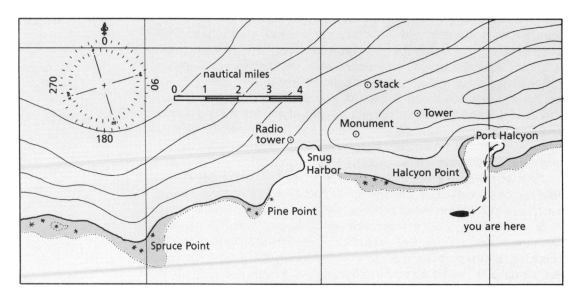

FIGURE 13-2. *The coast between Port Halcyon and Spruce Point.*

the presence of leeway and possible current, which may push him toward a hostile shore. For a variety of reasons then the sailboat skipper may want to keep track of his progress along the coast and his distance from shore. In general—electronic aids and lucky buoy sightings aside—he can only achieve this by getting fixes from shore objects.

The best time to begin conning the coast and identifying its shore objects is well before you need this information. If after a series of tacks—which can be very disorienting—you suddenly realize you may be too close to shore, or you see a squall coming up, you won't have the time or detachment to do a good job of identification. It is much better, before you start on a coastal passage, to try to visualize from the chart what the land and its reference points will look like. You won't always be right in your visualization, but by virtue of having focused on the problems you will help the learning process—you will learn by your mistakes as well. Look at the chart's various landmarks and navaids and tentatively sort out those that appear to be useful. Then look at the proper angles along the coast with binoculars and see which of them you can see, albeit imperfectly, even now, and you will have made a good beginning toward obviating any unpleasant navigational surprises.

I'll be writing about what one can and can't see ashore, and this obviously depends on the weather and the conditions of visibility. For my remarks to make sense they must be understood as referring to some specific state of visibility. Roughly speaking, I'll assume that the day is an "average," clear one. To make this a little more precise I refer to the ever-useful Light List which, in connection with the range of lights at night, categorizes different states of meteorological visibility. Its seven, admittedly approximate categories are: exceptionally clear, very clear, clear, light haze, haze, light fog, fog. The range of visibility goes to over 27 miles for "exceptionally clear" to 0.54 mile or less in "light fog." On a clear day, which is what I will assume, you can't quite see forever, but you can, according to the classification, see things at up to about 11 miles.

Back then to Figure 13-2, and the boat's position off Halcyon Point. We want to get to Spruce Point. If we can identify Spruce Point at this distance it is much easier and less wearing to sail to it as a visual target than to be hunched over a compass for several hours. The question is: Can Spruce Point be seen from the boat's position as shown?

The general answer to the question of when one can see a point—what the British call a *headland*—is complicated. I wanted to have a chapter about it, partly so I could call it "Getting To The Point"; alas, although the problem is complicated it does not merit a chapter's length.

There are several factors that determine whether a point is visible from a given location. Each can only be imprecisely assessed, so one can't make an infallible prediction from them as a whole. But here are some of the factors. The first is self-explanatory: meteorological visibility. You can't see a distant point in a heavy fog. Beyond visibility, a second factor is the height of the point itself. If it is of low relief, essentially a large sand or rock spit perhaps 10 or 20 feet above the water, it will tend to merge into or disappear beyond the horizon, and so not be seen beyond a few miles. If it is higher and more bluff-like, perhaps 50 or 100 feet high or even more, then whether you see it depends to a certain extent on its background. If the coast, having curved in beyond the point, quickly curves out again so that land can be seen in the further distance, then that land may camouflage the point itself. If however the coast beyond the point doesn't curve out again, or if it does but with a lower relief, then the point may be visible and stand out clearly although perhaps not appearing higher than the thickness of a pencil line.

You can't then tell from the chart whether Spruce Point can be seen. The first step in determining whether it can be seen is—to look for it. But if it is not very conspicuous, and if in looking your eye wanders more or less aimlessly over a large arc of the horizon, you can easily miss it. Here the protractor can help, by telling you where to look, and that can be crucial in finding it. Drop the protractor on the chart with its corner at the boat's position and orient it—by eye will be accurate enough—so that its edge is parallel to a parallel of latitude (Figure 13-3). The protractor's edge on the chart then corresponds to the centerline of the boat. Measure on the chart the bow angle of Spruce Point and, while you are at it, perhaps of other objects of interest as well. Then back on deck with the boat pointed in a true westerly direction look for Spruce Point, and anything else you like, at the angles the protractor has determined.

Not to overelaborate this scenario, let's assume you find Spruce Point and that perhaps you don't see Pine Point, even though you know where

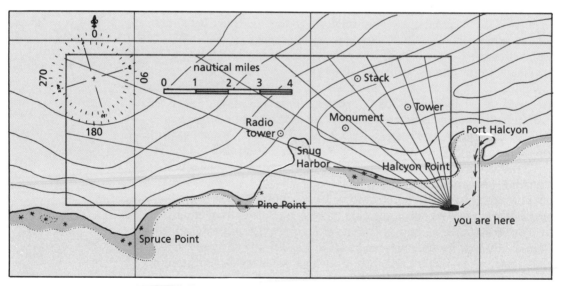

FIGURE 13-3. *With the boat pointed due west, Spruce Point is about 5° off the port bow; Pine Point is about 2° off the starboard bow; and Radio Tower and Snug Harbor are at about 23°. Monument, Stack, and Tower are, respectively, at about 38°, 54°, and 68°.*

to look for it, since it merges visually with the land behind it. Let's then come back up the coast and look at some other landmarks that might turn out to be useful. One such landmark would appear to be the radio tower behind Snug Harbor—a fine indicator of the location of the harbor itself. But as we scan the coast casually there is no radio tower to be seen. Let's look more carefully. The protractor has told us that we should look at a bow angle of about 25°, and if we do look at that angle, but now with binoculars, we do see a faint, tall, elongated outline. Radio towers are formidable close up, and they are often among the tallest structures on the coast; one would think that they always stand out clearly from afar. In fact, these spidery structures are among the first of the major landmarks to disappear in the distance when the visibility worsens or the sun strikes them from an unfavorable direction. They are not quite such good landmarks as one might first suppose.

But finding Radio Tower has served another purpose. We see close to it and clearly visible, if not clearly identifiable, rectangular white shapes or structures. (These will turn out to be new condominiums and a dual outdoor movie screen in the town of Snug Harbor.) Even though we don't know what they are it is a good idea to mark them on the chart (White bldgs? Conspic.) as an aid in finding Snug Harbor when its relatively skinny Radio Tower has disappeared into the mist.

Now looking at the coast closer to us we see what appear to be two tiny vertical cylinders on the land and on the chart *three* objects that might look like little vertical cylinders at a distance—Monument, Stack, and Tower. Although these objects aren't important for piloting to Spruce Point, you will be coming back up the coast later and will probably do yourself a favor by sorting them out now. How then are the *two* vertical specks seen from deck related to the *three* markings on the chart?

See what binoculars reveal. With them the left-hand structure does look like a monument—perhaps. A granite column with a general on a horse atop it? Or is it a brick stack with an antipollution device that looks like a general on a horse? Hard to say. But the protractor measurement clears up the dilemma. Upon measuring on deck the bow angle of the left-hand cylinder, it turns out to be the 38° that corresponds to Monument and not the 54° for Stack. In fact Stack is not seen at all, since the right-hand cylinder appears a full 30° to the right of Monument at a bow angle of 68°, so it must be Tower and not Stack. Why is Stack not seen? It may have been torn down since the chart was printed, or the visibility may be worse in its direction. Most likely it is hidden by intervening topography or foliage.

In the discussion above I have concentrated on bow angles mainly to give a variety of examples, but I could equally well have used some relative angles as well. In fact it is best to use relative angles when you can, since you don't have to point the boat in a particular direction to measure them. Once you have unambiguously identified one landmark or navaid, measuring relative angles with respect to it is the fastest way of identifying the little specks and lines on the horizon that are sometimes the deck view of the chart's markings.

Here is an example (Figure 13-4). Suppose you have visited Boston and are just about to emerge from Boston Inner Harbor to pick your way through the islands and shallows of Boston Harbor itself, and eventually head south down the coast. Finding the way out of the harbor is not very difficult, but it is not trivially easy either and you *can* run aground—it happens every day. For prudence you can, as you emerge from the Inner Harbor, use knuckles, Telefix, or both, and the big protractor on the chart, to identify a few prominent landmarks and navaids that will help keep you off the rocks and out of the mud. One prominent, centrally located landmark is Deer Island Light, so let's start with it. If you take a few sec-

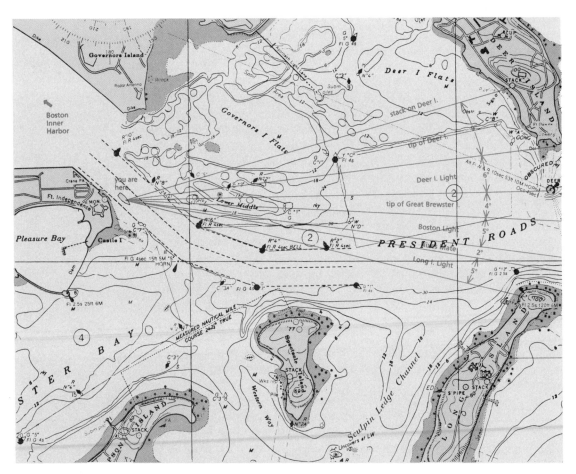

FIGURE 13-4. *Part of the chart of Boston Harbor, and some relative angles found on it.*

onds at your location to point the boat due east you will find that Deer Island Light is almost directly ahead. It is, in fact, about 2 degrees off the port bow, so that it is almost impossible to miss. Once you have identified it, measure relative angles to other useful landmarks on the chart, look for them at these angles on deck, put binoculars on them to get all the detail you can, and in a few minutes you will have a local knowledge that some skippers in the harbor will not acquire in their lifetime (Figure 13-5).

For example, at 4 degrees from Deer Island Light, pick out the northern tip of Great Brewster, the highest and most prominent island in the harbor. From this northern tip you can pick out Boston Light at 5°—it will be small but quite clearly seen when you know where to look. This is an

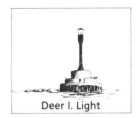

Deer I. Light

Long I. Light

Boston Light

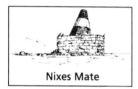

Nixes Mate

important navaid if you are leaving the harbor by a southern route, and the sooner you get to know it the better. If you identify it now you will never confuse it with Graves Light, which is about two miles farther north. You might think it impossible to confuse Graves with Boston Light, but in coastal piloting people regularly do the impossible.

An important navaid for the visitor departing toward the south is Nixes Mate, since it is at the beginning of the two commonly used channels for a southern exit—Nubble Channel and The Narrows. Unfortunately, from the viewing point shown on the chart, Nixes Mate appears directly in front of Lovell's Island, which serves to camouflage it nicely, so that if you don't know where to look you may find it hard to see. But if you *do* know where to look—2° to the right of Boston Light or 5° to the left of Long Island Light—you can probably pick it up with the naked eye and almost certainly see it with binoculars.

There may be another reason for not finding Nixes Mate if you look for it in front of Lovell's Island—you may not be looking at Lovell's at all. This can happen because Great Brewster as a whole looks like two islands—a high northern "island" and a low southern one. Having identified the northern tip of Great Brewster, it is natural to think that this is the entire island. If you then look at the chart you can easily convince yourself that the southern "island" is Lovell's. The error is easily detected if you measure the angular width of Great Brewster on the chart—about 4°—and then see that this 4° on deck includes *both* of the separate-seeming lumps on the horizon.

That's it. When confronted with a new navigational vista it is almost always worthwhile to take a few minutes to identify unambiguously a few landmarks or navaids. Everything else then tends to fall into place. Once you know Great Brewster it is obvious where to look for the chimneys on Calf Island, and immediately after recognizing Boston Light you can identify Tower on the mainland opposite. By increments you build up a pic-

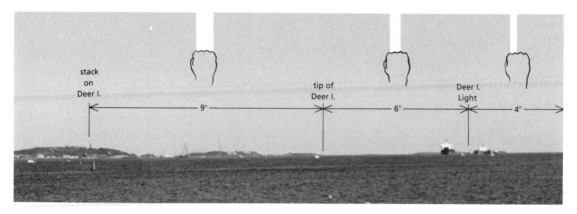

FIGURE 13-5. *A deck view of the chart area of Figure 13-4 with relative angles measured with knuckles or, if greater accuracy is required, by Telefix.*

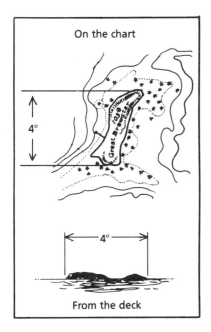

On the chart

4°

4°

From the deck

ture which is more and more complete and intuitive. As with other puzzles—crossword, jigsaw—if you get a good beginning and keep adding to it, things get simpler and simpler. But if you start poorly, with misconceptions, the confusion just mounts. If you think the southern part of Great Brewster is Lovell's Island, and so can't find the channel marker, the puzzle never sorts itself out but tends to get worse and worse. Finally you have to slow down or stop and make a concerted effort to undo the errors and replace them with the truth, and that almost always takes longer than it would have taken to get it right from the beginning.

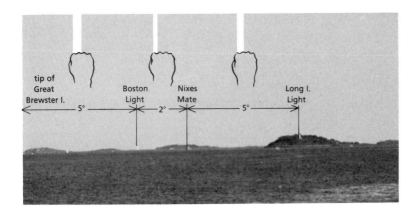

tip of Great Brewster I.   Boston Light   Nixes Mate   Long I. Light

5°   2°   5°

SECTION IV

Marine
Compasses

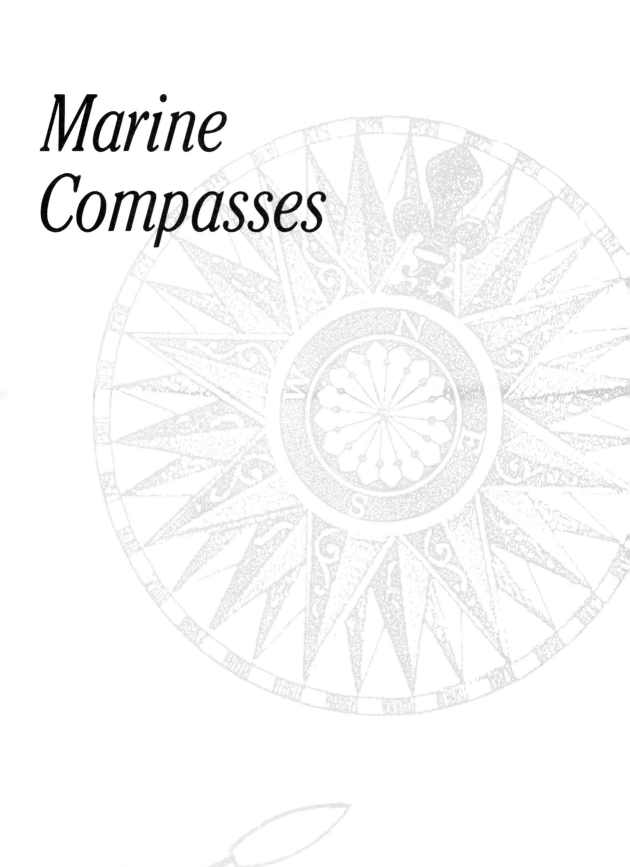

14

The Earth's Magnetic Field

It is likely that every reader of this book will have seen a compass or a picture of one, or used one, or been confused by one, or sworn by one, or sworn at one. He will also probably be aware in a broad, general sense that a compass works because it has a magnetic needle that is aligned in the earth's magnetic field. I hope to fill in the conceptual details in this section of the book on marine compasses, and in this chapter on the basic enabling fact behind them—the earth's magnetic field.

But what is a magnetic field? It is hard not to be circular in the definition. A magnetic field is what is produced by a magnet. And what is a magnet? It is something that produces a magnetic field. Let's break into the semantic circle by calling on everyday practical experience. Almost certainly every reader of this book has seen a magnet—a bar magnet or horseshoe magnet in a science lab, a magnet that attaches notes to refrigerator doors, an electromagnet in a car engine or radio speaker. Magnets everywhere. What is common to all these magnets is that they can exert a *magnetic force* on certain kinds of materials, which then come to be called *magnetic materials.* Iron is one of the oldest examples of a magnetic material, and although there are many other modern ones, I'll use iron as a generic name for them all. We have all seen examples of this magnetic force: iron filings made to line up in characteristic patterns; paper clips that jump out of their box to cling to the magnet waved above them.

magnetic materials

A magnet can exert not one, but two kinds of magnetic force. One is simply an attraction; the magnet *attracts* the paper clips out of the jar. But beyond this force, the force of crucial importance for the compass is the magnet's *aligning force* on a magnetic needle. A magnetic needle is a

aligning force of magnetism

120

long, slim piece of magnetized iron that is pivoted at its center and so is free to rotate horizontally. Magnetic needles can be of any shape. An ancient and traditional one is the long thin diamond you see illustrated at the right. When brought near a magnet, a magnetic needle will align itself in a certain direction, due to the action of the magnet—due to its *aligning force*. Taken away and brought back time and again to the same place, the needle will always align itself in the same direction. We can check that it is the magnet that effects the aligning since if it is taken away the needle will align itself randomly. *Why* the magnet exerts an aligning force is beyond us here; we would need a Ph.D. in physics to begin to appreciate the basic reasons. But instead of enrolling for that degree let's look at a superficial but illuminating analogy with another kind of aligning force. It is this.

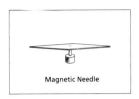

Magnetic Needle

In a certain country a yacht club is on the bank of a wide, swiftly flowing river (Figure 14-1). Boats are moored at the river's edge and for some distance out. They are acted on by the current, which pushes or pulls on them. They don't move downstream since they are moored in place, but they do swing to line up with the current—the current is an *aligning force* for them. A drawing of the boats as seen from a height might look like Figure 14-1a. If, starting from the left in that figure, lines were drawn from the stern of one boat to the bow of the one behind it, then through its stern to the bow of the one behind it, etc., and the boats themselves were erased, we would have left the lines shown in Figure 14-1b. These might be called the lines of direction of the current flow, or current force, or simply the *lines of force of the current.*

Figure 14-2 shows a magnetic analogue of these moored boats. A multiplicity of magnetic needles has been set down in the vicinity of a bar magnet, and they orient themselves as in Figure 14-2a. If we were to draw the lines connecting each needle to the one in front of it, and then erase the needles, we would end up with a picture like Figure 14-2b, a series of lines giving the direction of the magnetic force at any point. We

magnetic lines of force

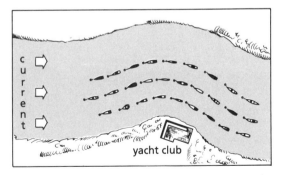

FIGURE 14-1a. *Current is an aligning force for moored boats that are free to swing.*

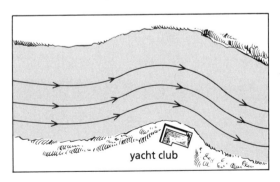

FIGURE 14-1b. *Lines along the direction of the current's force—the "lines of force" of the current.*

might call these *magnetic lines of force*. Each line has no more esoteric meaning than to show the direction along which a magnetic needle would align itself. Now these lines also have arrowheads on them; they point in a certain direction and not in the opposite direction. What does that mean?

The answer is given in terms of the magnetic needles that map them. To the eye, each needle is a symmetric thin diamond, one end the same as the other. *Magnetically,* the two ends are different. If a needle is aligned in a magnetic field and you turn it end for end—rotate it through 180°— it *looks* the same, but it doesn't *act* the same; it spontaneously rotates throught 180° to come back to its original position. The two ends are different, so we must distinguish between them. For historical reasons one is labeled the north end (pole) and the other the south end (pole). The labeling has its origin in the use of the magnetic *lodestones* that were the predecessors of the slim magnetic needle. It was found that when a lodestone aligned itself in the earth's magnetic field, one particular end, and not the other, always pointed to (was closer to) the geographic north pole. This end was then called the *north pole* of the magnet, and this designation has persisted; the opposite end is, of course, the south pole.

FIGURE 14-2a (left).

Magnetism is an aligning force for magnetic needles—pivoted iron needles that are free to rotate.

FIGURE 14-2b (right).

Lines along the direction of the magnetic force— the "lines of force" of the magnet.

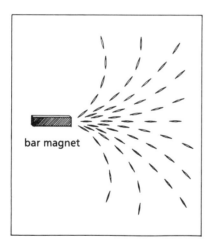

bar magnet

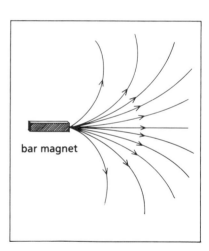

bar magnet

So much for the magnetic needles and lines of force that are associated with the magnetic field. Now, what is the field *itself*?

The definition begins operationally. We say there is a magnetic field in a certain region of space if there is the potential in that region for aligning a magnetic needle—*if* a needle is introduced at any point it *will* orient itself in a unique direction. The first characteristic of a field is then its direction at a point. Another characteristic that I have not emphasized thus far is its *strength*. Two magnets can look identical, have the same size and shape and hence the same pattern of lines of force, and yet be different. If one is made of a more powerful magnetic material than the other, if it is *stronger,* it will make the paper clips jump higher and will cling more tightly to the refrigerator door. A magnetic field has then a *strength* as well as a direction at every point.

The lines of force, by themselves, merely indicate direction; they say nothing about the strength. To indicate the strength graphically we can use, instead of a continuous line, a series of line segments which point in the direction of the field, with the *length* of each segment being proportional to the field strength (Figure 14-3b). You wil notice that the line segments farthest from the magnet are the shortest. (Obviously, the field strength diminishes as distance from the magnet increases.) Each directed line segment in Figure 14-3b is called a *vector.*

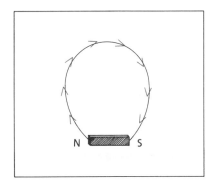 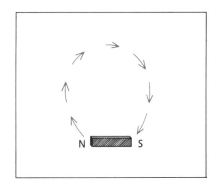

FIGURE 14-3a (left).
A line of force represents the direction of the magnetic field.

FIGURE 14-3b (right).
Directed line segments (vectors) also represent the direction of the field, and their lengths are proportional to local field strength.

Vectors are important, even indispensable, in dealing with a common problem—the magnetic field due to two (or more) sources. Imagine two magnets relatively close together. Each by itself would produce a field with lines of force and strength peculiar to it. Jointly, the magnets produce a net or resultant field—a field that somehow combines the two individual fields but is different from either. How is the combining done; how can we calculate the resultant field, given the two individual fields?

The answer is that the resultant field is calculated in a special way called *vector addition.* It is illustrated in Figure 14-4. If the term strikes terror in your heart call it something else—field combination or net field computation, or whatever. The process of vector addition will surface later in a discussion of correcting the ship's compass. Exactly this problem of the combined effect of two fields comes up. The one is the magnetic field of the earth, which acts on a compass needle; the other is the field due to shipboard sources of magnetism—the deviating field—which makes for compass error.

Finally let's return to the magnetic field that triggered all this discussion—the field of the earth. There is one simple thing that can be said about it—it is complicated. It is probably due to a rotating liquid iron core deep toward the center of the earth, but its details are not well known. There is then no simple model that predicts the earth's magnetic field with any accuracy. But roughly, very roughly, the field resembles the

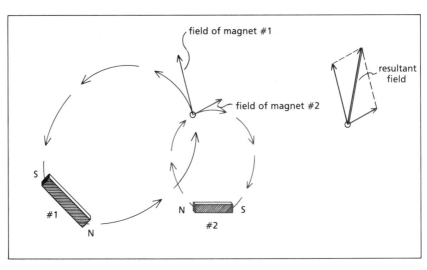

FIGURE 14-4.

The magnetic field at a point due to magnets 1 and 2, and the resultant or net field. The resultant field, the vector sum of the two fields, is the diagonal of the parallelogram defined by the two individual fields.

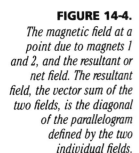

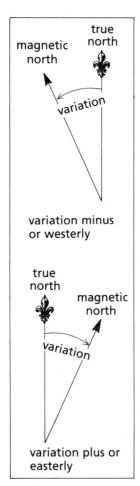

field that would be produced by a bar magnet in the earth's interior, inclined at an angle of some 15° to 20° to the north-south axis of the earth (Figure 14-5). The earth's field, however, is much more complicated than this simple model predicts. The lines of force are not as regular as for a bar magnet; they change with time, etc. The only reason for mentioning this model is because, even in all its crudeness, it exhibits two important features of the earth's magnetic field: *dip* and *variation.*

Dip refers to the fact that, as Figure 14-5 shows, the lines of force are generally not horizontal at the earth's surface; they poke into the surface at an angle. A magnetic needle pivoted on a universal joint and so capable of aligning itself along that line of force would then tend to have one end higher than the other. If the needle were on a compass card this tilt of the card would obviously impair accuracy. To prevent this, the better commercial compasses have their cards balanced to compensate for magnetic dip. The strength of the dip is, however, different in different parts of the world, so that balancing that is effective in one part may be less than perfect in another. To get around this, compasses are balanced differently for different geographic areas, sometimes only the northern and southern hemispheres, sometimes several different areas.

The second phenomenon illustrated by the model of Figure 14-5 is *variation.* Since the magnet is at an angle to the earth's axis its lines of force at the surface of the earth do not run in a true north-south direction. The direction they define at the surface, the direction of magnetic north, then generally makes an angle at any point with the direction of true north—the direction of northerly travel along the meridian through the point. This angle between magnetic and true north is called the *variation.* It has a sign, plus or minus. The arc of the angle is drawn as starting from the line of true north and moving in the direction that takes it to the magnetic line. If that direction is clockwise the variation is plus or easterly; if counterclockwise the variation is minus or westerly. It follows that an angle that is defined with respect to the magnetic reference line (magnetic angle) can be expressed as an angle referred to the true reference line (true angle), by the formula:

$$\text{True angle} = \text{Magnetic angle} + \text{Variation.}$$

The bottom line

I hope all the above is not too theoretical. Happily, compasses work whether one understands the earth's magnetic field superficially or profoundly. The bottom line is that the earth's magnetic field provides a reference direction, *magnetic north*. The cartographer has drawn that direction on the chart. If you want to sail from your present position to Port Contentment you can measure the angle on the chart between that reference direction and the course line to Port Contentment. On deck you have another instrument, called the ship's compass, which measures the angle between that same reference direction and the direction in which the ship is pointing. If you keep that deck angle equal to the chart angle, you will get to Port Contentment, all things else being equal (which they never are), even though you may not know the latest geophysical theories about the earth's magnetic field.

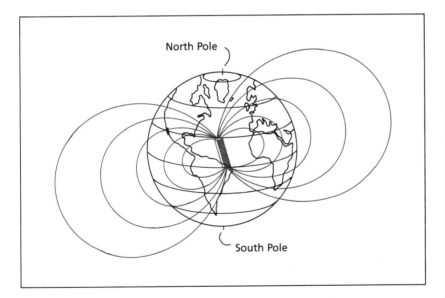

FIGURE 14-5. *The earth's magnetic field is roughly similar to one that would be produced by an inclined bar magnet in its interior.*

Examples of vector addition of two fields

first field
second field
resultant

15

Handbearing and Ship's Compasses

There are two superficially different kinds of marine compass: the handbearing compass and the ship's compass. The former term is a contraction for handheld *bearing compass*—a compass designed for convenience while taking magnetic bearings to navaids, and marks, etc. The *ship's* or *steering* compass measures the angle between the centerline of the ship and the direction of magnetic north. It is designed primarily for steering, for keeping to a magnetic course. These two kinds of compass are basically the same in their innards; they differ mainly in their sighting systems. They are to be thought of as conventional or traditional compasses, which use a pivoted magnetic needle that orients itself in a magnetic field; I leave aside the recently developed "fluxgate" compasses, electronic compasses that dispense with the needle.

handbearing compass   In books on big-boat piloting the handbearing compass is usually given short shrift, not because bearings are unimportant for large-ship piloting, but because, on a large ship, there are devices such as bearing circles and peloruses for taking those bearings. Moreover, in using a handbearing compass you must be sure that it is well removed from extraneous shipboard sources of magnetism—frequently a tough requirement on a large steel ship, which is a rich source of magnetic perturbations that may in fact change with time as the ship as a whole magnetizes or demagnetizes. On a small fiberglass, wooden, or aluminum boat it is usually much easier to find a location free of magnetic perturbation, and having found it you can be reasonably sure that it will remain satisfactory unless you carelessly introduce nearby magnetic sources.

One of the ways of checking the ship's compass is by comparing it with a good handbearing compass (Chapter 18), and a handbearing com-

126

pass can in fact pinch-hit for the ship's compass if necessary. For these reasons, as well as for its primary purpose of taking bearings for piloting, I think a good handbearing compass is a most useful tool to have aboard, second only to the ship's compass.

To help clarify why the marine compass is what it is, let's look at a brief "history" of a predecessor that is still in use today—the woodsman's, trail, or Boy Scout compass.

An early kind of compass consisted of a magnetized needle inserted into a piece of straw that floated on some liquid and hence was able to rotate toward magnetic north (Figure 15-1a). Some of its obvious limitations were removed by dispensing with the straw and instead balancing the needle at its center, so that it could rotate more freely (Figure 15-1b). If every compass user wanted only to go in a northerly direction, compass development could have stopped there. But users often wanted to head in some other direction than north, so a card with markings for the different cardinal directions—north, south, east, and west—and possibly intermediate directions as well—was placed under the needle (Figure 15-1c). By sighting over the card one could at least *roughly* determine a direction with respect to magnetic north. This crude sighting is not very accurate, so a pair of sights—sighting vanes, slits, or whatever—was added to improve the accuracy, and for the same reason the card was calibrated in degrees (Figure 15-1d). The resultant model has all the elements of a modern woodsman or trail compass; add some design features to make it rugged and compact and you have such a compass (Figure 15-1e). The sighting system of this compass is not usually the simple sighting vanes shown in Figure 15-1d, but there is always an equivalent system.

This is a practical kind of compass, and it is still used on land. What is wrong with it for marine use? Why does a skipper rarely take a magnetic bearing with a trail compass?

There are two reasons. In order to use it to take a magnetic bearing you must make sure that the North–South line on the compass card is aligned with the needle over it. This doesn't happen automatically. If you take such a compass off the shelf or out of your pocket, and put it on the table, the needle will of course swing and finally settle down to point toward magnetic north, but only by accident will the card be so oriented that the North–South reference line is exactly under the needle. You must rotate the card to get the line under the needle, and do it slowly so as

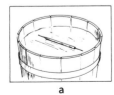 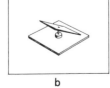 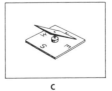 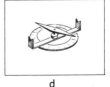 

a   b   c   d   e

FIGURE 15-1. *How to invent the land compass; or, from medieval mariner to Boy Scout in five steps.*

not to start the needle swinging again. Then and only then can you use the sighting system to find direction.

This is a slow and fussy procedure, but for the hiker who uses his compass only occasionally, it is not unfeasible. It is, however, clumsy to the point of impracticality for the frequent checking of the steering compass on a boat. The marine compass must be invented.

The first stage of this invention was provided by an unknown genius who attached the needle directly to the card—of course orienting it along the card's North–South line so that needle and line were always properly aligned. Then he put needle and card as a whole on the pivot (Figure 15-2a).

But a card with an attached needle has its own problems; the earth's magnetism is not a very strong force, and it is one thing for that force to make a light needle by itself rotate, and another for it to make the much more massive needle-plus-card rotate. The cards had then to be made as light as possible; they were often made of tissue or rice paper stretched on a wire frame. Such *dry card compasses* were still in use up to perhaps a hundred years ago, but being so light they were skittish. With little inertia, they were easily affected by the motion of the boat, and if the sea was at all rough they swung and oscillated and didn't settle down readily.

Some other clever person then had the idea of immersing the pivoted card, now made not of paper but of some very thin, light nonmagnetic metal in a clear liquid. This had two desirable effects: First, the buoyancy of the liquid acting on needle-plus-card in effect reduced the weight of the card, and hence reduced friction at the pivot; the card could then rotate relatively easily. Second, the liquid provided a damping mechanism that inhibited the card's sudden tilting and wild swinging, even in rough seas.

The pivoted needle-plus-card in a liquid is now the basic mariner's compass, both handbearing and ship's. Of course there can be many variations and elaborations of these basic components. The card can be flat or dished or half-spherical; a sighting system is added for a handbearing compass; compensating magnets to cancel out extraneous shipboard

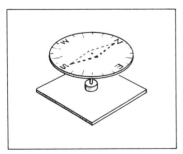

Attach needle under card; pivot assembly on bearing

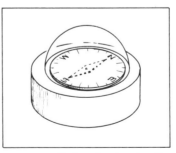

Encase needled card; add liquid for damping

For *handbearing compass,* add sighting system—vanes, wires, notches, etc.

For *ship's compass,* add reference line (lubber's line) that is an extension of ship's centerline

FIGURE 15-2. *From land compass to marine compass in three steps.*

sources of magnetism are added for the ship's compass; there may be lights for night work; etc. But the two basics are as above, a needled card in a damping liquid. The only exception that I know of is the handbearing compass manufactured by the E. S. Ritchie Company that has no liquid but is damped by electromagnetic "eddy currents."

All liquid-damped marine compasses are basically the same, but they may look different. Handbearing compasses in particular can have a variety of sighting systems, which impart a different appearance to different models. The point is illustrated in Figure 15-3, which shows three popular styles.

The first of the three is as basic as can be. The card-plus-needle is actually a hemispheric inverted bowl-plus-needle. It rotates on its bearing in the liquid encased in a transparent dome, attached to which are a handle and two sighting vanes. In use you rotate the handle, hence the sighting vanes—the card remaining stationary, in principle—until the object in question is lined up in the two sights; then you read the angle.

The second compass is also designed to be held at arm's length, but the sighting system is different. The optical system has, among other things, a lens or prism that produces a *magnified* image of the card markings. It is then practical to have the markings at every degree instead of every five degrees, as is common with the first, basic compass.

A third popular type is the "hockey puck" Mini, shown in Figure 15-3c. It has the ubiquitous liquid-damped card, and it too has an optical system that magnifies the card's degree markings, but the system also projects the image of the card markings to infinity. Thus you can hold the compass next to your eye and still be able to focus on the markings. Since

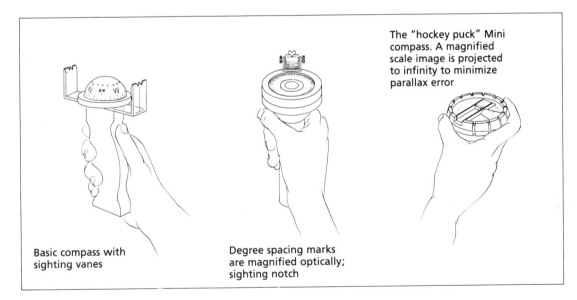

The "hockey puck" Mini compass. A magnified scale image is projected to infinity to minimize parallax error

Basic compass with sighting vanes

Degree spacing marks are magnified optically; sighting notch

FIGURE 15-3. *Three standard models of handbearing compasses.*

ship's compass

the sighted object and the image of the markings are both essentially at infinity there is no parallax error, and the fact that you can stabilize this kind of compass by holding it against your eye is also an advantage.

There are two differences between handbearing and ship's compasses. First, I remarked earlier that one is free to use a handbearing compass anywhere on the boat and so can search out a place without extraneous magnetic fields produced by shipboard equipment or objects. With a ship's compass you don't have that liberty; it is where it is, usually in the cockpit, perhaps close to an iron engine, instruments, or wiring, any of which may produce a local error-causing magnetic field. In the ship's compass one attempts to *negate* this field by built-in compensating magnets that can be adjusted (one hopes) to produce a field that is exactly opposite to the perturbing field, and so cancels it out. This process is called *compensating the compass;* one example of compensating magnets is shown in Figure 15-4b; I'll have more to say about them later.

The second difference between handbearing and ship's compasses is that the handbearing uses the sightline to an object as a reference line, whereas the ship's compass uses a *lubber's line.* This term can be confusing, since the lubber's line on a modern compass is not a line at all; I'll try to clarify it with some history.

A common type of marine compass many years ago had a flat circular glass top (Figure 15-4a). A line was scratched or marked through the center of this top; this was the *lubber's line,* and as you looked down on the compass you could read the angle between the zero degree line on the card (magnetic north) and the lubber's line. If then the compass was carefully installed so that the lubber's line was along the centerline of the boat—or parallel to it—the angle between lubber's line and magnetic

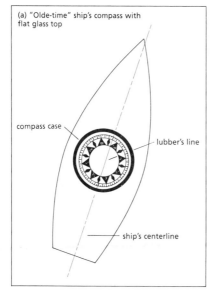

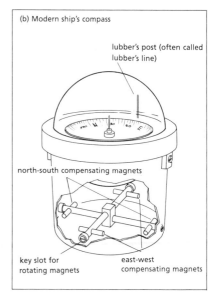

FIGURE 15-4.
The ship's compass, old and new.

north would be the angle between centerline and magnetic north, which is just what a ship's compass should measure.

In reading the angle on the compass of Figure 15-4a you don't need the whole lubber's line. When you look down on the compass all you need is that small part of the lubber's line that is directly over the edge of the compass card. You can dispense with most of the lubber's line, leaving only a small fragment of it, and still read the compass perfectly well. The same remark applies to the compasses with hemispherical glass cases, which were developed later. Lubber's lines were marked on these tops, then they were replaced by fragments of lines, which were in turn replaced by bent wires or strips whose shape conformed to the interior shape of the compass dome. These curved strips still were called the "lubber's lines." In fact, in many modern compasses the curved strip has evolved into a simple straight vertical post—still the "lubber's line." You may read that the compass should be installed so that the lubber's line is parallel to the centerline, but if the lubber's line is a vertical post and the centerline is a horizontal line you have every right to be puzzled. Tradition aside then, I think it is best to call the vestigial vertical post that used to be the lubber's line by what it is, a vertical post, or in deference to its origin a *lubber's post.* I have done just that in Figure 15-4b. The true lubber's line is of course the line through the base of the post and the center of the compass, and it is this line that is parallel to the centerline of the ship in a properly installed compass.

16

Checking a Handbearing Compass

A handbearing compass is very useful aboard a small boat—but only if it is accurate. This chapter is about ways of checking its accuracy.

A useful spinoff of the discussion is that it will make it easier to explain in Chapter 17 how to check a ship's compass. There is more to checking a ship's compass than a handbearing one: there are problems of alignment, of deviation due to extraneous shipboard-produced magnetic fields, etc. But there is also much in common, so I hope this discussion of handbearing problems will whittle down the problems of ship's compass checking and make it easier to understand them later.

What is there to check in a handbearing compass; what can possibly go wrong? I am not an expert, but I have talked with some experts and gathered that some of the possibilities are these.

what can go wrong

The pivot on its jeweled bearing can wear unevenly, possibly after many years, so that the card doesn't move freely—a circumstance obviously detrimental to accuracy. Sometimes a needle may be misaligned. A bubble may form in the fluid, which won't affect accuracy if the bubble is small, but there is always the question of how small is "small." It is possible that the compass one has is not balanced correctly for the magnetic dip of the region in which it is used (Chapter 14), so if you are in the Northern hemisphere, say, buy your compass locally and not from an itinerant Australian seaman. These are, to repeat, merely possibilities. On the whole I think you can count on a new factory-checked handbearing compass of good design—for example, a "hockey puck" Mini—to be accurate to a degree or so.

If you use any of the techniques about to be described for checking a handbearing compass, there is one precaution to be observed. You must be sure that at the place where you use the compass only the earth's magnetic field acts on it; there must be no extraneous interaction from local magnetic sources. On a boat you must be certain that no sources of magnetism—the engine, current-carrying wires, magnets in speakers and instruments, etc.—affect the compass. Choose your location with common sense; farther from the cockpit, with its engine and instruments, is usually better than nearer. Even away from a boat you have to be alert to unexpected magnetic perturbations; a floating pier might seem innocuous magnetically, but it won't necessarily be so if it floats on large iron drums.

check for magnetic interference

One way of checking for extraneous magnetic effects on a boat is to take the magnetic bearing of a distant shore object for different boat orientations. For example, if the boat is at a mooring or on an anchor and, due to changing tides, swings in different directions at different times, take the bearing of the shore object for a half dozen or so different directions. If all the readings are the same it is likely that there is no local magnetic perturbation.

If you are not on a boat, but are, say, on a pier, you can't swing the pier in different directions. But if you take the bearing of some distant shore object from several different locations on the pier, always getting the same result, it is unlikely that there is any local source of magnetic field. If such a source existed it is hard to imagine how it could produce the same effect in several different locations.

Given a suitable location, checking a handbearing compass means measuring a bearing with it and comparing the result with the same bearing as measured accurately in some other way by some reliable citizen. Two very reliable classes of citizenry are first, astronomers, and second, cartographers—the makers of charts. Let's see how we can use their work for our purposes.

checking a bearing

I will begin with an astronomical technique, but discuss it only briefly, since it provides a check at only two points of the compass. It also requires some knowledge outside the necessary ken of the coastal pilot. But the method is accurate and interesting. If you are thinking of branching out beyond coastal into celestial navigation it provides an easy if limited introduction to some aspects of that art.

There is a publication, *The Nautical Almanac*, that tabulates data from which the true bearing of the sun can be found at any instant of the year. (More precisely, the bearing is of the so-called *ground point* of the sun—that spot on the earth's surface that is directly under the sun.) If you could deduce from the Almanac the bearing of the sun at some time of day and compare the result with the bearing measured at the same time with your handbearing compass, you would have a check on the latter. (The true bearing would of course have to be converted to a magnetic bearing using the local variation.)

Performing this check at most times of the day requires a more than elementary knowledge of celestial navigation. It requires tilting the compass up to measure the bearing of the elevated sun, and no handbearing compass is accurate when it is tilted substantially. But there are two special times when life becomes easier: when the sun is rising and when it is setting. Then the sun is on the horizon, and you can point the level compass easily and accurately toward it. The astronomical calculations become easier at those times, too. The technique then is to shoot the bearing of the sun when it is peeping over the horizon in the morning or disappearing below it in the evening and compare that bearing with astronomical predictions. Note that these bearings are not necessarily true east in the morning nor true west in the evening, except at two times of the year. You can sometimes win bar bets with these facts. "Hey listen, this guy thinks the sun didn't rise in the east this morning."

One virtue of checking only at sunrise and sunset is that then you don't need the whole *Nautical Almanac;* only limited extracts from it are required, and coastal piloting references often have these. For example, in Eldridge's *East Coast Tide and Pilot Book* there is a table called "Sun's True Bearing on Rising and Setting," and instructions on how to use it. This true bearing depends on the date, or more precisely on the sun's *declination,* a basic celestial navigation concept, so you have to use the table in conjunction with still another one that gives the sun's declination. But this latter, one-page table is clearly explained and easy to use, even if you don't know what declination is.

Other reference books besides Eldridge give similar information in a different format. For example, in *Reed's Nautical Almanac* there are tables of the "Sun's Bearing at Sunrise and Sunset," along with rather more complete tables from which the sun's declination can be found for any time of day or year.

Let's look now at checking a compass against the chart. There are two different approaches. I will describe them as if you were located on a boat, but you needn't necessarily be aboard one. You can do these checks on land, even far from the sea, and everything that is said about comparing with charts can be applied on land to comparing with topographic maps.

In the first mode of comparing compass with chart you rely on finding two objects *in transit.* I will have more to say about transits later (Chapter 21); all that is needed now is to know that two objects are said to be in transit when the one is seen from deck to be directly behind the other—when they "line up." Then you know that your position on the chart is somewhere on the extension of the line drawn on the chart between the two. With your favorite protractor you can then measure on the chart the bearing of this transit line—its angle with magnetic north. Then, on deck, measure the compass bearing of the nearest of the two objects, when they are in transit, and compare the result with the "exact" result from the chart.

checking against a transit

This is an accurate and convenient way to check a handbearing compass, and it takes a minimum of effort. In fact, if before a day's sailing you take a few minutes to seek out on the chart the transits you are going to pass, and if you take their bearings on deck when you do pass them, you will often have painlessly collected enough data to check your compass at a goodly number of points.

If you are really feeling laid back you don't even have to draw a line on the chart and use your protractor on it. When two objects are in transit they are said to constitute a *range*. Ranges are useful enough navigationally that they are tabulated in the Light List along with their (true) bearings. These can be converted to magnetic bearings, which then can be compared with on-deck measurements obtained with your handbearing compass. In fact these bearings are sometimes listed to an accuracy of minutes of arc, which is far better accuracy than you can achieve by drawing lines. I don't know how the Coast Guard achieves such accuracy, but more power to them. Here are three examples of range bearings from Light List #1.

> Kennebec River (ME)—Doubling Point Range: 359°
> Salem Channel (MA)—Hospital Point Range: 276° 16′
> Cape Fear River (NC)—Keg Island Range: 003° 19′

A second way of using the chart to check a handbearing compass begins with finding your precise location on the chart—that is, with getting an accurate fix. Then find on the chart some distant landmark or navaid and draw the line on the chart from your location to it. Measure the magnetic bearing of that line. Then from deck seek out the real landmark, measure its bearing with your handbearing compass, and compare the result with the result from the chart.

checking against a charted bearing

This method is usually less accurate than use of a transit line, due to the inevitable inaccuracy in the initial fix. We can estimate how the position inaccuracy affects the bearing by using the Rule of Sixty (Figure 16-1). The illustration shows first the bearing line drawn from the exact position of the ship to the landmark. This exact position is not known; all that is known is the assumed position, derived by some inevitably inaccurate method of position fixing. The error in position, the distance between exact and assumed position, is S; the distance away of the landmark is L. The error in the bearing depends of course on what direction S takes; if S happens to lie *along* the bearing line to the landmark it will not generate an error in the bearing angle. In the worst case S is at right angles to the bearing line, and the resultant bearing error is the small angle of the triangle with sides S and L in Figure 16-1; by the rule of Sixty,

$$\text{Error in bearing} = 60\,\frac{S}{L}.$$

For example, if the uncertainty S is 100 feet and the landmark is a nautical mile away (L = 6080 feet), the error in angle is $60° \times {}^{100}\!/_{6080} = 1°$. Sometimes one sees the categorical statement that the object should be 3 miles, 6 miles or some other arbitrary distance away to get adequate

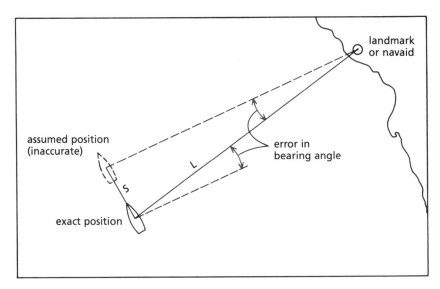

FIGURE 16-1.
*Error in bearing due to
inaccuracy in position.*

accuracy, but if the error of the observer's position is not stated this is
nonsense. If you could fix position to within a few feet or yards, say, you
could use objects much less than a mile away and still introduce less
than 1° error.

How then can the ship's position be fixed as accurately as possible?
There are precision techniques using horizontal sextant angles, but the
average coastal pilot won't want to bother with them. Usually he will fix
his position approximately by locating himself as closely as he can to
some landmark or navaid on the chart. If this is done it is best to find, if
possible, a fixed navaid rather than a floating one. Floating navaids are,
as you know, moored with a chain to an anchor or mooring block on the
sea bottom, but this anchor or block can be dragged out of position. But
even if it keeps its position the navaid on the surface can swing in a circle
under the effect of tide and current. The chain that connects navaid to
anchor/block is usually at least three times the depth of the water. Suppose the depth of water is, say, 30 to 35 feet; The swinging circle on the
surface is then not quite a hundred feet in radius, but it is not much less
than this. For best accuracy in this method choose objects as far away as
possible, and station yourself next to fixed navaids.

17

Aiming the Boat

A peculiar title for a chapter—Aiming the Boat. And the chapter is in a peculiar place. This section of the book is about compasses. The preceding chapter is on handbearing compasses; the succeeding chapter is on ship's compasses. What has aiming the boat to do with compasses? Is there some kind of printer's error here?

No error—at least no printer's error. I discussed the checking of a handbearing compass in the last chapter; I want to do the same for a ship's compass in the next chapter. The handbearing compass was checked by measuring bearings with it and comparing them with more accurate values deduced from the chart or the *Nautical Almanac.* Basically the same technique of measuring and comparing can be applied to the ship's compass. But—and it is a large but—the small boat's compass is rarely set up to take accurate bearings. A large boat's compass is sometimes fitted with a *bearing circle,* a device that enables it to take accurate bearings, but this is not often seen on small boats. So to use the techniques of measuring and comparing bearings with a ship's compass, one must somehow be able to take accurate bearings with it.

A handbearing compass measures the angle between magnetic north and a sighting line; the ship's compass measures the angle between magnetic north and the centerline of the boat. You can make a ship's compass into a bearing compass if you can "aim the boat" accurately—that is, if you can use the centerline as an accurate sighting line. The point of this chapter is to show how to do just that. In fact it will turn out that one wants to aim the boat accurately not only for checking a compass, but also in correcting for a current (Chapter 26), so this discussion will give us one leg up on current correction.

how not to aim

The process of aiming the boat is not difficult, as I'll try to show, but I think it is often not given its due and is described too cavalierly. We read, for example, in various piloting books, that in taking the bearing of an object with the ship's compass one should "point the bow" at the object or "steer toward the object." But to say "point the bow" without saying where the observer is located is incomplete and ambiguous. You can't just stand anywhere in the boat, steer it so the bow appears to be right in front of the object, and then take the compass reading. If you are on the port cockpit seat and see a lighthouse lined up with the bow, and I am on the starboard seat, I will *not* see it lined up, since our lines of sight through the bow are different. When you point the bow at a landmark to take a bearing you must be sure that your eye is on the centerline. In other words, you must think of the centerline as a rifle barrel, and have that rifle barrel aimed at the landmark when you read the ship's compass. If you don't do this carefully you can generate errors of a few degrees. These are unfortunate but may not be intolerable if you are measuring a bearing to get a fix; they make the fix less accurate but it will probably still be useful. But a few degrees of error is, of course, completely out of the question if you are trying to check a compass to a degree or two.

possible error

To see how a few degrees of error can arise, imagine yourself in the cockpit of a 30-foot sailboat as you line up the very center of the bow with some distant landmark. You can't sight through the mast, so to see that center you have to sight around it. Now if the mast is, say, 6 inches in transverse cross section and 10 or 12 feet from the bow, this offset sighting introduces an error of over a degree, as the Rule of Sixty demonstrates. Even if the mast weren't there and if you placed your feet carefully to straddle the centerline, it is almost inevitable (and hard to detect) that your upper body tilts one way or another so that your eye would not be centered. I have found it not unusual to have the eye offset by a few to several inches in these circumstances. If you are standing in the cockpit, say 20 feet or so from the bow, and your eye is displaced by 6 inches from the centerline, your line of sight will be, again from the Rule of Sixty, at an angle of about 2 degrees from the accurate centerline. Best not to try to check a deviation table to a few degrees with this handicap to begin.

aiming with centerline sights

You must then aim the boat carefully, and there are various ways to do this, depending on the kind of boat. For example, in an open cockpit outboard with a center console you could make a mark on the middle of the console and from it sight across the bow. You might improve on this (Figure 17-1) by using rods or dowels to make a vertical sight at the console (observer's sight) and one at the bow (forward sight), and so have a crude rifle sight. But this technique may not be possible on boats where the centerline is blocked visually. On a sailboat, for example, you can't stand in the cockpit on the centerline and sight on the forestay—the mast is in the way.

Happily, there is a simple alternative to sighting along the centerline. You can sight, not along it, but along a *displaced centerline,* parallel to it and a foot or two away. The error involved in sighting along a centerline displaced, say, a foot from the real one is the same as if you sighted along the real one and the landmark were miraculously displaced by a foot. This error is ordinarily very small and can be estimated by the Rule of Sixty. For example, if you are sighting an object 120 feet away using a centerline displaced one foot from the real one, the error incurred is just ½°. (Set S = 1 foot, L = 120 feet in the Rule.) Double the displacement and you double the error; double the distance and you *halve* the error. So for a centerline displaced by one foot the sighting error for an object 480 feet away is ⅛ of a degree, completely negligible for our practical purposes.

aiming with off-center sights

If this argument from the Rule of Sixty doesn't leave you completely satisfied, you can see how small the error is from a drawing to scale. The drawing below shows the centerline of a 30-foot boat pointing at a buoy 3 feet in diameter and 500 feet away. To the scale shown, the buoy is represented by a dot one millimeter in diameter. A displaced centerline

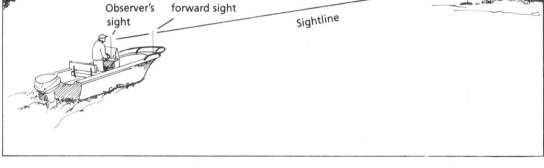

FIGURE 17-1.   *Aiming the boat with a pair of vertical sights on the centerline.*

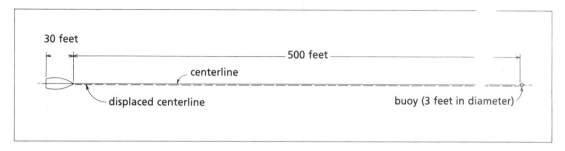

FIGURE 17-2.   *Error introduced by a displaced centerline, to scale.*

one foot away would be represented by a line a third of a millimeter distant from the true centerline. One-third of a millimeter is about the thickness of a fine pencil line; the displaced centerline is so close to the real one that it is hard to draw it satisfactorily. But that very fact indicates how small an error is incurred by sighting along the displaced centerline; in this example it is about 0.2°.

To set up a displaced centerline you must first, of course, set up the real centerline—easily done with a string stretched between mast and forestay or backstay. At two places along it measure outward the chosen perpendicular distance. The two resultant points define the displaced centerline. If you put sights at these two points you have an accurate displaced centerline at your disposal.

A word about the possibilities for these sights. Two vertical rods are adequate (as in Figure 17-1), or the observer's sight can be a slit a few millimeters wide in a vertical strip of thin plywood or aluminum (Figure 17-3), fixed at some convenient place in the cockpit. It can be combined with a forward sight of anything readily seen—say a bit of white tape or red wool on the bow pulpit. The virtue of having a slit rather than a peephole is that you can choose to sight close to the top or bottom of it and in effect get the displaced centerline to point higher or lower; this facilitates sighting on objects at different heights. You *can* use a peephole for the observer's sight, but then the forward sight is best taken to be a vertical rod or wire so that you can still sight higher or lower as necessary.

I have tried both kinds of sights, with no problem, but I favor still another type. It is illustrated below in the specific context of a sailboat

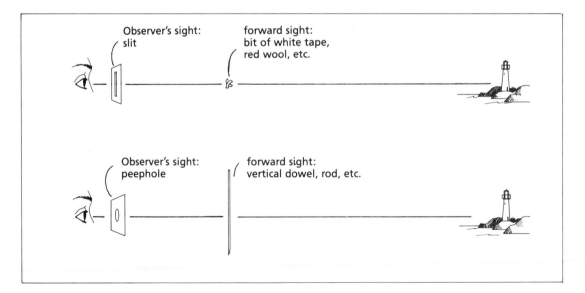

FIGURE 17-3. *The slit sight and the peephole sight.*

cockpit, but there are of course many variants possible. Basically it consists of two lines—of ⅛-inch Dacron, polypropylene, or whatever—attached to a flat piece of plywood or metal with a sighting hole in it. The lengths of the lines are so chosen that when the pair of lines is taut the sighting hole is the desired distance from the centerline; then a forward marker is also fixed at that same distance. The lines can terminate in cliphooks so that they can be attached to fittings on the coamings in a matter of seconds. With Dacron lines, which stretch minimally, the transverse position is repeatable from use to use to within an inch or so—more than adequate accuracy. Moreover the sight is easily stowed and is unbreakable. It also has another useful feature: If the plane defined by the two stretched lines is vertical, the sight is of course at its maximum height. But if you push the sighting hole forward or pull it back, keeping the lines taut, it lowers from that height, still keeping the correct distance from the centerline. In effect, then, you can move the displaced centerline up or down to accommodate different target heights.

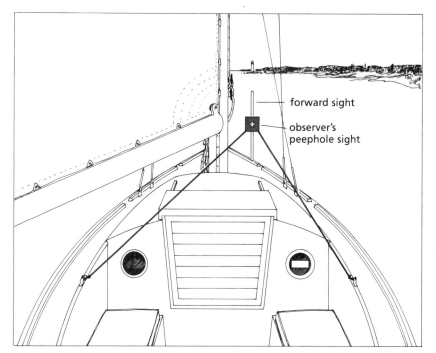

forward sight

observer's peephole sight

FIGURE 17-4.
Sightline parallel to the centerline. Two taut lines of different lengths fix the peephole at the desired distance from the centerline; the forward vertical sight is at that same distance.

18

Checking the Ship's Compass

I started the chapter on Checking a Handbearing Compass with this banal remark: "A handbearing compass is very useful aboard a small boat—but only if it is accurate. This chapter is about ways of checking its accuracy." Banal as it may be, it is unassailable, so I will retread it.

A ship's compass is very useful aboard a small boat—but only if it is accurate. This chapter is about ways of checking its accuracy.

Despite these almost identical statements this chapter is more complicated than the previous one, since a ship's compass can be defective in all the ways of the handbearing compass and some of its own as well.

sources of compass error
It can have the same kinds of "internal" problems—bearings, pivots, etc.—but may also have three "external" problems:

- *Misalignment.* The compass may be so installed that the lubber's line is not parallel to the centerline of the boat.

- *Shipboard magnetism.* There may be extraneous magnetic fields produced by shipboard sources—instruments, engine iron, wiring, etc.—that erroneously deflect the compass needle.

- *Maladjusted compensating magnets.* The internal magnets that are intended to improve accuracy by canceling shipboard magnetism can equally impair accuracy if they are not properly adjusted.

142

Internal compass problems are usually ones for the repair shop; not many skippers can cope with them. But remedies for external problems *are* accessible to the skipper, and he should be able to improve the alignment of the compass, adjust the compensating magnets correctly, etc. These processes as a whole are called *correcting* or *compensating the compass,* the subject of the next chapter.

Alternatively he can learn to live with the errors in his compass. He can, for example, make a table of such errors—a *deviation table*—which enables him to look up, and hence correct for, the error for any boat heading. It may tell him, for example, that the compass reads too high by four degrees near easterly courses, so if he wants to sail at 92° the compass should read 96°. Using a deviation table is obviously less elegant than having a perfectly adjusted compass, but it is much better than simply using an incorrect one. And there may be times when it is not possible or appropriate to compensate a compass starting from scratch. You may be on a cruise and pressed for time; you may be on a chartered or borrowed boat where one simply does not tamper with the compass; you may just be lazy. But you can still be a prudent skipper if you use a deviation table. Here are some ways of making one.

deviation tables

A practical deviation table for the ship's compass must list the compass error at enough points to enable accurate interpolation between them. To find the error at any one point there are the same possibilities as for the handbearing compass; call on the astronomer for help, or on the chartmaker. In Chapter 16 I pointed out how, with a minimal knowledge of astronomy, one can use simple tables to find the true bearing of the sun at sunrise and sunset. Applying local variation converts these to magnetic bearings to compare with compass measurements. That gives two points toward a deviation table, but, of course, many more are required. You can get these points by measuring the bearing of the sun at other times of day than sunrise or sunset, but doing this requires a compass with a "shadow pin," not common on small boats, and familiarity with celestial navigation, so I will bypass this method. It is, however, accurate and can be applied offshore, out of sight of landmarks, and so is uniquely useful. It is often used by professional compass adjusters.

checking deviation with the sun

The two other techniques used to check a handbearing compass are to measure on deck the bearing of a transit line, or of a charted shore object, and compare these with the chart's predictions. Both these techniques can be used with a ship's compass, but less conveniently. A handbearing compass is set up to take bearings; its sighting system is suited to the task. But a ship's compass is set up to measure the angle between the centerline of the ship and magnetic north, and if you want to convert it to a bearing compass you must use the centerline as a sighting line; you must *aim the boat.* These last three words are, I hope, familiar to you, since Chapter 17 is devoted to them, partly in anticipation of this chapter. I won't repeat the words of Chapter 17 here except to remind you that if you want to take a bearing with the ship's compass you can't stand just

taking bearings with the ship's compass

anywhere in the boat and "point the bow" at a shore object—you must use the centerline as a rifle sight.

Checking the ship's compass by measuring the bearing of the transit line of two charted objects is a painless technique, especially if you are in no hurry. It is great for opportunists and the indolent. If, in the course of a day's sailing, you take care to exploit all the transits you encounter, you may well have enough points to make a deviation curve. It will be just as useful as if you constructed the table all at one time. There is however one point to be alert to in taking the bearing of a transit line. You have first to maneuver and steer the boat so that the two objects are *seen* to be in transit. That takes some concentration, and it is easy to forget that seeing the objects line up is only half the problem. In addition, when they are lined up you must aim the boat at them.

The second method for checking a handbearing compass was to take bearings of a shore object from some accurately pinpointed location and compare with the chart's predictions. The same can be done with the ship's compass, but since many points are needed for the deviation table a location with as many charted objects as possible should be chosen. Minimally, a dozen or so are needed, spaced at about 30 degrees; such ideal locations are not common.

However many objects there are, you must measure the bearing of each in its turn. There are two ways of doing this. First, you can get underway and aim the boat simply by steering. In doing this you must be alert not to stray too far from your accurate location. It is easy to so concentrate on sighting the shore object that you move too far for accuracy from the correct location. If you are moored or can anchor at the location there is another possibility. If there is enough wind or current to force the boat to swing in a definite direction, you can put out a bow and stern line to the anchor or mooring. By adjusting the relative lengths of these lines the boat can be made to point in any direction you like. Held by bow line only it points in one direction; by stern line only, at 180° from that direction; by bow and stern lines combined at any intermediate direction. With this method the taking of shore bearings becomes a relatively easy one-man job.

Another method for checking a ship's compass is to compare it with an accurate handbearing compass, and there are a couple of ways of doing this. In the first you dispense with the chart and the need to pinpoint your location, and simply measure the bearing of any object, charted or not, with handbearing and then with ship's compass, and compare. This is an obvious method, but there is a still simpler one. You can compare handbearing and ship's compass directly, without the intermediate step of measuring the same bearing with one and then the other and comparing the results. Here is an analogy. Suppose I have two centimeter scales, one known to be accurate and one in need of testing. To do the testing I could get a series of blocks, measure their lengths with the accurate ruler, write down the results, do the same with the other ruler, and compare the answers. But why bother? Why not simply put one ruler

checking ship's compass by bearings of transit lines

checking ship's compass by bearings of charted shore objects

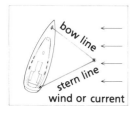

swinging boat by adjusting lengths of bow and stern lines

checking ship's compass with handbearing compass by measuring bearing of same object

against the other and see how their markings compare? Does the 10-centimeter mark on the accurate ruler coincide with that on the other ruler? As simple as that.

From a point on the cockpit exactly on the centerline (perhaps as determined by a string stretched between mast and backstay), measure with the handbearing compass the bearing of the center of the mast. This bearing is the angle between magnetic north and the sightline between compass and the mast; in the present case the sightline is obviously the centerline of the boat. But that is just what the ship's compass purports to measure—the angle between magnetic north and the centerline of the boat. You are then comparing directly handbearing (assumed exact) and ship's compass readings. They should agree; if they don't, the deviation is:

comparing ship's and handbearing compass directly

$$\text{Deviation} = \frac{\text{Exact (hand-}}{\text{bearing) reading}} - \frac{\text{Approximate (Ship's}}{\text{compass) reading}}$$

The deviation has a sign, plus or minus.

In using this method you must of course find a sighting location on the centerline that is free of shipboard-generated magnetic fields. This may be difficult in that the cockpit is usually close to the engine and other sources of magnetic perturbation. But there is no reason for limiting yourself to a centerline location. The bearing of a line parallel to the centerline—a displaced centerline—will be the same as the bearing of the centerline; a measurement of it can be compared with the ship's compass reading. The great advantage of using a displaced centerline is that you can choose a sighting location that is not only free of magnetic perturbation but is physically convenient.

To establish a displaced centerline, choose a sighting location for the handbearing compass, then measure its offset distance from the ship's centerline. Some 10 or 15 feet forward measure outward from the centerline the same offset distance, and put a mark there to be sighted. As I mentioned in Chapter 17 it is not hard to get accuracy of parallelism of the displaced and real centerlines to ½° or so. If in addition you have a handbearing compass accurate to about a degree you are well on your way to easily finding as many points as you need for an accurate deviation curve.

Once again this can be an opportunist's method. You must take readings for the boat heading in different directions, but you can simply take them incidentally to a day's sail as the boat naturally moves on different courses. Whenever there is a course change, steady on the new course and read the ship's compass; then sight the sighting mark and read the handbearing compass. If it takes more than 20 seconds you are doing something wrong. Or you can take readings when anchored or at a mooring, with adjustable bow and stern lines, as described above in connection with taking bearings of charted shore objects.

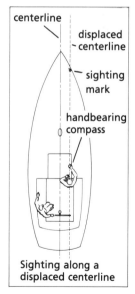

centerline

displaced centerline

sighting mark

handbearing compass

Sighting along a displaced centerline

In the next chapter I will show a deviation curve obtained by this method, but for the moment let's look at the question of what to expect in a deviation curve. What should it look like?

In this discussion I will not consider internal problems as a source of error. If there is a problem with the bearing or pivot it is usually random and irregular—the needle will sometimes stick or bind in one way, sometimes in another. The deviation that I discuss is due to the effect of shipboard-produced magnetic perturbation. The ship's compass needle responds to the magnetic field of the earth. Other local fields, due to shipboard instruments, equipment, or whatever, also affect the needle. The problem is basically one of vector addition. The earth's magnetic field and the shipboard field add (combine) vectorially to produce a net field that is not in the direction of magnetic north.

Vector addition is not exactly a sexy subject. People don't leap out of bed in the morning crying "Whee, I am going to add vectors today." Books on vector analysis quickly get heavy and are easy to put down. Vector addition is, in short, dull, dull, dull. But to understand its rudiments is useful, useful, useful, and I have speculated on how to make it interesting, gripping, even dramatic. On the printed page it is usually people, their characters and personalities, that are interesting. You remember Tom Swift, Dr. Doolittle, Hamlet, or David Copperfield in a way that you don't remember the binomial theorem. It would seem hard to populate the world of vector addition with interesting characters, but I thought it was worth a try.

My attempt took the form of looking for a hero in whose fate we might be interested—and it occurred to me that the compass needle is just such a hero. It is (he is?), as we all are, acted on by different forces that tend to pull him in different directions, and he must achieve some resolution or balance under those forces. So I worked up the "drama" below, in which Compass Needle is the main protagonist. I hope I don't have to add that the whimsy in this (drama?) is in the characters, not in the technical matters.

DEVIATION
or
The Secret of the Shape of the Deviation Curve
A Magnetic Drama in Six Acts

Cast of Characters

Earth's Magnetic Field (also called EARTHFIELD)   The magnetic field of the earth, that acts on the ship's compass. It happens to be drawn here at a certain angle, called the *variation,* with respect to

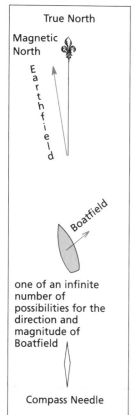

True North

Magnetic North

Earthfield

Boatfield

one of an infinite number of possibilities for the direction and magnitude of Boatfield

Compass Needle

True North, but at another point of the globe the angle might be different. Whatever the angle, EARTHFIELD has the same character: reliable, steady, strong.

Boat's Magnetic Field (or BOATFIELD)   The magnetic field at the ship's compass produced by magnetic sources on the boat: wires carrying current, magnets in speakers, the magnetism of the engine, electronic equipment, etc. Whatever the sources, the fields they produce all add up to one net BOATFIELD, which can point in any direction and can have any magnitude. Usually it is smaller than EARTHFIELD. (If it is not, the compass adjuster is in *big* trouble.) BOATFIELD is devious, cunning, sneaky, not to be trusted. But it has one redeeming feature—its loyalty. BOATFIELD is firmly attached to the boat, and if the boat turns, BOATFIELD faithfully turns with it.

Compass Needle   A weak, oscillating character with no sense of direction of its own—it is influenced by any magnetic field it meets. Its innermost desire is to be one with EARTHFIELD and point in EARTHFIELD'S direction (Magnetic North). This desire is often frustrated by BOATFIELD, who cunningly makes NEEDLE *deviate* from this deepest wish.

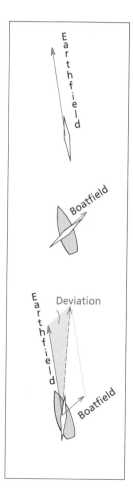

ACT I

The scene is an ideal world in which BOATFIELD does not exist, so COMPASS NEEDLE happily points in the exact direction of EARTH-FIELD.

ACT II

The scene is an imaginary world from which EARTHFIELD has been banished so COMPASS NEEDLE must snuggle up (Yuk!) to BOAT-FIELD only.

ACT III

The scene returns to the real world where both EARTHFIELD and BOATFIELD exist. NEEDLE wants desperately to point in EARTH-FIELD'S direction, but BOATFIELD inexorably turns him aside. He must compromise, and so points in a direction between the two that is determined by a Law of the Land known as VECTOR ADDITION. The angle between the direction in which NEEDLE points and the direction of EARTHFIELD is the loathsome *deviation*.

ACT IV

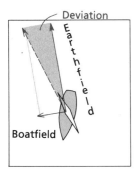

NEEDLE secretly hopes that some other orientation of the boat will give him the freedom to line up with EARTHFIELD. He tries again when the boat has rotated but, alas, to no avail. Although the boat has changed its orientation, the toadying BOATFIELD has followed it right around. In the new orientation a compromise must again be made and NEEDLE lines up not with EARTHFIELD but in a direction somewhere between it and BOATFIELD. Deviation again. Deviation in a different direction, deviation of a different magnitude and different sign—but deviation!

ACT V

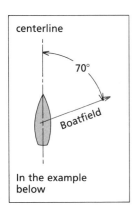

NEEDLE is in despair. "Is there no orientation of the boat that will let me line up with EARTHFIELD?" he cries plaintively to the air. To his surprise he hears an answer from a Friendly Sage who has come on stage unseen. "Yes, there is. I am a Friendly Sage who understands the laws of VECTOR ADDITION. There are two orientations of the boat for which you will point in EARTHFIELD'S direction. They are when the boat is so rotated that BOATFIELD either points in the same direction as EARTHFIELD or in precisely the opposite direction. That is the good news. The bad news is that for every *other* orientation of the boat there will be deviation according to the laws of VECTOR ADDITION." NEEDLE is overjoyed at the good news and arranges for a succession of boat orientations, differing by 45° from one to the next, to check on the bad news. He finds, as you see from the drawing below, that Friendly Sage was exactly right. The number above each diagram is the deviation for that orientation.

(For this example the angle between BOATFIELD and centerline has been taken to be 70°, but it might have been chosen to be anywhere between 0° and 360°.)

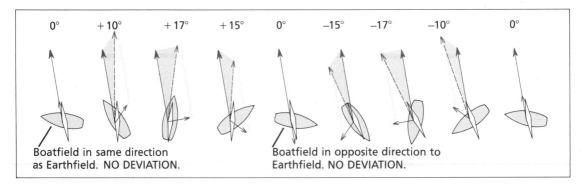

18-1. *Origin of the deviation curve.*

ACT VI

But his happiness is shortlived. When he realizes that there can never be more than two orientations in which he achieves his heart's desire, he again becomes discouraged. Happily, Friendly Sage is there to advise him. "This is an imperfect world," he says, "and you can't expect to find perfection in it. Now I have plotted on a graph your results for deviation as a function of the angle between the directions of BOATFIELD and EARTHFIELD. (The reader will see the graph in Figure 18-2). See how smooth, how symmetric, how graceful the curve is. Yes, you deviate, but you deviate in such a balanced, elegant, and pleasing way that you should be proud of it." And NEEDLE looked. And NEEDLE saw. And it was as the Sage had spoken. And he at once became contented with his lot and accepted his fate—and pivoted happily ever after.

CURTAIN

End of drama, but not quite end of explanation. The curve of Figure 18–2 is not a conventional deviation curve. It is correct enough, but usually one doesn't make a plot of deviation against Earthfield-Boatfield angle, since it is not useful in practice. What *is* useful is a plot (or table) of deviation against magnetic heading (the angle between magnetic north and the centerline). Suppose you want to sail on a course of 37° magnetic. What will the compass read on that course? If you have a plot or, as in

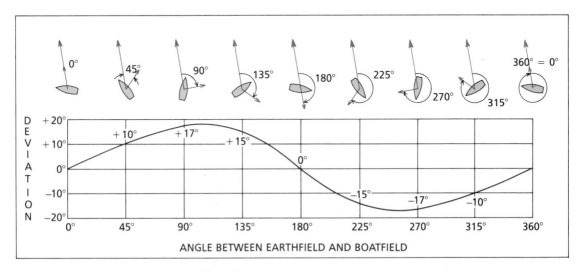

Figure 18-2. *Deviation vs. Earthfield-Boatfield angle.*

the margin to the left, a table of deviation versus magnetic heading, you simply look up the deviation for 37° and calculate the compass reading from

$$\text{Compass reading} = \text{Magnetic heading} - \text{Deviation};$$
$$34° = 37° - 3°.$$

Magnetic Deviation
heading

Magnetic heading	Deviation
0°	+6
15°	+5
30°	+3
45°	+3
60°	0
75°	−2
90°	−3
.	.
.	.
.	.

You could of course do the same thing with a plot, and would then find interpolation even easier.

The curve in Figure 18-2 can be made into one of deviation versus magnetic heading, and I will go into that in a moment, but first note some features of that curve; it is redrawn to smaller scale as the left-hand curve A of Figure 18-3 below. In that curve the point at 0 degrees is the same as the point at 360 degrees, since 0° and 360° are the same angle. Now suppose I were to cut the curve vertically along the line shown, and move the leftmost part of the curve to the right so that the point at 0° coincided with the point at 360°. I would get the new curve B, which *looks* quite different from curve A but is really not. It conveys exactly the same information as the original.

Why bother to take a nicely symmetrical curve and make it into an asymmetrical but basically identical one? The method in this madness is that it permits us to convert the curve of Figure 18-2 to the much more useful curve of *deviation* versus *magnetic heading*. To do this I will cut that curve at 70° and make a new curve of it, according to the prescription of Figure 18-3. I choose 70° because Figure 18-2 has been drawn for an assumed angle between centerline and boatfield of 70°. Given that fact you can easily convince yourself with a diagram that 70° on the curve of Figure 18-2 corresponds to a magnetic heading of zero. In short, the cut curve can be considered to start at zero on the magnetic heading scale, and with this labeling it becomes the desired curve Figure 18-4 of *deviation* versus *magnetic heading*.

Figure 18-4 shows then the possible shape of a deviation curve for a 17° maximum deviation. Incidentally, 17° is a larger deviation than is common on small boats; I chose this relatively large number not because it is typical but because it makes the drawings clearer. But that aside,

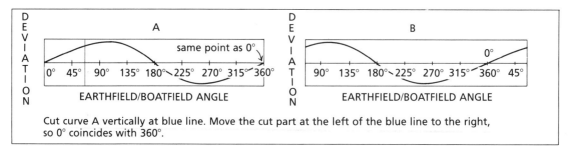

Cut curve A vertically at blue line. Move the cut part at the left of the blue line to the right, so 0° coincides with 360°.

FIGURE 18-3. *Converting the curve A to the different-looking but basically identical curve B.*

note that for 17° there is an infinite variety of other possible shapes generated by cutting Figure 18-2 not at the arbitrarily chosen 70°, but at any other point: 26°, 134°, 273°, whatever. There are as many different 17° deviation curves as there are places to cut Figure 18-2, which is another way of saying that there are as many different 17° deviation curves as there are angles between the shipboard-generated magnetic field and earth's magnetic field.

What about other maximum deviation angles? If I have a deviation angle of 14°, I do exactly the same thing—construct a curve like Figure 18-2 for 14°, cut it, and rearrange it to get all possible 14° deviation curves. I could do the same thing for 13°, say, or any other number I chose. Four possible deviation curves for different maximum deviations, out of the infinite number possible, are shown in Figure 18-5.

I have been assuming that the compass is aligned properly—that is, that the lubber's line and centerline are parallel. If they are not, the misalignment introduces an error. As the figure in the margin shows, if the lubber's line is rotated clockwise with respect to the centerline (on looking down on the compass), the compass reading will be too high; if counterclockwise, too low. This error is constant, the same for every direction (heading) of the boat. For example, if it amounted to 3°, then even if there were no magnetic deviation error, the compass would read high by three degrees whatever the ship's course might be. If there were deviation due to magnetic sources this error adds to the magnetic deviation error, with the effect of raising or lowering the deviation curve so that it is not the same height above and below the horizontal axis. Consider a deviation curve with maximum positive deviation of 10° and negative of −10°. A 3° misalignment error would make the total positive deviation into 10° + 3° = 13°, and would make the 10° negative deviation into

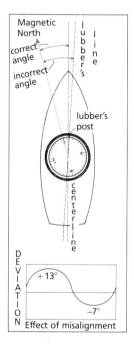

I have been assuming that the compass is aligned properly—that is,

D
E
V
I
A
T
I
O
N

Effect of misalignment

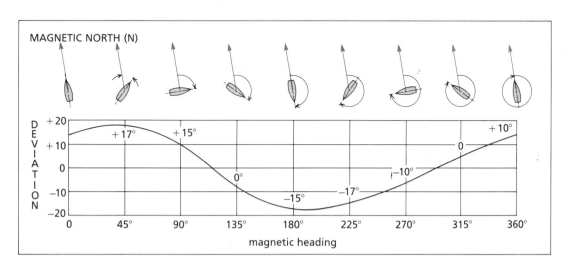

FIGURE 18-4. *Deviation versus magnetic heading as derived from the curve of Figure 18-2.*

$-10° + 3° = -7°$. The curve would no longer be symmetrical above and below the horizontal axis, as the drawing in the margin shows. This lack of symmetry is then a sensitive test for misalignment. One of the curves in Figure 18-5 shows the effect of misalignment.

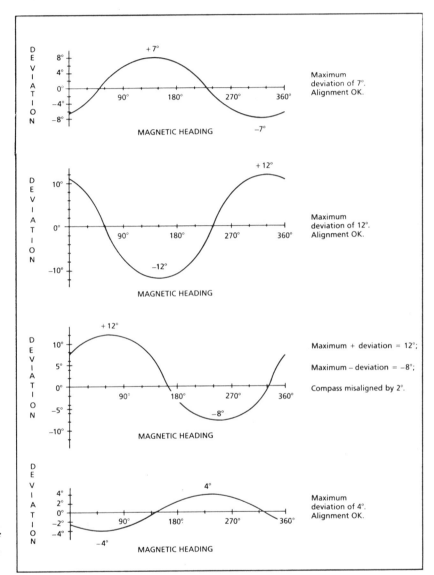

FIGURE 18-5.

A small selection of representative deviation curves.

19

Compensating the Ship's Compass

       A reliable ship's compass with an accurate deviation table makes for a happy skipper. Only one thing can make for more happiness—a reliable, perfectly compensated ship's compass that requires no deviation table at all. This chapter is about the pursuit of such happiness.

We want then not merely to check a compass but to systematically eliminate the sources of error in it. As I outlined in Chapter 18, there are at least four sources: the internal problem of defective bearings, pivots, etc., and the three external problems of misalignment, incorrectly adjusted compensating magnets, and shipboard-produced magnetic fields.

There is a variety of procedures for compensating a compass, and I will present two of them later. But all the procedures start with the same two steps: checking for internal problems and checking that the compensating magnets are "in neutral." Both these steps should be done with the compass off the boat and on some flat surface well clear of perturbing fields—for example, on a wooden tabletop.

You can test for internal problems by checking reproducibility. Read the compass when it is stationary on a table, then deflect the card by bringing a small magnet close to the compass so the card swings; take the magnet away and see if you get back the original reading. If you do this with the compass oriented in a few different directions, and the readings are always reproducible, you can be pretty sure that there is nothing wrong with the compass's internal organs.

There is another way of testing reproducibility, which I think is more realistic and also more stringent in that I have seen compasses pass the magnetic deflection test but fail this one. First, devise some way of setting

testing reproducibility

the compass on the tabletop so that it can be picked up and put back down in exactly its original position and orientation. One way of doing this is simply to tape a strip of stiff paper or thin cardboard to the base of the compass, with one edge of the strip along a diameter (Figure 19-1). Then orient the strip with respect to a line drawn on the tabletop. Lift the compass and wave and twirl it to simulate boat motion, then put it back in its original orientation and see if you get back the original reading. Do this for lines in a few different directions, and if the readings are always reproducible there is probably nothing wrong with the compass's innards.

I mentioned in Chapter 15 the general rationale of compensating magnets. They are intended to cancel, negate, or *compensate* the magnetic field produced at the compass needle by shipboard sources. The second step in compensating a compass is to check that these compensators have, of themselves, no effect on the compass needle. Their effect is reserved for canceling unwanted fields.

I have until now mentioned only the built-in compensators (B.I.C.'s) shown in Figure 15-4, because they are almost universally used these days. Before they became common, however, compensation was usually done with two *external* compensating magnets. These are simply bar magnets placed near the compass, with one along the centerline and the other along a line through the center of the compass and perpendicular to the centerline—the *athwartship line* (Figure 19-2). The centerline magnet (called the North-South corrector) is at right angles to the centerline, just as the other magnet (called the East-West corrector) is at right angles to the athwartship line. The reason for these names will become clear soon.

Although external compensating magnets are not common these days I will begin discussing compensation in their terms, since it is rela-

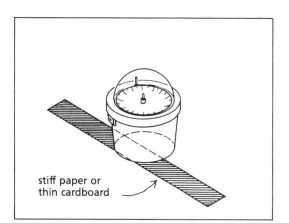

stiff paper or
thin cardboard

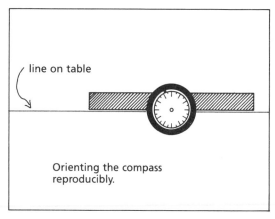

line on table

Orienting the compass
reproducibly.

FIGURE 19-1. *A thin piece of cardboard taped to the base of a compass, with an edge of the cardboard along a diameter of the base.*

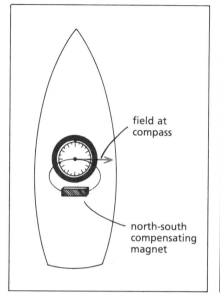
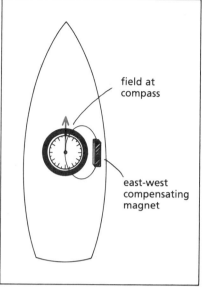

field at
compass

north-south
compensating
magnet

field at
compass

east-west
compensating
magnet

FIGURE 19-2.
External compensating magnets and the fields they produce at the compass needle. Built-in correctors (B.I.C.'s) produce the same kinds of fields, but with different arrangements of magnets.

tively easy to understand how they work. The fields they produce are simple to visualize compared with the fields of the rotating, built-in correctors. In fact, rotating correctors produce the same kinds of fields as the external ones, but with a different and less intuitive mechanism. You have to be a good visualizer of magnetic fields in space to follow how the rotating magnet's field changes as the magnet goes from horizontal to vertical and back again, so it is good to get one leg up by looking at these fields as produced relatively simply by external compensators.

Let's look first at names. Why is one of the magnets in Figure 19-2 called the N-S corrector and the other the E-W corrector? (Note that these names imply magnetic, not true, directions.) The answer can be read from Figure 19-3. When the ship is pointing due north—that is, when its centerline is in the direction of the earth's magnetic field—the field of the E-W corrector is along that line as well. The corrector then tends to line up the needle in the direction in which it is already lined up—in short, it has no effect on the needle. The field of the N-S corrector *does* have an effect. It is at right angles to the earth's field, and so tends to make the needle rotate in its direction, away from the centerline. If you were trying to correct the compass with the ship on a north-south course you would need only to adjust the N-S compensator, and that is the origin of its name; similarly for the E-W compensator on an east-west course.

The shipboard-produced deviating fields that the compensators are intended to negate are of course different in strength and direction for every boat. To adapt to the requirements of different boats the compensating magnets must be able to produce fields of a variety of strengths and fields that can change sign so that, pointing in one direction, they can also be made to point in the other direction. With external compen-

compensating magnet fields

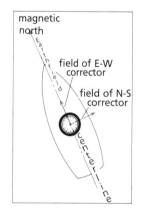

FIGURE 19-3.
When the ship is pointing toward magnetic north, only the N-S compensator has an effect on the compass.

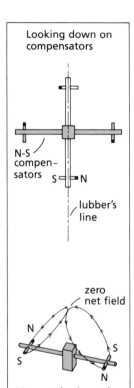

Looking down on compensators

N-S compen- sators

lubber's line

zero net field

Magnets horizontal. Field of one opposite to field of other. Zero net field.

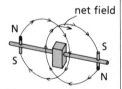

net field

Magnets vertical. Field of one adds to field of other to produce net field.

sators the varying field strength is achieved by moving them closer to or farther from the compass. Obviously the farther away, the less compensation; if you take the compensator off the boat and put it in your gear locker you will get no compensation at all. The direction of an external compensator's field is changed by switching it end for end.

Let's see now how the built-in compensators do the same job. The N-S and E-W pair are seen in Figure 15-4, and are shown again in the drawing at the left. Each compensator consists of a pair of magnets at the opposite ends of a shaft that can be made to rotate. The magnets have opposite polarity—viewed from above, the south pole of one magnet is on the same side of the shaft as the north pole of the other. This opposite polarity is a key feature in the workings of the compensators. The shaft of the N-S corrector is at right angles to the lubber's line, hence to the centerline of the boat; that of the E-W corrector is parallel to the centerline. The shafts can be rotated through 360° by the external slots, but we shall see that 180° of this rotation is redundant—that is, all the correction a compensator can provide is obtained by rotating it through a 180-degree arc.

To set a compensator in "neutral," so it has no effect on the compass needle, you rotate the shaft until the two magnets are horizontal. Then the field produced at the compass needle by one magnet in effect cancels that due to the other; the two fields are equal and opposite, so the net field is zero. The margin drawing shows the cancellation of the fields only at the center of the compass needle, but basically the same thing happens over the needle as a whole.

A compensator produces its *maximum* effect when its shaft is rotated so that the magnets are vertical. Then the fields of the two magnets are in the same sense—point more or less in the same direction—so they add to produce a greater net field. You see this illustrated in the drawing at the left for the field at the center of the needle, but again, essentially the same effect occurs over the needle as a whole.

If you start with horizontal magnets and rotate the compensator clockwise through 90° you get a maximum field, pointing in a certain direction. If from the same starting point you rotate the magnets through 90° counterclockwise (Figure 19-4), you get the same maximum field, but pointing in the opposite direction. So a 180-degree range of rotation gives all the correction the compensator can provide. If, having rotated clockwise from 0° to 90°, you continued through 90° to 180°, you would gain nothing. The fields between 90° and 180° simply repeat those between 0° and 90°; the field obtained when the magnet is rotated, say, to 110°, is the same as when it is rotated to 70°.

Fine. You put a compensator in neutral by rotating its magnets to be horizontal. But how do you know they are horizontal? You can't see through the base of the compass, but you *can* see the slot at the end of the compensator shaft, and if you know how the orientation of that slot is correlated to the magnet's orientation, you are home free. In most compasses the magnets are horizontal when the slot is horizontal, but there are just enough mavericks for which vertical slots imply horizontal magnets that you can't be sure. The manufacturer's literature, if you have it, probably will tell you what goes with what. If not it is easy enough to find out once and for all by the following method.

Affix to the compass the orientation aid shown in Figure 19-1. Set the slots of the N-S and E-W compensators accurately horizontal or vertical, according to your whim. Mark a reference line on the tabletop, orient the compass along that line (Figure 19-5), and read it. Then rotate the compass 180° using the same reference line and read it again. If your chosen slot orientation happened to put the compensators in neutral, the difference between the two readings will, reasonably enough, be 180°. If the compensators were not in neutral you're not likely to get 180°. The reason is not obvious—it has to do with the vector addition of the earth and compensating magnet's fields—and does not merit explanation; I will simply ask you to accept it.

Thus, a 180-degree difference between readings tells you whether the magnets are horizontal. There is just one caveat, in that there happens to be one special direction of the orientation line for which, even with the

setting compensators to neutral

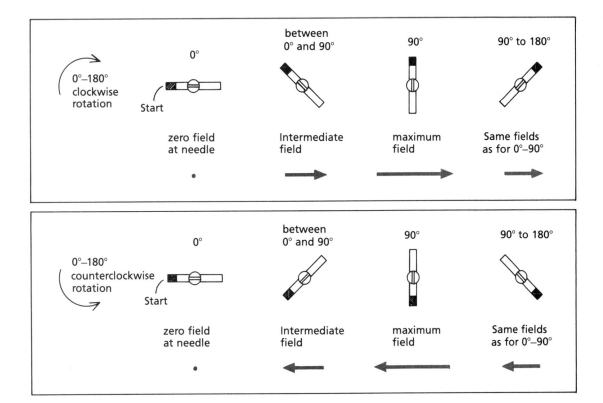

FIGURE 19-4. *Effect of rotating a compensator; view looking down the shaft.*

compensators not in neutral, you will get a 180-degrees difference. It is unlikely, but possible, that you could happen to choose that line, so to rule out the possibility do the same experiment with an orientation line at right angles to the first. If you still get a 180-degrees difference, then you may be sure the compensators are in neutral.

With compensators set to neutral let's turn to the final problem of actually compensating the compass. There are many ways of doing this; they are constantly being rediscovered and redescribed in the boating literature. I will mention only two.

The first, which may be called the *method of reciprocal courses,* is often presented in magazine articles and books, including the latest (58th) edition of Chapman's *Piloting, Seamanship, and Small Boat Handling.* It is based on essentially the approach of a 180-degree compass rotation that was described above for checking the compensators in a compass on a tabletop. Suppose now the compass is back in the boat with compensators in neutral, but with the possibility of some deviation. This deviation can be detected if the compass can be rotated through 180 degrees, but since the compass is attached to the boat, to effect this the

method of reciprocal courses boat itself must rotate (change course) by 180°. If there is *no* deviation and the boat changes course by exactly 180° (changes to the *reciprocal course*) the compass reading will change by 180°. If there *is* deviation the difference between the initial compass reading and that on the reciprocal

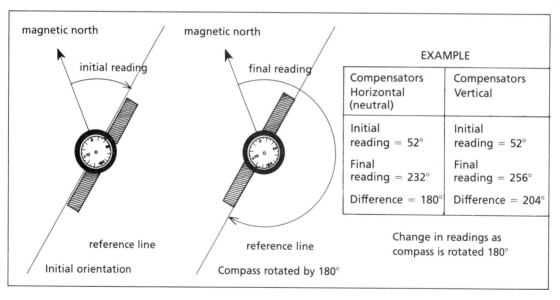

	EXAMPLE	
	Compensators Horizontal (neutral)	Compensators Vertical
	Initial reading = 52°	Initial reading = 52°
	Final reading = 232°	Final reading = 256°
	Difference = 180°	Difference = 204°

Change in readings as compass is rotated 180°

FIGURE 19-5.   *Orient the compass along the reference line and read. Rotate the compass 180° and read again. If the difference between the two readings is also 180°, compensators are probably in neutral. Do the same for another reference line at right angles to the first. If you still get a 180 degrees difference, the compensators are certainly in neutral.*

course will be different from 180°; the difference will be twice the deviation on the initial heading.

In principle then you can find out the deviation, and so be in a position to compensate it, by putting the boat first on one course and then on the reciprocal course and subtracting 180° from the difference of compass readings. But this is easier to describe than to do. It is much more difficult to reverse a boat's direction by exactly 180° than it is to rotate a compass on a tabletop. What is usually recommended is to set up a course involving temporary buoys—wadded paper, or weighted plastic jugs. The ship is directed along the course and then along the reciprocal course. Even a very modest amount of current or leeway will spoil the results, however, and the steering has to be very accurate indeed; in order to compensate a compass to a degree's accuracy you must be able to keep a course and its reciprocal with like precision. The method doesn't tell you whether the compass is misaligned, and there are other sources of inaccuracy; on the whole, to my mind, it is best forgotten.

The technique I advocate begins with the making of a deviation curve. Any of the methods discussed in the last chapter can be used, but I favor the one in which a handbearing compass is used to sight along a displaced centerline. This has the great advantage of convenience. Whenever the boat, either underway or at anchor, faces a direction for which you have no reading, whip out your table of the kind shown at the right and make another entry in it. When you get 20 to 30 readings, you can begin to plot them. Or if you want to get the job over with get yourself to a mooring. As in the last chapter, affix bow and stern lines to control the direction of the boat, if it is held by tide or current. If there is neither tide nor current you can put the engine in gentle reverse to substitute for them.

Figure 19-6 is an example of a deviation curve produced by this method. The readings were taken one day when I was doing odd jobs on my boat, which was held by bow and stern lines to its mooring. To minimize line handling I took the various readings at different times of the day, relying more on tide and wind changes than on muscle to pull the boat in different directions. I taped the handbearing compass in place, so it was a quick and easy business to simply bend over it and take a reading. Each reading took perhaps 10 to 20 seconds, time spent mainly in waiting for the boat to come to the end of the small swings it undergoes even on quiet days. But the total time for a reading was certainly less than a minute, and the total time for all the readings added up to about a half hour. The points on the curve are somewhat scattered, but still they define a perfectly usable curve. There is no doubt that the curve would have been tighter with two people aboard—one compass-reader per compass.

Now to use the curve to correct the compass. First, the misalignment. The maximum positive deviation shown on the curve is 10°, and the maximum negative is −6°, so that, as I mentioned above, the compass should be rotated by 2° to split the difference. The effect on the curve is to raise

HEADING	BEARING	SHIPS COMPASS	COMPASS	DEVIATION
11		7		4
31		20		11
67		57		10
.		.		.
.		.		.
.		.		.
161		163		−2
212		216		−4
251		256		−5
.		.		.
.		.		.
.		.		.

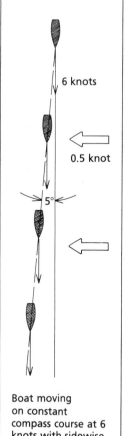

6 knots

0.5 knot

5°

Boat moving on constant compass course at 6 knots with sidewise current of 0.5 knot.

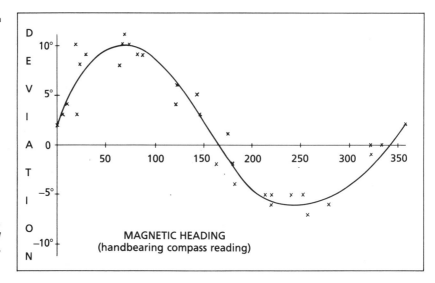

FIGURE 19-6.
Deviation curve produced by using an accurate handbearing compass.

correcting from a deviation curve

the baseline 2° so that it becomes symmetrical, with maximum plus and minus deviations of 8°. The next step is to take out these deviations by adjusting the compensating magnets. In general, there are two ways of doing this. You can put the boat on the heading of maximum deviation, arbitrarily choose one compensator, and by turning it one way or the other take out as much deviation as you can. Then use the other compensator to take out the rest. The second, more systematic procedure is to put the boat on a north-south course and take out the deviation on that course with the north-south compensator, then do the same with the east-west course and compensator. The advantage of this procedure is that you know from the beginning exactly which compensator to use. In the example of Figure 19-6 it turns out that both these methods are basically the same since the maximum deviation comes at about 80°, so that it is mainly the east-west compensator that must be used. When I did use this compensator to correct I was able to do it perfectly, so far as I could tell, and ended up with a deviation-free compass.

The Bottom Line
To minimize or correct the deviation of a ship's compass:

> 1. Test reproducibility, either with a small magnet (see text) or by the method of Figure 19-1.

> 2. Put the compensators "in neutral" either following the manufacturer's instructions or using the method of Figure 19-5.

3. Make a deviation table, using any of the methods described in Chapter 18. I prefer the one that directly compares an accurate handbearing compass with the ship's compass.

4. If the maximum positive and negative deviations are not of the same size, adjust the compass alignment (make the lubber's line parallel to centerline).

5. With the compass properly aligned, use the compensators to take out whatever deviation remains.

This last step can be done in either of two ways. One way is to put the boat on the heading of maximum deviation (either + or −) and take out as much deviation as you can by tweaking one compensator; the rest should come out by using the other compensator. Alternatively, put the boat on a north-south heading and use the N-S compensator to take out the deviation on that heading; then do the same with the other compensator on an east-west heading. These headings need not be exact for this purpose; within five to ten degrees is good enough.

On most fiberglass or wooden boats this technique should produce a close to deviation-free compass. But when you have done, of course check a few points of the presumably corrected compass; for sailboats, also check when the boat is heeled.

SECTION V

Where Is the Boat Now?

20

Lines and Curves of Position

Here are three fragments of overheard conversation. What do they have in common?

"Meet me at the corner of Broadway and 42nd Street."

"Let's put the canoe in on Snake River near the bridge on Route 36."

"The lighthouse bears 83° magnetic and we are two miles away by rangefinder, so here is our position on the chart."

The common denominator in each case is that a position is defined or fixed as the point of *intersection* of two straight lines, or a line and a curve, or two curves. On a street map of New York there is a line that represents 42nd Street and a line that is Broadway. The meeting place is to be the intersection of these two lines. (Forget for a moment that Broadway and 42nd Street have a finite width and two different sides. Think of them as lines on a map.)

In the second case the canoe is to be launched at the point on the map represented by the intersection of the curved Snake River with the curved Route 36.

In the third example the position on the chart is known because the compass bearing tells us that we are somewhere on a line at 83° magnetic that passes through the lighthouse. The rangefinder tells us that the boat is at some point two miles from the lighthouse and so could be anywhere on a circle of radius two miles. We must then be at a point which is simultaneously on the bearing line *and* the circle; this can only be at their intersection.

The lines and curves in these three cases are examples of *lines* and *curves of position.* In general, a curve of position is a curve on the chart along which you know you are located. Thus, if you paddle lazily along Snake River, not trying to identify places on it and not knowing how far you have come, then Snake River on the chart is a curve of position for you. Similarly, if you are strolling up Broadway without noting the cross streets, and so know only that you are *somewhere* on Broadway, then the line representing Broadway on the street map is a line of position for you.

It is obvious that the concept of line of position is basically identical with that of curve of position—a line is in fact a special case of a curve. For brevity I'll refer from here on only to curves of position, with the understanding that they are intended to include lines of position as a special case.

This chapter is then about curves of position and their uses. I will first lay out all the curves of position that are potentially useful, and in the chapters that follow I will try to sort out which ones are the most convenient and practical. Even the more esoteric and infrequently used curves of position are worth mentioning at least once, because there may be circumstances in which they will come in handy.

Following is a list of five different curves of position. Some have been mentioned earlier in the book, but I include them all now on an equal footing, even at the expense of some redundancy. They are:

1. Magnetic line of position

2. Transit line of position

3. Distance-circle of position

4. Angle-circle of position

5. Curve of constant soundings

Although these are the most important curves of position for coastal piloting, others are used regularly in offshore navigation and may on occasion be used along the coast. It is fair to say that every position fix on the surface of the earth is the intersection of two curves of position of one kind or another. For example, Loran curves of position are the hyperbolas associated with the carefully coordinated emission of radio signals from a pair of Loran stations. The Loran fix is the intersection of two such hyperbolas from two pairs of stations. Celestial navigation is based on circles of position on the surface of the globe. The center of a celestial circle is the so-called *ground point,* the point on the earth "directly under" the sun, moon, star, or planet being sighted. The radius of the circle is determined by the altitude of the object as measured by a sextant, and one of the intersection points of a pair of such circles yields the fix—in principle. In fact, the actual practice of celestial navigation is not quite so simple. One doesn't carry a globe of the earth in the cabin on which to draw the circles directly, but the specialized techniques of the art of celestial navigation do in effect draw their crucial segments indirectly.

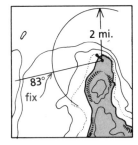

Back then to coastal piloting. I'll define the five curves of position listed above operationally—that is, in terms of what one has to do to get

LOP = line of position

COP = circle of position

them. Note the abbreviations: Line of position = LOP, and circle of position = COP. Curve of position is not abbreviated.

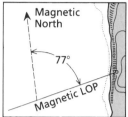

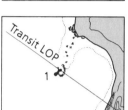

Magnetic line of position
Measure with compass on deck the magnetic bearing (say 77°) of an object, and on the chart you are somewhere on a line through the object making an angle of 77° with magnetic north.

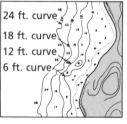

Transit line of position
Observe from deck that two objects (1 and 2) are in line (one seen directly behind the other), and on the chart you are on the (extended) line drawn between them.

Distance-circle of position
With rangefinder on deck find your distance from, say, Tower. Suppose it is 2 miles. Then on the chart you are somewhere on a circle of radius 2 miles with Tower at its center.

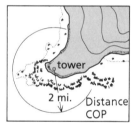

Curve of constant soundings
If from the deck you manage to steer so that successive depth sounder readings are constant (for example, 27 feet), then on the chart you are on a curve for which every point corresponds to that depth.

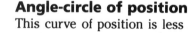

Angle-circle of position
This curve of position is less intuitive than any of the four above, and requires more explanation. It is mentioned in Chapter 11 and is illustrated in Figure 20-1. Operationally you measure on deck the angle between two objects—their horizontal angle—and this implies that you are somewhere on a circle that passes through the two objects, the *angle-circle of position*.

The fact that a horizontal angle implies a COP is basically a geometrical theorem, but I'll not pull Euclid on you to try to prove it. It is more instructive to deal in examples, so you see in Figure 20-1 two circles of position for the same distance between the two objects; one for a 30-degree angle and the other for a 7-degree angle. On each of these circles I have drawn three possible positions of the observer on the circumference of the circle. These are of course only three out of an infinite number—from *every* point on the circle the same angle will be found between the two objects. It is instructive to verify this for yourself. For the 30-degree circle for example, get a 30-degree drafting triangle or cut out a 30-degree angle from a piece of cardboard. Put the vertex of the angle anywhere on the circumference of the circle, and from that point you will find that one edge of the angle will pass through the one landmark when the other edge passes through the other.

I should note that for any given angle between a pair of landmarks there are really *two* circles of the same size. On one of them the one landmark is seen to the right of the other; on the other circle that landmark is seen to the left, as the drawing in the margin of the next page shows. In the future I will always draw only one circle, since in practice we always know which object is to the left or right of the other.

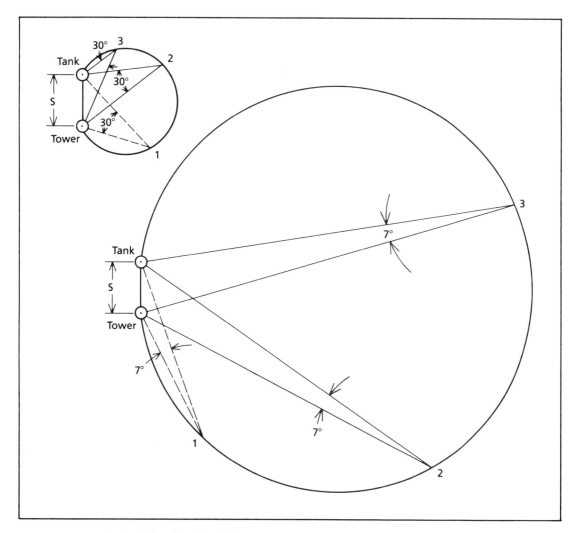

FIGURE 20-1. *Angle-circles of position for horizontal angles of 30 degrees and 7 degrees between Tank and Tower. For each circle three possible positions of the observer out of an infinite number are shown.*

Figure 20-1 shows that for a given distance between objects the radius R of the circle is larger for the smaller angle. This fact can also be seen from a formula for the radius:

$$R = S/2 \sin A°,$$

where S is the spacing or distance between the two objects and A° is the angle. In this formula the radius has the same units as the spacing: spacing in centimeters, radius in centimeters; spacing in miles, radius in miles.

As an example, from the formula we find that for a "typical" chart spacing of 10 cm (about 4 inches) the radii for 30°, 7°, and 2° are:

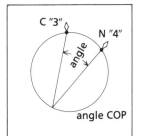

Angle A	Radius R
30°	10 cm
7°	41 cm
2°	143 cm

You see that the radius not only gets large, but gets *impractically* large for small angles; you can't draw a 143 cm circle with an ordinary compass. On the other hand these small angles are important in coastal piloting, so Chapter 22 will be devoted to techniques for using them without having to draw the circle as a whole.

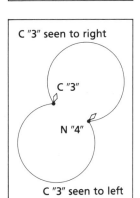

Each of the five most important curves of position can be used in any of three ways: as a position fixing aid, as a course to follow, or as a danger curve to avoid. In effect we have 15 different piloting aids, or tools. They are not all equally accurate, practical, or useful, and they need to be sorted out and evaluated along these lines. The remaining three chapters of this section do just that. For the moment, however, I will merely amplify on the above uses to make sure I have made clear what they are.

curves of position as aids to a fix

The first use of a curve of position, as a position fixing aid, served to introduce this chapter. The several illustrations that were provided of a fix as an intersection of two curves of position make this use clear enough. If two curves of position cross, the observer is at the point of crossing.

curves of position as course lines

I'll use the magnetic line of position to illustrate the second use of a curve of position—as a *course line* to follow. We use this LOP to define a desired course which we keep to by steering with an eye on the compass. Thus we observe on the chart that a line drawn from our present position to Snug Harbor makes an angle of 147° with magnetic north. This is a course line, which we stay on by making sure that the compass holds steady at 147°.

Another example, and one of the most useful curves of position when a course line is needed, is the transit line, which is the subject of the next chapter. The three other curves of position mentioned above are less commonly used as course lines than these two, so I'll leave this use of curves of position at that.

The third use of a curve of position is neither as an aid to a fix nor a course curve, but as a *danger curve*. In fact this use is just the opposite of a course curve; one wants to stay *on* a course curve but *off* a danger curve. Let's take a circle of position as an example. Suppose a lighthouse has scattered rocks and shallows that extend about a mile out from it. A circle of radius one mile with the lighthouse at its center is then a *danger circle*. If you steer to keep outside it, and never touch it, you keep off the rocks and reefs. Similarly, a transit line can be a danger line. If, looking from seaward, the transit line between two objects has dangers to the left but not the right of it, you stay off those dangers by keeping that line to port as you sail toward shore. It is not hard to imagine situations in which the other kinds of curve of position are danger curves, but since I'll be returning to this subject later I'll close it out for now.

curves of position as danger curves

21

The Transit Line of Position

When two objects—landmarks, navaids, whatever—are seen from the deck to line up one behind the other, they are said to be in transit (Chapter 20). If the objects are also found on the chart, the observer must then be on the extension of the line drawn on the chart between the objects; this is called the transit line of position, transit LOP, or simply the *transit line*. In Chapter 20 the two objects were called "1" and "2". Less abstractly, Figure 21-1 shows a transit line of two real-life objects, Flagpole and Lighthouse. When the view from deck is as in the left half of the figure, the transit line will be as in the right half.

Flagpoles and lighthouses are, of course, only two of the many kinds of objects that can serve to define a transit line. Chapter 6 described the structures called rangemarks that are set in place to define a transit line, often the centerline of a long, narrow channel. In this case the transit line may be called a *range*. But other objects can be used—tanks, towers, stacks, building edges, etc. In fact, "objects" is too narrow a word. Any identifiable point on the landscape will do—the end of an island, the peak of a hill, the saddle between two hills. Even the vertical plume of smoke from an unseen smokestack may be useful.

These examples suggest—correctly—that whatever defines a transit line need not be on the chart for the line to be useful. Stated differently, you don't have to be able to plot a transit line for it to do you good. For example, suppose you have just anchored and want to be able to check whether the anchor is dragging. You can, with some luck, define the ship's position by noting that it is at the intersection of two transit lines, each of which is defined by two objects, charted or uncharted—a boulder, a spruce tree, a tank, a house chimney, etc. In fact you won't *always* be able to find such lines, but the example does make the point that uncharted objects *can* be useful.

Whether plotted on the chart or not, transit lines are ideal for the practical pilot. To find them requires no instrumentation except the eye; the measurement is quick, truly taking no more time than the blink of an eye; as we shall see later the accuracy is high. And if the transit line is to be plotted on the chart the plotting is simplicity itself: Draw a line on the chart between the two objects. Better still, don't mark up the chart at all; drop onto the chart a straightedge that touches the two objects, and the line is defined.

Let's look first at transit lines as plotted on the chart. Chapter 20 showed that there are at least three ways of using any curve of position on the chart: as an ingredient in a fix; as a course curve; or as a danger curve. Consider the first use, a fix, which is the intersection of two curves of position, at least one of which is now a transit line. What is desirable in a fix, among other things, is that it be accurate and convenient. The accuracy of the fix as a whole depends not only on the nature of the individual curves that make it up, but on how they intersect. This latter question is best left for later, and is discussed in Chapter 23. But this is the time to examine the merits and demerits of transit lines as an ingredient in a fix.

I have already pointed out that a transit line is, in general, convenient to measure and to plot, and it is no less so when used as an aid to a fix. It gets high marks in the convenience department. What about accuracy? No curve of position is completely accurate. There is always some uncertainty in it, usually due to instrument error in the deck measurement. The rangefinder you use to measure the distance to a lighthouse may not be accurate to better than a few percent, and at a distance of a mile, this

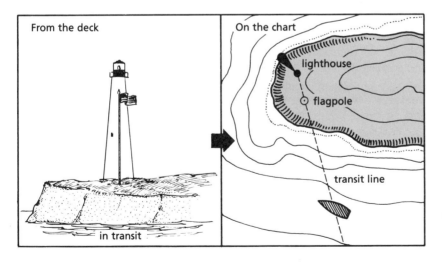

FIGURE 21-1.
Flagpole and Lighthouse in transit, and the transit line on the chart.

*transit lines
and a position
fix*

means an error of a few hundred feet in the radius of the circle of position. A magnetic line of position, even when taken with a good handbearing compass, is probably not accurate to better than a degree, and this can easily imply errors in position of hundreds of feet if the bearing is of an object a few miles away. As it will turn out, the transit line is one of the most accurate if not *the* most accurate curve of position, with the possible exception of the horizontal angle-circle derived from a sextant measurement. I simply state this fact here; to discuss it in detail I must introduce another concept, the small-angle circle of position, in the next chapter. We will find there that it is quite possible for a transit line to be off by not more than 50 to 75 feet for transit objects a few miles away, and this is a high accuracy indeed.

That is the good news about transit lines as aids to a fix plotted on the chart. The bad news is their availability. Other curves of position can be found whenever you want them from wherever you happen to be. With a rangefinder you can get a distance-circle of position from any suitable object within the range of the instrument. With a compass you can get a magnetic line of position from any object that can be seen, and is on the chart. Not so with transits. You may see two objects that potentially define a transit line, but you can't use them from wherever you are; you must wait until the boat is so positioned that they are in fact in transit. So there is a certain amount of waiting in using transit lines. On the other hand, a pilot who is oriented toward their use often finds more possibilities than a first untutored sight might indicate, and with a little experience the waiting time between transit line determinations can be kept small.

So much for transits in conventional fixes, plotted on the chart. Sometimes one may want what is basically a fix, but not on the chart. One may simply want to return to or identify a certain place on the unmarked water. For example, a diver may want to come back to a place on the water over a certain wreck, without leaving a revealing buoy. Similarly for a fisherman and a discovered fishing hole. In an example already cited, the skipper who has anchored may want to make sure that his anchor is in the same place a few hours later. All have the same problem, and with some luck their problems can be solved in the same way, by finding a first pair of objects in transit—boulder, spruce tree, sand pile, whatever—then finding a similar, second pair, and later ensuring that both pairs are still or once again in transit.

It is easier to write about this than to do it; you can't always find suitable pairs of objects. But it is worth remembering as a possible technique; if it works it works, and if it doesn't nothing is lost. Note that in checking for a dragging anchor there is still another problem. You may have found two beautiful transit lines at night with which to fix the boat's position, and wake in the morning to observe a completely different shore scene and find that you are off both transits. Don't panic. More likely than not the boat has merely swung on its rode due to a wind or current shift. But if the ship's compass reading has not changed from the previous night's, the tidal height is about the same, and you are not on the transit lines, then you may reasonably infer that the anchor has dragged.

The second of the three possible uses mentioned in Chapter 20 for any curve of position is as a course line. Let's see how the transit line in particular works in this capacity.

As with a transit line in a fix, a transit line as course line can be defined by charted or uncharted objects. An important example of a course line based on charted objects is the range, specifically identified by rangemarks noted on the chart and usually defining a danger-free path in the center of some narrow channel. There exist of course charted objects that do not specifically designate a range but may be so used by the resourceful skipper.

You want to steer to keep the transit objects lined up perfectly, but inevitably, you won't achieve this 100 percent of the time—they will tend to drift out of alignment. To bring them back in, you must steer in the direction of the closer object. If for example the closer object is seen to the right of the farther one, steer to the right to bring it back in transit; steer to the left if the closer object is seen to the left. The validity of this rule should be evident from Figure 21-1, perhaps even more so from Figures 21-2 and 21-3.

Course lines defined by uncharted objects can be of service, for example, when steering in currents. Suppose you want to sail several miles across the bay to a destination that is visible from your starting point. Nothing could appear easier, but what if a current pushes the boat in a transverse direction, at right angles to the desired course line? Then even if you keep the boat pointed at the destination it will be swept sidewise, moving not in a straight line but in a curved path. If that path leads over hidden dangers you may get into real trouble just by steering straight for your destination on a clear day.

If you suspect currents and know there are dangers, try to find an identifiable point or object behind the destination that combines with it to make a transit line. You won't always succeed—the landscape may be blank and featureless—but it is worth a look. If you do find such a point and steer along the transit line between it and the destination, you will be moving along your desired course line. Your *course made good* will be in the proper direction even though your *course steered* will not be. Your boat's bow will in fact point somewhere upcurrent of the destination, and the boat will progress with a crabbing motion, pointing in one direction but moving in another.

The same problem can arise if you are sailing on a compass course in the presence of currents. You may find that a course line of 173° magnetic on the chart takes you from starting point to destination, and on deck you may keep the boat scrupulously on 173°, but if there are transverse currents you will be swept sidewise and the actual track of the boat will not be the course line on the chart. Again the solution is to try to find a transit line, to define your course. (If your destination is not in sight,

transits and course lines

perhaps, as discussed later in this chapter, a transit line over the stern can be found.)

Transit lines and currents are treated in more detail in Chapter 26, and if you find the above explanations too cursory you may be helped by the illustrations there.

The third use of a curve of position is as a danger curve, and a transit line provides a fine specific example. If a charted transit line has rocks, shallows, or wrecks on one side of it but not on the other, steering to favor the safe side will keep you out of trouble. You have merely to keep one of the transit objects to the right or left of the other, as the case may be (Figures 21-2 and 21-3). As you see, Flagpole seen to the right of Lighthouse implies that the ship is to the left of the transit line; Flagpole to the left, ship to the right. If there are dangers to the right of the transit line, steer to keep Flagpole to the right of Lighthouse. This is sometimes called, especially in British writings, keeping the flagpole "open" with respect to the lighthouse.

danger lines

Transits can also be used, much as a danger line is used, to signal the need for a course change. If your course from one point to another can't be a straight one for whatever reason, but is a series of short legs, a transit line is often useful in signaling the change from one leg to the next. You may want to steer 134° magnetic until end of island and Tower are in transit, then change to 98° magnetic.

transit lines signaling a course change

This trick was well known to skippers generations ago. I have had much pleasure in reading a small historical pamphlet, recently reprinted in its original 1821 format and typography, entitled *Directions for Buzzards Bay and New Bedford.* It contains a set of sailing directions for a skipper of 150 years ago going up the southeast coast of Massachusetts to New Bedford, and much use is made of transits. Here, for example, are instructions for a course change generated by the disappearance—or "shutting in"—of Gay Head Light on Martha's Vineyard when the western tip of "Cutterhunk" (now Cuttyhunk) comes between the ship and the light:

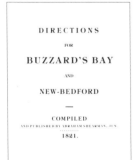

> It may be well to observe, that if when you have stood in from Seaconnet Point towards Cutterhunk, and the Light on Clark's Point is not to be seen, but you can see Gay Head Light, you may stand on your course E. ½ S. till you shut it in behind the West end of Cutterhunk, but must then immediately change your course to N.N.E.—If neither Light is to be seen, the soundings are the only dependence, and must be very carefully attended to.

The usefulness of transits, both in general and as course-change signals, hasn't gone out with the clipper ship. Many parts of the world—the Caribbean and the South Pacific, for example—are much less well supplied with navaids and buoys than the well-tended U.S. coastlines. Transits there can be crucial in keeping the mariner out of trouble.

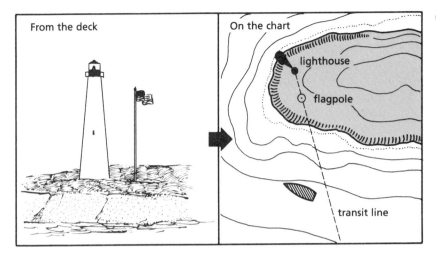

FIGURE 21-2.
If the flagpole is seen to the right of the lighthouse, the ship is to the left of the transit line.

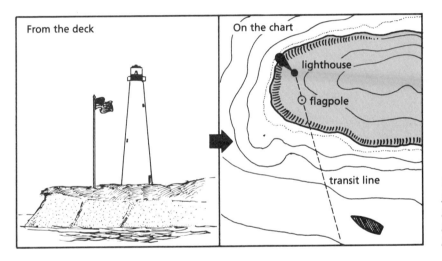

FIGURE 21-3.
If the flagpole is seen to the left of the lighthouse, the ship is to the right of the transit line.

Figure 21-4 shows one such example in the British Virgin Islands. The sailor in the open ocean at the northern entrance to Gorda Sound wants to find his way to the secluded Drake's anchorage off Mosquito Island, and the *piña colada* that can be had there at the bar of the pleasant hotel. The problem is getting past Colquhoun's Reef off Mosquito, and the reef off Prickly Pear, and rounding up into the anchorage. In fact there is no real problem at the beginning, between the two reefs, since they break at all states of the tide and are easily visible. The real problem is not to round up too soon, since Colquhoun's Reef ceases to break toward its southern end. It is then not so easily visible but is still very much there, ready to trap the unwary. Not everyone avoids this trap; Don Street in his

Cruising Guide to the Greater Antilles reports that in one year 50 groundings were observed.

One way of not adding to grounding statistics is to exploit three transits. You enter at about 135° magnetic into the passage between the reefs and eyeball them carefully to stay clear. Continue until you see the western points of Necker Island and Prickly Pear in transit, then and only then changing course to due south. You know you have gone far enough south when you see Anguilla Point and the center of the largest Seal Dogs rocks in transit. Then head west along that transit line until Necker emerges from behind Prickly Pear—that is, until their ends are again in transit. Then you change course to the center of the island, drop the hook in Drake's anchorage, breathe a sigh of relief, and break out the potables.

back transits

The uses of transits outlined above assume that the transit is to be seen in front of the boat, or possibly abeam. But there is no reason not to use, on occasion, a *back transit,* defined by objects aft of the boat. For

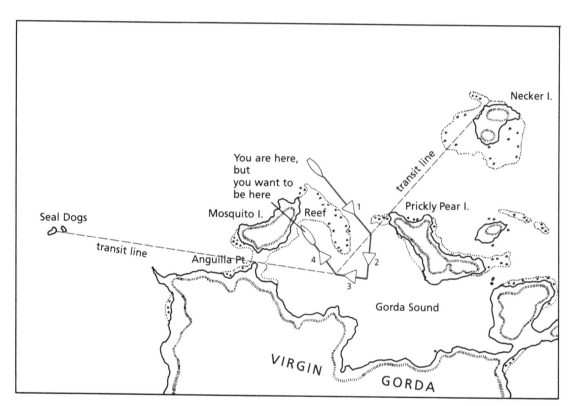

FIGURE 21-4. *To get safely into the anchorage off Mosquito Island:* **(1)** *Sail at about 135° magnetic between the breaking reefs off Mosquito and Prickly Pear islands, eyeballing them carefully.* **(2)** *When the westernmost ends of Prickly Pear and Necker are in transit, change course to due south.* **(3)** *When Anguilla Point and the largest of the Seal Dogs rocks are in transit, change course to sail along that transit line.* **(4)** *When Necker Island just reappears behind Prickly Pear—that is, when their ends are again in transit—round up toward the center of Mosquito.*

example, you may be departing a harbor with nothing before you but water, but with a rich landscape behind you, full of potential transits. These too can be used as fix lines, course lines, or danger lines, although admittedly it is less convenient to have to glance backward to exploit them. Sometimes they may be uniquely useful, and they are worth remembering.

I have discovered a final use of transits: as a Means of Establishing the Skipper's Authority. If you are skipper of your own boat, as I am, and invite the occasional friend or acquaintance for a sail, you will know that it is important to establish quickly who is boss. That sounds crude, but I don't mean by it that you should reincarnate Captain Bligh's personality. Rather, I mean it should be made clear from the beginning that the skipper knows what he is doing and should be obeyed without fuss. This makes for a pleasant and efficient voyage and may be crucial in emergencies, and it provides the skipper with an agreeable ego trip. Why not.

There are obvious ways of impressing the new crew. A trip to the masthead in wild seas is effective but not without disadvantages. I have found a simpler and less flamboyant way.

My boat rides at a mooring off the yacht club dock, and I row out to it with crew and passengers in my own dinghy. Now, first impressions are everything. If the rowing is done in a lubberly fashion involving near collisions with other boats, much arm waving by the passengers, and advice to lean harder on the left (right) oar, then all chance of asserting dominance is lost. The guests have got the upper hand with their pathetic little pointings and strident cries of "Watch out—mooring chain ahead." To be avoided at any cost.

The solution, as you have guessed, is to use a transit to row out in an impeccably seamanlike fashion that aborts attempts at criticism or comment. Before the season begins find two objects that, as you row—backward, of course—give a perfect transit for a course to your boat. They may be the end of the dock and a flagpole, a cleat on the dock and the gas pump, etc. Practice rowing on this transit until you are absolutely perfect. Then, when the first passengers arrive, load them in and retrace your route to the boat with (this is important) impassive face and stony features. With your previous practice you will be able to row without blinking an eye or twisting your neck. When your boat appears out of the side of your eye, say casually, "Well, here we are." And you *will* be there; it will be your boat; you will be in command.

Happy Sailing. Good Transits. Power to the Skipper.

22

Small-Angle Circles of Position

Transit lines of position seem invented for the small-boat pilot: They are very accurate, and they need as tools only the eye on deck and a straightedge on the chart. But they also have a defect in that they are only intermittently available. If two objects on the coast define a potential transit line, you must wait to use it until the two objects do indeed line up. Wouldn't it be great if you didn't have to wait, if you could exploit them before and after they come into transit, as their visual separation gets smaller, then becomes zero when they are in transit, and finally increases again?

In fact, it *is* great. You can exploit the magnitude of the visual separation of two objects to get very useful piloting information, and that is what this chapter is about. By "magnitude of visual separation" I simply mean the size of the horizontal angle between two objects as seen by an observer. The concept of horizontal angle is not new. It is mentioned in Chapter 20 and earlier in Chapter 11, and is illustrated in Figure 11-2. The angle we consider now is smaller than that in Figure 11-2, say less than 10 degrees, and it comprises two objects that are almost lined up (Figure 22-1).

Since we'll be dealing with small angles it is good to have some intuition about their size. You can get this intuition by using your knuckles or some other angle-measuring device to observe and measure many small angles and then storing the experience in your memory databank, but you can't have too much intuition, and the pictures of Church and Flagpole on the facing page provide another way to get a feeling for the appearance of small angles. If you hold the book page at normal reading distance from the eye, about 16 inches, then the angles between Church and Flagpole will be as marked.

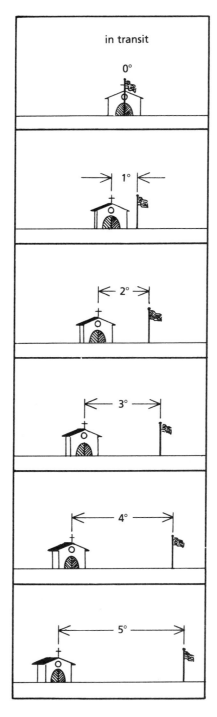

Holding the page about 16 inches from your eye will produce the indicated angles.

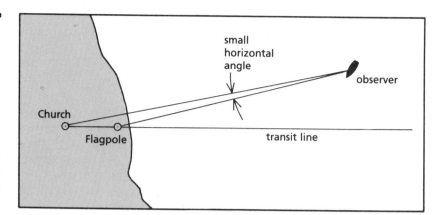

FIGURE 22-1.
*When Flagpole and Church
are almost in transit, there
is a small horizontal angle
between them.*

In Chapter 20 I discussed the horizontal angle observed between two objects and showed, or rather stated, that whether the angle is large or small it implies a circle of position for the observer. Figure 20-1 showed the circle of position generated by a 7-degree angle between a tank and a tower. There is nothing wrong in the abstract about that circle (it would be perfectly acceptable to Euclid), but it does fail to emphasize two aspects of a small-angle circle that are important for this chapter. The first is that here we are interested mainly in that part of the circle for which the observer is closest to the objects. Stated differently, we are interested in that part of the circle in which the two objects are almost in transit, since we will be looking at the small-angle circle as a generalization of the transit line. Conversely, we'll consider that the transit line is a small-angle circle of angle zero. To give some further insight, Figure 22-2 shows how the relevant arc of a small-angle circle might be generated point by point. Think of the vertex (point) of this angle as the observer's position and the two edges of the angle as the sightlines to the objects. If the angle were to be cut out of cardboard and put on the chart in different orientations in which the edges pass through two objects, the arc seen at the bottom of the figure might be generated.

In Figure 22-3 I have drawn ten such arcs for angles of 1 to 10 degrees. To do this I have bypassed the intuitive but tedious method of Figure 22-2 in favor of a mathematical formula that defines the circle arcs in terms of offsets (distances) from the transit line. The formula itself need not concern us, but you should note that the scale in Figure 22-3 is universal; all quantities are expressed in terms of a *unit length,* which is taken to be the distance between the objects. As you see, both the horizontal and the vertical axes are labeled in terms of this length. To use the chart is simple; just substitute for the unit length the actual distance between the objects. For example, if you wanted to use Figure 22-3 to help plot a 7° circle when the charted distance between the two objects (not necessarily a church and a flagpole!) was 8 centimeters, then the length **1** on the horizontal axis would be 8 centimenters, the length **2** would be 16 centimeters, etc., and similarly for the vertical axis. If on the other hand you

The Angle

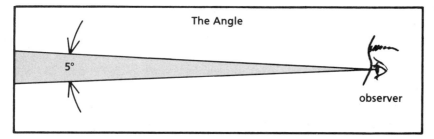

5°

observer

The Circle

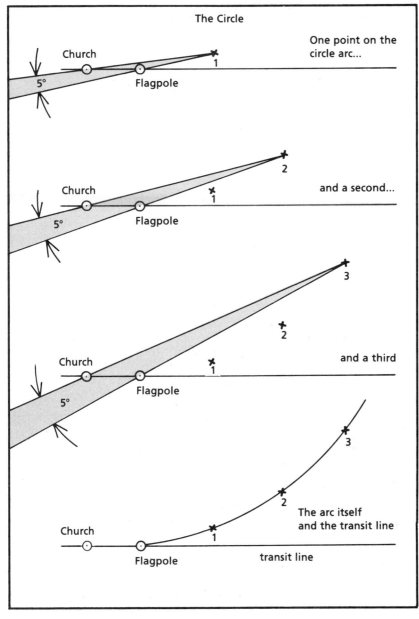

One point on the
circle arc...

Church

Flagpole

5°

1

and a second...

Church

Flagpole

5°

2

1

and a third

Church

Flagpole

5°

3

2

1

The arc itself
and the transit line

Church

Flagpole

transit line

3

2

1

FIGURE 22-2.
*Point-by-point generation
of part of the circle of
position for a 5-degree
angle seen between
Flagpole and Church.*

wanted to apply Figure 22-3 to a full-size curve of position for which the distance between objects was 1.5 miles, then **1** would be 1.5 miles, **2** would be 3 miles, and so on.

One point still needs to be made. From Figure 22-3 it is clear that an observer on any of the circles shown, for example the 5° one, will see Church to the *right* of Flagpole. But he could equally well measure 5° between Church and Flagpole when Church is to the *left* of Flagpole. There would then be a corresponding circle of position which, a little thought will convince you, is the mirror image of the first circle. Thus, for a given angle between two objects there are *two* circles, corresponding

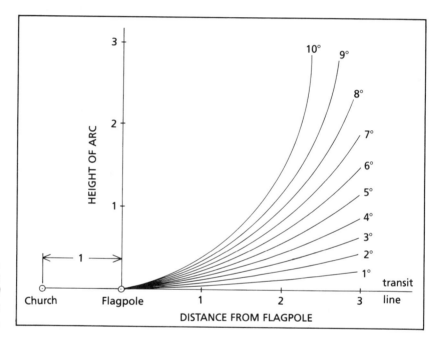

FIGURE 22-3.

Arcs of circles of position for angles from 1 to 10 degrees and Church seen to the right of Flagpole.

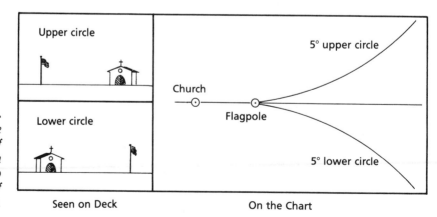

FIGURE 22-4.

For a given angle there are two different circles of position, depending on whether Church is seen to the left or right of Flagpole.

to the two relative positions of the objects. These are illustrated in Figure 22-4 for a 5° angle.

Both to illustrate the use of the curves in Figure 22-3, and to examine an interesting question, I'll use them to discuss the accuracy of a transit line of position. The idea is this. Two objects are in transit when the angle between them is zero. But our judgment is not perfect, and when the eye says the angle is zero a more accurate instrument might say that it was merely small. There are really two questions here: How accurate is the estimate of zero angle? How does the error in this estimate affect a position determination?

The first question can't be answered generally; many factors are involved. Nonetheless I will, rather arbitrarily, take an average accuracy to be about one-tenth of a degree. The crude justification for this is found in the drawings in the margin, which show the appearance of two objects with varying small angles between them. I think it likely that almost everyone can detect a 0.5° error in a transit; many can detect a 0.2° error. But with less than perfect visibility in a moving boat, a 0.1° error is difficult to discern, so 0.1° seems a not unreasonable average error. What then is the positional inaccuracy?

If two landmarks are 0.1° apart as determined by a precision instrument, the observer is of course on a 0.1° circle of position. Had he merely looked at the landmarks and guessed incorrectly that they were in transit, he would have drawn the transit line as his curve of position, and the error in his position would then be the distance from the transit line to the 0.1° circle. Let's see what that amounts to in realistic cases.

We want to use a curve like those in Figure 3, but for the 0.1° circle, which is not drawn there. That is no problem. In the present context the 0.1° circle is everywhere just one-tenth as high as the 1° circle. We can now take some typical spacings between landmarks and find the deviation of the 0.1° circle from the transit line at various distances from the nearer landmark. For example, we might take the spacing as one mile and ask for the error at a distance of one mile from the nearer landmark. I have worked out some examples like these, and they are presented in the following table.

in transit

0°

0.1°

0.2°

0.5°

Holding the page about 16 inches from your eye will produce the indicated angles.

Position errors in feet for a transit line the determination of which is in error by 0.1°	Distance from nearer landmark (nautical miles)		
	1	**2**	**3**
Spacing of landmarks (nautical miles) **1**	21	37	127
2	64	42	35
3	127	79	63

The table highlights the remarkable accuracy of the transit line. By contrast, if one took the magnetic bearing of the nearer landmark, and it were off by 3° (a not atypical figure), the error in position would be 300 feet at one mile from the landmark and 600 and 900 feet at two and three miles.

Let's return now to the primary use of the curves of Figure 22-3—as circles of position in their own right. They can be used in any of the three ways common to all curves of position (Chapter 20): as a course to steer; as a danger circle to be avoided; or as a position circle to be crossed with another curve of position for a fix. Transit lines have these uses as well, but when using the circles you don't have to wait for the two landmarks to line up. Over a whole range of angles, which translates into a whole range of positions of the craft, they are ready to be exploited. But you gets nothing for nothing, and they have the disadvantage that you must measure the angle with an instrument. And drawing the circles on the chart is clearly more complicated than drawing a transit line. In fact, the difficulty of drawing small-angle COPs on the chart is their major disadvantage. For the moment, however, I put that aside to illustrate how useful they can be, once drawn. Here in Figure 22-5 are three examples of the practical uses of small-angle COPs.

The 5° COP in Figure 22-5 is an example of a *danger circle* for the rocks off Spruce Point. If you steer to keep the angle between Lighthouse and Bird Island less than 5°, you keep off them. If the angle is less than 2° you may find yourself on the sands of Brewster Spit. Thus, 2° also defines a danger circle.

Instead of thinking about avoiding two danger circles in this passage you might simply seize on one of the intermediate circles as a *course line* to follow. For example, if you choose the conservative, middle-of-the road 3.5° circle, you can, by monitoring the angle on deck, stay clear of the dangers to either side.

Finally, any of the COPs shown can be used as a *position line.* If you were sailing northward, say, leaving Brewster Spit to port, you wouldn't be concerned with either danger or course lines for the passage between the spit and the point. You might well be interested, however, in getting a fix, and could use any of the COPs on Figure 22-5 to cross with some other curve of position to that end.

plotting small-angle COPs

Small-angle COPs are clearly useful—but only if they can be drawn on the chart. Let's look at the plotting problem now. I mention briefly one solution, a drafting instrument used by railway and highway engineers, who often have occasion to draw large-radius circles. The instrument is available in some drafting supply outlets, but I mention it with some reservation since the version I have is relatively expensive and fairly fragile. But if you can locate one you may find it more satisfactory than I do.

A second possibility is to somehow mark points that are on the circle and then use ordinary drafting curves to draw the arc between the points. I have done just that in Figure 22-2 for a 5° circle, but a crucial observation must be made. In the arc of Figure 22-2 I marked several points, but mainly for pedagogic reasons, to show how the small-angle COP evolves. Pedagogy aside, these several points on the arc were not required. I needed to draw only *one* point to determine the arc of the circle of 5°. Here is the reason.

You may recall this theorem from your geometry class: Three points determine a circle uniquely. That is, if you put three marks on a piece of paper, one and only one circle can be drawn through them. If then we want to draw, say, a 7° COP for two objects, we need three points on it. But here is the good news. The objects, or more precisely the points marking their positions, are *themselves* two points on the circle, as you can confirm by looking back at Figure 20-1. To draw a 7° COP for two objects, then, I simply have to find one other point on the circle in addition to the objects themselves. But that is easy. I set a small-angle protractor to 7, adjust it on the chart until the two edges of that 7° angle pass through the objects, and I have the third point.

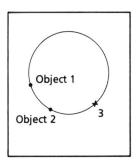

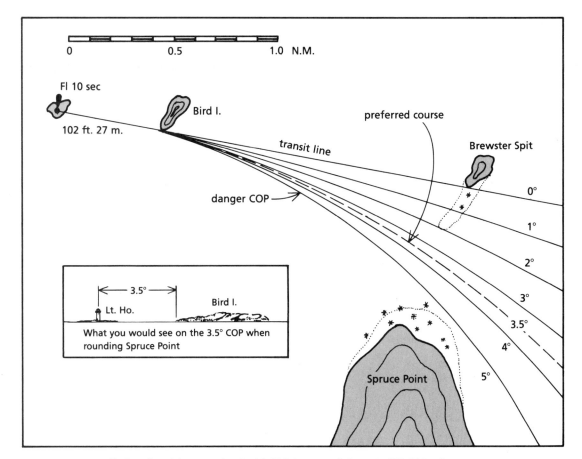

FIGURE 22-5. *Circles of position associated with Lighthouse and the end of Bird Island.*

Given the three points it is sometimes accurate enough to swing a freehand circle through them. But if more precision is wanted, one way of doing better is illustrated in Figure 22-6. This shows a slim strip of springy material, perhaps plastic, a few millimeters thick, a centimeter or two wide, and as long as is convenient. The strip is bent like a bow—perhaps with a bowstring or, as in the drawing, with a piece of flat tape. The "bowstring" is tightened or loosened and then held in place with the clip. This strip does *not* assume the shape of a circular arc over its whole length; rather it assumes the shape of a sine curve. But I have found that, provided the bending is not excessive, the shape of the central part of the curve is the arc of a circle, and this central half provides the template you need to plot a circle. If you develop your own bent strip, check out its accuracy before you use it for navigation. I have tried out quite a few strips of different dimensions and materials, and they always seem to work as I have described, but it would be prudent to take nothing for granted.

It is clear that I think small-angle COPs are potentially excellent navigational tools, but given the problems of plotting them I can't claim they are particularly useful to the small-boat skipper if he must draw them on the chart in the cockpit. Since these COPs have so many advantages, however, it is a shame to abandon them completely. There is a way out of this dilemma: Preplot them. For example, it may be that when you take your boat from its slip or mooring to more open water you have to pass a navigational trouble spot. At your leisure, take a few minutes to plot a few small-angle COPs and see which one, considered as a courseline, keeps you out of trouble. The 3.5° preferred courseline in Figure 22-5 is an example of this. Draw it in lightly on the chart and you have, once and for all, a railroad track on the water that you can adhere to simply by monitoring with a Telefix or your knuckles.

Or it may be that you are doing the morning's planning of a days' trip down the coast, and you are shorthanded, and the weather looks dubious.

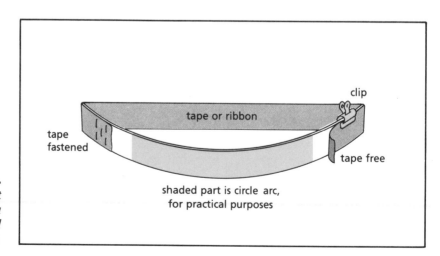

FIGURE 22-6.
The middle part of a bent thin strip is an arc of a circle, for practical purposes.

Draw lightly on the chart a series of small-angle COPs for some suitable pair of landmarks or navaids. The five circles of Figure 22-5 are an example. With these circles you can cover quite a few miles, easier in your mind from knowing that your progress and position will be monitored periodically as you cross the 5°, 4°, 3°, 2°, and 1° circles. The advantage of this kind of preparation is inversely proportional to the size of the boat. For the sea kayaker, for example, with no facilities for onboard plotting, preplotting can be very advantageous.

You can, of course, preplot other curves of position. If there is an object of known height down the coast you can draw on the chart its distance COPs for several distances from it, perhaps radii of 1, 2, 3, and 4 or more miles. Or you can draw magnetic lines of position fanning out from it at 5- or 10-degree intervals. Among these possibilities, small-angle COPs remain one of the best candidates for preplotting. Distance circles are fine, but objects of known height are not very common. Magnetic LOPs are fine, but you must use a compass and take a bearing to exploit them. This may not be very accurate and indeed may be difficult when substantial boat motion causes the compass card to swirl. But boat motion must be quite marked to prevent you from measuring a small angle with a Telefix, and must be boisterous indeed to preclude your holding out a clenched fist and sighting over your knuckles.

23

Fixes

So far I have emphasized a continual, easy scrutiny of the land and its landmarks, along with a constant comparison with the chart, so as to form an approximate idea of your ship's position. But there are times when more is needed. For example, when passing a featureless coast, or at night when only scattered lights are visible, you may go long distances without finding much that enables you to estimate your position. In these cases coastal piloting begins to lean less on observation and more on calculation.

In such a situation, at the beginning leg of a trip note carefully on the chart the position of the boat, its direction as given by the compass reading, and its speed. Then, using the formulas detailed in Chapter 26, calculate where the boat will be (its *calculated position*) after some time interval that will put it near new landmarks or navaids. Once you've arrived at that place, you'll use these objects to get a *position fix.*

A fix is simply a determination of the location of the boat—a mark on the chart that tells you where the boat is. More often than not the calculated position will be different from the fix, which is usually presumed to be more accurate. If so, you correct the calculated position on the chart, try to figure out why there is a discrepancy between the calculated position and the fix, and perhaps use this discrepancy to revise your estimates of speed, current, leeway, and so forth. Then you begin another leg of the course, at a known speed and direction, to be corrected later with a fix, and so it goes. This process of calculating a later position *dead reckoning* from initial speed and direction is called *dead reckoning* (presumably from *ded*uced reckoning). Obviously, the fixes used to monitor coastal piloting by dead reckoning should be accurate as possible.

Even apart from a series of dead reckoning legs, there may be times when you want an accurate fix. Perhaps you are going to a harbor up the coast and know where you are approximately, but would like to know more precisely so that you can calculate whether you will get there before dark. Or, in an emergency, you may want to report to the Coast Guard your location or that of another boat as exactly as possible.

The following discussion is laid out in two parts. In the first part, we'll classify the kinds of fixes that can be derived by pairing the various curves of position described in Chapter 20, without particular reference to small boats. In fact, this part might be called "position fixing for big boats," since most of the techniques require a flat surface for spreading out a chart, plotting instruments, pencil, compass, etc.—just the requirements this book eschews in general. The reason I've temporarily set aside our general goal of piloting from the cockpit is that there may arise situations crucial enough that the skipper is willing to take the time to go below and use tools and techniques not especially adapted to small boats. Even if such an occasion comes only once a year, it will have been worth taking the time to learn these techniques. In the second part of the chapter, we'll sort out those fixes which *are* especially appropriate for small boats.

Every fix is the intersection of two curves of position. For each of these curves there are these questions: How convenient is it to do the deck measurements for the curve? How easy is it to draw the curve on the chart? How accurate is the curve?

In Chapter 20, we listed five different curves of position, of which one was the circle of position (COP) derived from a horizontal angle. Let's now divide these angle COPs into two categories: the *small-angle COP* (arbitrarily defined to be one for an angle of less than about 10 degrees), and the *large-angle COP* (for angles of, say, larger than 30 degrees). The exact angles that define small and large COPs are arbitrary, but it is important to distinguish between them somehow; although they are the same in geometrical principle, small- and large-angle COPs are quite different in practice. For instance, the radii of small-angle COPs may be so large that they can't be drawn on the chart with an ordinary pencil compass, in contrast to the large-angle COPs.

With this splitting up, there are then these six different kinds of curves of position.

Magnetic LOP

Transit LOP

Distance COP

Small-angle COP

Large-angle COP

Constant-soundings curve of position

Let's look at these curves of position with four criteria in mind: accuracy; convenience of the deck measurement; convenience of plotting on the chart; and universality (that is, how often in the course of normal coastal piloting there would be an opportunity to find this kind of curve of position).

magnetic LOP

Magnetic line of position. The accuracy of this LOP depends on the accuracy of the measurement of the bearing angle, and the distance away of the object. For a given inaccuracy in angle measurement, the position inaccuracy is larger when far from the object than when close in (see margin illustration). Look for bearings from nearby objects when you have a choice. If the LOP is found with a good handbearing compass, convenience on deck is high except in rough sea conditions. For the small boat, the convenience of plotting on the chart is poor, but not so for large boats. But the magnetic LOP scores high in universality, since whenever you can see an object, you can take its bearing.

transit LOP

The *transit line of position* scores high on the first three criteria: it is accurate, convenient to find on deck, and easy to plot on the chart. It scores low on universality, though, since it may be employed only from special viewing points.

distance COP

The *distance COP*'s accuracy depends, of course, on the accuracy of the height measurement. With a Telefix or a sextant this can vary from a few percent to a fraction of one percent. The convenience of measuring on deck is good with a Telefix. Plotting on the chart requires a pencil compass and a flat chart on which to swing it. The universality leaves something to be desired. You need an object whose height is shown on the chart, *and* you must be close enough so that its vertical angle is not too small to measure.

small-angle COP

The *small-angle circle of position* is, next to the transit line, probably the most accurate of the curves of position. This COP is convenient to measure on deck with a Telefix or even knuckles, but it is in the plotting on the chart that it loses points. Here you need a spread-out chart and some of the specialized techniques discussed in the last chapter that require more than one person. However, the small-angle COP is reasonably universal; although two objects are required, you can exploit the COP from anywhere that they can be seen.

large-angle COP

The *large-angle COP* is used by the Coast Guard in setting buoys and in position fixing in geodetic surveying. However, the extreme accuracy of this method is realized only if the angle is measured with a sextant, which is almost impossible on a small boat. It's true that the measurement can be made reasonably well with a simple crosstaff (see Chapter 11), but then the plotting is somewhat fussy. Universality is high, since there is almost always a pair of objects on the chart that subtend a large angle.

constant sounding

The *constant-soundings curve of position* is not very accurate if the depth of the seabed varies slowly. Also, it may be ambiguous due to the presence of more than one curve of a given depth on the chart. The unique virtue of soundings is that they don't depend on visibility; you can use them in the night or in the fog. They are the poor man's Loran.

Given two curves of position that define a fix, an important question is the accuracy of the fix as a whole. How close to being correct is the position defined by the intersection of the two curves? Apart from errors in the individual curves, this accuracy is determined to a large extent by the angle at which the curves of position cross. The highest accuracy is achieved when they cross at a right angle, the least when they cross at a small angle. (The crossing angle is sometimes called the *angle of cut* or simply the *cut.*)

This point is illustrated in Figure 23-1, which shows two magnetic LOPs intersecting, first at a large angle (90°), and then at a small angle, to produce a fix. It is obvious that the small angle is much less advantageous. Although the illustration is for magnetic lines of position, the same principle holds true for any other intersecting pair of curves.

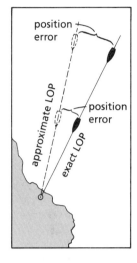

If the accuracy of a two-bearing fix is in doubt, the bearing of a third object may be taken; ideally, its position line should pass through the point of intersection of the other two. It almost never does in practice, but instead the three bearing lines define a small triangle that is often called a *cocked hat* (see margin illustration). It is natural to assume that the correct position is somewhere within the cocked hat, and often it is, but not always. In the absence of evidence to the contrary such an assumption is convenient, and probably more often right than wrong. The size of the cocked hat is usually a good index of the accuracy of the fix; the smaller it is, the more accurate the fix.

In principle, a fix can be obtained through the intersection of any two of the six kinds of curves of position listed above. In practice, a good angle of cut makes some of those more accurate than others. Indeed, for some pairs there is no angle of cut at all. Let's look at some examples.

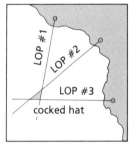

Suppose a distance COP for, say, a lighthouse of known height is combined with a magnetic LOP for the same lighthouse. At their point of intersection the circle and the line are at right angles to each other, so the fix is potentially accurate. Now suppose a tank behind the lighthouse were in transit with it. In that case, the lighthouse-tank transit line cannot be crossed with the magnetic LOP of the lighthouse, since the transit line and the LOP are identical. If the lighthouse and tank weren't quite in transit, but had a small angle between them, the small-angle COP *would* cut the magnetic LOP for the lighthouse and a fix would be possible in principle. In practice, though, the angle of cut would be so small that the accuracy would be poor.

Two separate objects are generally required to provide the two simultaneous curves of position that define a fix, the only exception mentioned thus far being the fix obtained from a single object of known height by combining a measurement of its distance with a measurement of its magnetic bearing. There is, however, a general technique for getting a fix from a single charted object, even though its height is not known. It is basically a big-boat method, but I will mention it for completeness. This method is often described as one for *finding distance off* from an object, but it contains all the ingredients of a fix.

Suppose there is a single charted landmark on the shore some distance up the coast (see margin illustration). At point 1, some time before the ship is abeam of the landmark, measure its bow angle (A). Carefully

fix from single object

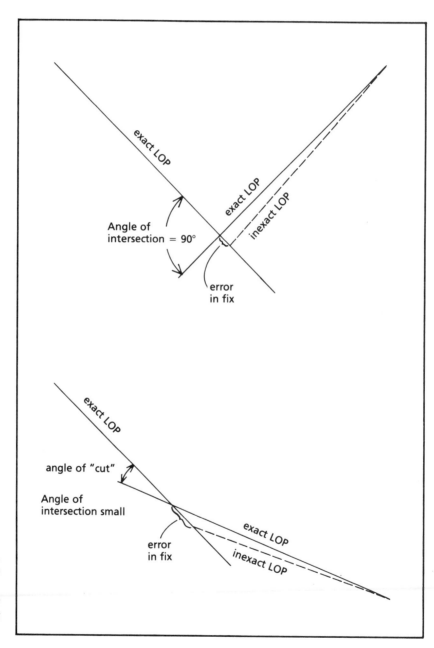

FIGURE 23-1.

Two magnetic LOPs intersect to produce a fix, which is most accurate when the intersection is at a right angle.

steer a compass course so that the boat keeps a straight track until some later point 2, when you again measure the bow angle A_2. In the run from 1 to 2, you have carefully monitored speed and time so that you can calculate the distance run, D_{run}, or you've used the odometer to find that figure. In either case, in the triangle in the margin figure, you now know the base D_{run} and the two interior angles A_1 and $180°-A_2$. If you remember high school geometry you will recall that the distance D can now be determined.

The actual calculation from scratch of D from two arbitrary angles requires more math than most coastal pilots will be able to muster, but there is a table in Bowditch called "Distance of an Object by Two Bearings" that enables one to bypass these calculations. Better still, calculations may be avoided altogether by according special values to the successive angles A_1 and A_2. For instance, A_1 could be 45°, and A_2, 90°, whereupon the method is called the *method of bow and beam bearings,* and D is equal to D_{run} (see margin illustration). Alternatively, A_2 could equal $2A_1$, whereupon the technique is called *doubling the angle on the bow* and again D is equal to D_{run} (see margin illustration).

As I remarked, these methods yield not only the distance D, but a fix as well. For if the angle A_2 is known, the bearing of the landmark can be found from A_2 and the compass heading, and bearing and distance yield a fix.

In general, these techniques of obtaining a fix from a single object are big-boat methods. In fact, they are good examples of why feasibility on a big boat may not be feasibility on a small boat, and I'll shortly elaborate on this. Why then have I described them? First, these methods are described in most books on piloting and I didn't want the reader to imagine they had been omitted here from ignorance or negligence! More important, I wanted the chance to set the record straight on their usefulness in a small boat.

Here is why these methods of finding distance off are basically for big boats. They require the keeping of a straight course between two points, accurately measuring the distance run, and measuring two bow angles. All these are far easier in a big boat, for several reasons. Its massiveness enables it to keep on a uniformly straight course even in chop or waves. A big boat probably has an accurate speed-rpm curve that can be used to deduce distance run. It may well have a permanently installed, well-aligned pelorus to measure the bow angles, or an accurate bearing circle so that one crew member can take a bearing while a second measures the ship's heading. It has a large, dry chart table on which fixes may easily be plotted. Finally, for a ship steaming at, say, 15 knots, a current of a knot or two may decrease the accuracy of the fix but won't vitiate it entirely.

Things are quite different on a small boat, even if it is a powerboat traveling fast enough to minimize the effect of current. The small seas that go unnoticed by the big boat may be enough to make the smaller

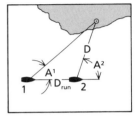

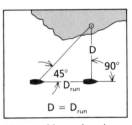

Bow and beam bearings

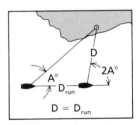

Doubling the angle on the bow

boat's course more sinuous and the calculation of distance run less accurate. More important, the measurement of the bow angles is less certain. There is most likely no pelorus aboard—and with good reason, as I have pointed out earlier. The bow angles must then be measured by combining a magnetic bearing of the landmark, taken perhaps with a hand-bearing compass, and a simultaneous reading of the ship's compass by another crew member—if there is another crew member. In general there is no question that the process will be less accurate than in a big boat, though the conclusions drawn may still have some validity if all conditions are favorable.

The obstacles against accuracy in a small sailboat are even greater. With a possible leeway of a few degrees and a speed of only a few knots, even a knot or two of deflecting current can set it well off the course the compass indicates. The possible variability of the wind, and hence of boat speed, can also complicate the calculation of the distance run. Add these potential sources of error to those the sailboat shares with a powerboat, and you will see why well-known British yachting writer and editor Des Sleightholme calls these methods of *distance off by bow angles* "monsters of possible inaccuracy."

Having looked at these methods, let's turn to ways of getting a fix that *are* feasible in the cockpit. Most of these ways will involve a small horizontal angle combined with any of several curves of position. Probably the most useful fix of this kind involves a small angle combined with a transit line, despite the fact that this kind of fix is not universally available.

transit line/ small angle fix

One kind of fix involving a transit line and a small angle requires two objects that define the transit line, and another, off to the side, that defines the small angle (Figure 23–2a). Such a configuration of landmarks or navaids is not uncommon. The small angle is measured on deck with a Telefix or your knuckles, say; then one or the other of the small-angle protractors described in Chapter 12 is used on the chart. For example, if you have the protractor shown in Figure 12-4, the edge of the instrument is laid along the transit line and then slid one way or another along it until the protractor measures the same angle between Tank and Tower that was measured on deck. The fix is then at the vertex (point) of the small angle—in this case, at the corner of the protractor.

island edges as landmarks

A similar fix can be obtained with an island in front of a more distant landmark (see Figure 23–2b) if the island has a reasonably bluff coastline so that its edges are well defined. In effect, instead of two landmarks, the two opposite edges of the island define the small angle; given that, the procedure is basically the same as for the fix above. Here this is illustrated with the second of the two small-angle protractors described in Chapter 12.

There are of course other possibilities than these two for a transit line and small-angle fix; indeed there are as many possibilities as there are kinds of transit lines. For example, with two islands, one partially behind the other, one might get a fix from the small angle the front of the island presents, and the transit line produced when the left end of the closer island lines up with the right end of the back island.

How practical are these fixes in the cockpit? Once the transit line has been sighted and the small-angle measurement made, they require a chart that is spread out reasonably flat so that you can press a protractor down on it and line up its edge with the two points that define the transit. They may further require the drawing on the chart of the *extended* line between the two objects. But these are requirements that can be met even in a modestly organized cockpit.

One virtue of this kind of fix is that you know the direction of the error in it. Since the transit line sighting is very accurate, you may be quite sure that you are very close to being on it. The error in the fix is then one-dimensional—it is essentially only your location *along* the line that is in error. By contrast, in a fix that involves, say, two crossed magnetic bearings, the error in the fix (there is always an error!) is one that compounds the possible errors in *each* of the two magnetic bearings into a total error. Moreover, you have no way of knowing in advance in what direction that total error will lie.

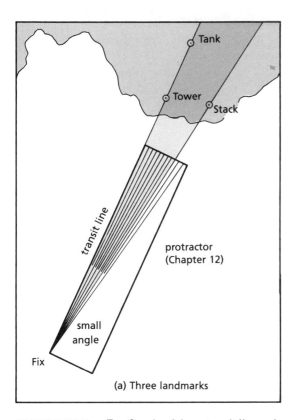

(a) Three landmarks

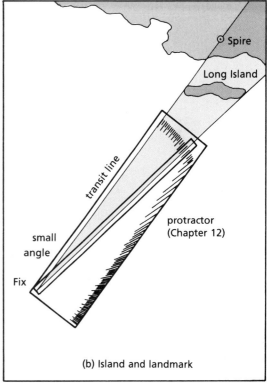

(b) Island and landmark

FIGURE 23-2.   *Two fixes involving a transit line and a small angle.*

*magnetic LOP
small-angle fix*

So much for a fix with transit line and small angle. It is clear that there may be a similar fix with a small angle and *any other* kind of curve of position. Consider in particular a magnetic LOP. Suppose you see two charted objects ashore with a small angle between them. With a hand-bearing compass, say, find the magnetic LOP for the first object and draw it on the chart. Measure the angle between the first and second objects on deck; on the chart slide one edge of a small-angle protractor against the magnetic LOP until the angle on the chart between the first and second objects is the same as the measured angle on deck. You have a fix. An illustration for this fix would be essentially identical to those in Figure 23-2. Simply substitute a magnetic LOP for the transit line there.

You may justly accuse me of backsliding here since I said I intended to concentrate on fixes that could be done in the cockpit. Instead, I have invoked a magnetic LOP whose plotting requires drawing instruments and space to spread out a chart. There are two reasons for my regression. First, the fix just described is a very useful one. When plotting on a chart is convenient, a standard and practical fix is found by crossing the *two* magnetic LOPs for each of two objects. But the accuracy is good only if the angle between the two LOPs is large—say greater than 30°. Two magnetic LOPs that intersect at small angles are hopelessly untrustworthy. But the fix just described, with one magnetic LOP and an angle, is not at all hopeless—it can be quite accurate. If you are willing to plot just *one* magnetic LOP and measure a small angle, you can salvage fixes with two objects that would otherwise be lost.

The reason this kind of small-angle fix is accurate is that it is really the intersection of a magnetic line of position and the small-angle circle generated by the measured angle between the objects. If the objects are not almost in transit, this circle crosses the magnetic LOP at a good angle of cut, ensuring good accuracy.

The second reason for introducing the fix that combines a magnetic LOP and a small angle is that it can on occasion be used in the cockpit *without* the usual problems connected with plotting a magnetic LOP on the chart. To do this requires a *beamsight,* which allows you to sight along a line perpendicular to the centerline. On every boat there is some way of rigging a sighting line to give a beamsight. You can, for example, sight along the mainsheet traveler, or across the face of the main cabin bulkhead, or across a shock cord that has been stretched from a port stanchion to its starboard companion (see Figure 26-5).

A beamsight of some object is called a *beam bearing;* if, for example, as you sight along the traveler or shock cord you see Tower on the sightline, you have a beam bearing of Tower. The method for a fix I am describing combines a beam bearing and a small angle.

It is not just any beam bearing that is taken, but one when the boat is oriented in a particular direction. As we saw in the Orientation Program of Chapter 13, it is often worthwhile to put the boat momentarily on a true north, south, east, or west course to help interpret bow angles and relate them to shore objects. Thus if the boat is moving in a more or less

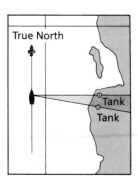

northerly direction, and you put it momentarily on an exact true north course to take a beam bearing of a shore object, you have found a *position line*—the east-west line through the object. The virtue here is that you can relate this line readily to the chart. Drop on the chart a straight-edge that passes through the object, judging by eye when it is parallel to a latitude line (the eye does this very accurately); you have in effect plotted a magnetic line of position without having left the cockpit.

Let's look now at an example of how a beam bearing and small angle combine to yield a fix. In the margin illustration, Tank and Tower are seen on shore. As the boat passes them you contrive to take a beam bearing of Tank when the boat is momentarily headed in an exact northerly direction, and you also measure the small angle between Tank and Tower. Then, with a small-angle protractor, you do much the same as with the transit line/small-angle fix—slide the protractor on the beam-bearing line until the angle between Tank and Tower is the same as the angle measured on deck, and there is the fix. Again, you can get this kind of fix from an island, with the two ends of the island serving the same functions as the landmarks Tank and Tower in the example above.

beam bearing/ small angle fix

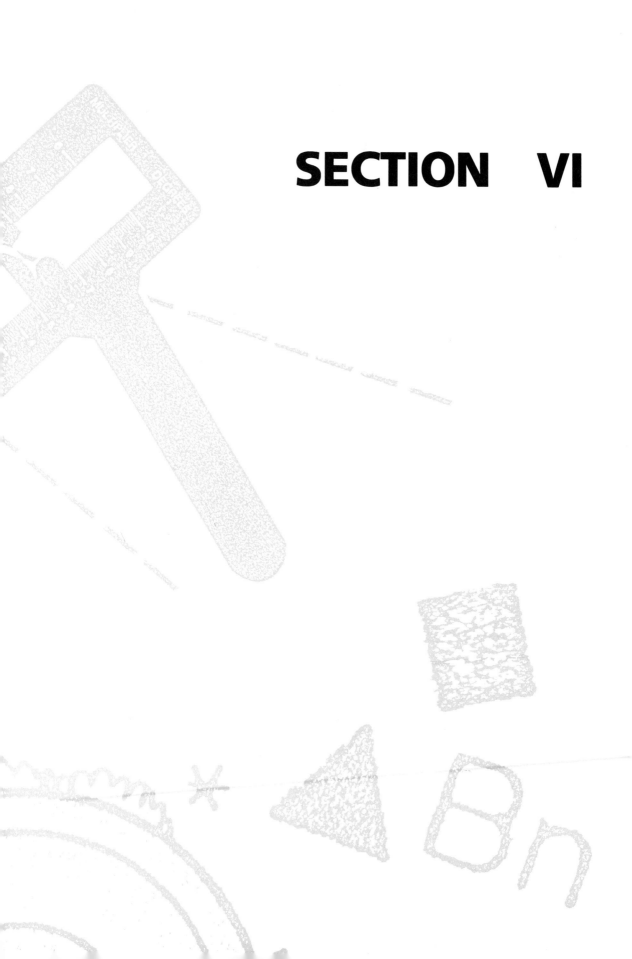

SECTION VI

Getting from
Here to There

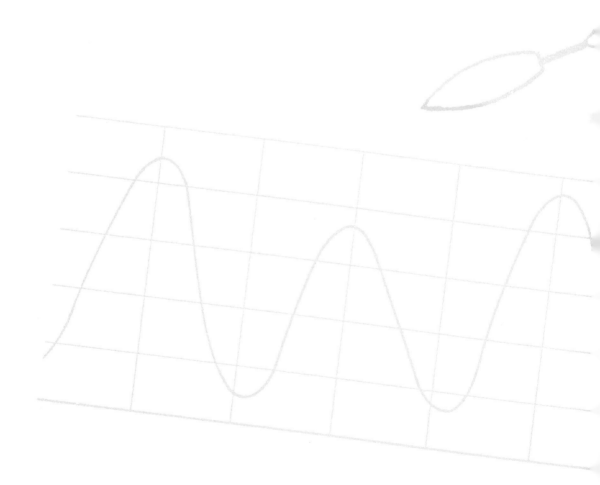

24

Can We See It from Here?

A major theme in this book has been the importance in good piloting of always correlating what you see on the chart with what you see on deck. When I discussed the orientation program in Chapter 13, I tried to show how to use angles of one kind or another to make this correlation. We were able to relate landmarks and navaids to each other by the relative angles between them. One question that I didn't emphasize, not wishing to complicate the explanation of angle usage, was: Which shore objects should we choose to correlate? We see on the chart Tank, Tower, Monument, etc., but before we try to correlate them with angles it would save time if we choose reasonable candidates from among them. If in fact Stack or Monument is too far away to be seen, or is otherwise hidden from sight, and if we can deduce this in advance so that we don't even try to find it, we shall be far ahead of the game.

This chapter is then about what can be seen from wherever you are. It would be natural to have put this chapter right after the one on the orientation program, but I have chosen to put it in this last section of the book, Getting from Here to There, for this reason: As one goes along the coast it is desirable—easier and more interesting—to steer toward something you can see in the distance instead of constantly bending over a swinging compass card. Granted, on a 30- or 40-mile trip you won't be able to see the final destination from the beginning; but if you can break the voyage into a series of several-mile legs, each with a target to be aimed at in turn, you will find the trip much less fatiguing.

The question that is the title of this chapter is perhaps more clearly framed in a slightly different form: Why are we sometimes unable to see things that are marked on the chart? Of course, there may be a simple

200

and obvious answer: We may not be able to see something because the visibility is poor—perhaps it is foggy. If the object is small, like a buoy, it may just be too far away. Even if it is large it may be beyond the horizon, hidden from us by the curvature of the earth.

But there are less obvious reasons for not seeing. We may be looking in good visibility for some large, charted object that is not beyond the horizon, and be unable to see it, or see it only with difficulty. In such cases it is easy, I have observed, to become indignant with the chart, as if it had deceived us with a lie. In fact I almost called this chapter "Do Charts Lie?" for just that reason. But of course they don't lie; they tell the truth— mainly. Huck Finn said of his author Mark Twain, "He told the truth, mainly. There was things which he stretched, but mainly he told the truth." Charts do tell the truth, mainly, but especially for the novice pilot they do stretch and tell him to look for more than he can actually see. In fairness, it is not the chart that is at fault. The inexperienced pilot deceives himself if he too cavalierly translates the chart into a mental picture of what can be seen. He comes to his task with a set of conceptions—and misconceptions—that make for the difference between what the chart seems to indicate and reality.

Here then are some of the reasons, obvious and less obvious, for not seeing what the chart says is there. I begin by listing them, and then return to discuss them in detail.

- Poor visibility.

- Landmark/navaid has ceased to exist—chart not up to date.

- Landmark/navaid is beyond the horizon—or a significant part of it is beyond the horizon.

- Landmark/navaid is too small to be seen at the distance in question.

- Landmark/navaid is camouflaged by the background— *camouflaged,* not hidden.

- Landmark/navaid is hidden by something that intervenes between it and the observer—*hidden,* not camouflaged.

- Landmark/navaid is large but not really conspicuous.

- Other reasons: Unfavorable direction of the light; effects of the tide; difference between what is seen coming and going; state of the sea; low viewing position.

poor visibility and a problem with good visibility

Poor visibility due to fog or haze needs no explication. We have all experienced it. But I have sometimes been surprised by the effects of exceptionally *good* visibility. I have sailed on the same waters now for 20 years and know the shoreline pretty well, but on occasion I have seen what appeared to be new construction on the shore—bungalows, larger buildings, etc.—seemingly having materialized overnight. In fact, as it turned out, there had been no overnight building. I saw the "new construction" on days, in the Light List's terminology, of "exceptionally clear visibility"—the highest category of good seeing. I saw what had in fact been there for years but had not previously been visible. It doesn't happen often—exceptionally clear days are by definition rare events—but you may save yourself some puzzlement one day if you remember how they can markedly change a well-known vista.

On the whole, chart markings change slowly over the years. The shape of the land, of course, changes little, if at all. Buildings, tanks, and towers do not come or go frequently. On the other hand, from time to time a structure *is* razed by natural causes or the hand of man, and the Coast Guard *does* modify, usually in small ways, the buoyage system from year to year. Charts do then get out of date, and things are noted on them which are in fact not there to be seen on land or sea. (This is of course, the purpose of the *Notices to Mariners.*) This possibility must be considered if you are having difficulty correlating the chart and deck view, but don't invoke this explanation too readily. In my experience it is the least frequent cause for confusion. Make sure you have exhausted all other possibilities before latching onto this one.

on the chart but non-existent in fact

To the coastal pilot, in contrast to the transoceanic voyager, the fact that the earth is a sphere is of little practical importance. But there is one crucial exception. The earth's sphericity limits the distance a pilot can see; there is always a horizon beyond which the earth's surface is hidden. This is illustrated in Figure 24-1 (not to scale!) of a man standing on the deck of a boat. His eye is at height h above the water. The greatest distance at which he can see an object on the earth's curved surface is found by drawing his line of sight so that it just touches or is tangent to the

beyond the horizon

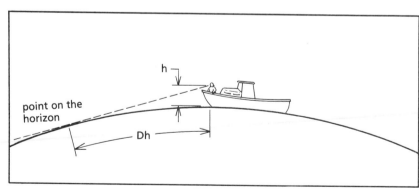

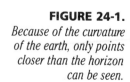

FIGURE 24-1.
Because of the curvature of the earth, only points closer than the horizon can be seen.

earth. The point where it touches is a point on the horizon. What is beyond the horizon might be intrinsically conspicuous—it could be the yellow floating dye patch of a distress signal—but the curvature of the earth prevents his seeing it.

It is obvious that the higher the observer is, the greater is the distance to his horizon, an intuition confirmed by the following formula for the distance D_h to the horizon from a height of an observer's eye h (in feet above sea level):

$$D_h \text{ (nautical miles)} = 1.14 \sqrt{h}.$$

Here is a table based on the formula.

h (feet)	D (nautical miles)
4	2.3
9	3.4
16	4.6
25	5.7
100	11.4

The coastal pilot is not usually interested in the distance to the horizon in its own right, but it does figure critically in the question that is the title of this chapter. He sees on the chart, at some distance along the coast he is about to traverse, a structure or bluff whose height can be deduced. Given good visibility, should he be able to see that structure or bluff from where he is, or is it hidden by the curvature of the earth?

Suppose what he has noted on the chart is a tank of height H. Figure 24-2 shows him straining to catch a glimpse of it. If the tank were just a bit farther away, his sightline would miss its top altogether and he would have no chance at all of seeing it. The absolute maximum distance, call it D_{max}, at which the tank can be seen is $D_{max} = D_h + D_H$. The geometry

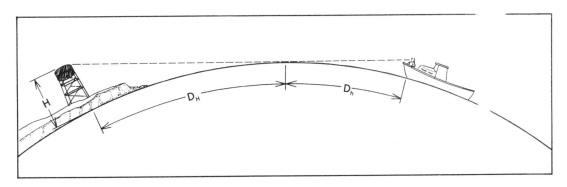

FIGURE 24-2. *The sightline of the observer just grazes the sea surface and touches the top of the tank. If the tank were any farther away, there would be no chance of seeing it.*

involving D_H is the same as that for D_h, so that $D_H = 1.14 \sqrt{H}$, and we can use this fact to calculate the absolute maximum distance. Here are some results for various heights H. The observer's height is taken to be 10 feet, and $D_h = 1.14 \sqrt{10} = 3.6$ nautical miles.

H (feet)	D_H (nautical miles)	D_{max} (nautical miles)
50	8.1	11.7
100	11.4	15.0
200	16.1	19.7

According to the laws of geometrical optics we can't then see the tank at distances beyond D_{max}. But there is a further question. Can we see it *at* that distance? The answer is probably not, for the following reason. To see anything that is visible by virtue of light from an external source falling on it (as opposed, say, to a searchlight, which is seen because it produces its own light) your field of view must include a certain portion of it. That portion may be only a few feet or a few meters high—many factors are involved—but it must be measurable. If your field of view includes only one line of sight that touches only one point of the object, you won't see it. So the distance at which a landmark can be seen is usually smaller than the maximum geometrical distance D_{max}, but just how much smaller is in general an unknown quantity.

On the other hand, if it were the *light* of a lighthouse that you were trying to see, and if H were now the height not of the entire structure, but of the light itself, then you probably could see it if the light were strong enough and the visibility good.

We all know that a buoy eventually disappears as we leave it behind us. Even on clear days and calm waters, and before it gets beyond the horizon, there is a distance at which the buoy becomes too small to see. What is that distance? Based on other writers' remarks and observations of my own, I think it is fair to say that a small buoy, say 4 or 5 feet high, can't usually be seen beyond perhaps a nautical mile.

This limitation of visibility may arise from the limited resolving power of the eye. Let's suppose you are seated in front of a white vertical surface on which are drawn two small, solid, black dots. There is an angle associated with your position and these dots—the angle between your line of sight to one dot and your line of sight to the other. If the dots are a few inches apart, the angle may be a few degrees. But if the dots are drawn closer and closer together, the angle will get smaller and smaller. Eventually there comes a spacing between them at which you can't really tell whether there are one or two dots; they begin to merge visually. The angle corresponding to that distance is called the angular resolving power of the eye, and it can differ a little or a lot from person to person. On average, that angle is about one sixtieth of a degree, or one minute of arc.

What has this to do with the distance at which a 4-foot buoy can be seen? My conjecture is that the buoy can't be seen unless a point on its top can be distinguished from a point on its base—that is, the angle subtended between the top and the base is at least equal to the resolving power of the human eye. It's doubtful, however, that the one-minute resolving power obtained in the ophthalmologist's office with contrasting black dots on a white background will still obtain for a green or even a red buoy against the water. A more realistic estimate of resolving power at sea might be two minutes of arc.

With this (somewhat arbitrary) value for the resolving power of the eye, let's calculate the distance at which a 4-foot buoy subtends an angle of two-sixtieths of a degree. The calculation is done with the Rule of Sixty which, as you recall, reads: $(Angle)° = 60 \times Height/Distance$. In this case the angle is $(2/60)°$, and the height is 4 feet, from which we get a distance of 7200 feet. This seems to be close enough to our earlier estimate of one nautical mile (6080 feet) for the limit of visibility.

Figure 24-3, in a more graphic and perhaps clearer way, represents the distances at which objects can be seen. Objects of different sizes are drawn to such a scale that their apparent height on the page (held from the eye at about the normal 16-inch reading distance) is the same as their real size at the listed distances. This picture gives a rough confirmation of the fact that a 4-foot buoy disappears at about a nautical mile. Even at half a mile, the height of the buoy on the page is about a half-millimeter, barely able to be printed, and at a mile it is half that again, a quarter of a millimeter high, too small to be shown.

An obvious reason for not seeing a landmark is that something else may intervene and block your sight. Sometimes this blocking is predictable from reading the contour lines on your chart. Sometimes, though, the blockage is unpredictable, either because the chart doesn't show contour lines or because the object may be hidden by trees or foliage.

Figure 24-5 makes this point, and also serves as a good example of the different visibilities of objects that are undifferentiated on the chart, all having the same size circle and dot. Tower (TR) to the left is small, but in good lighting it can be seen against its background. The Tank is superbly visible, perched on the highest point of the land. The Spire, on the other hand, is nowhere to be seen, although it should be very close to Tank. In fact, it does exist, and can be seen from the other side of the hill, but a combination of foliage and topography hides it completely from this side.

In clear weather, from a mile or two away, tall radio and television towers may be very prominent visually. One would think that they would continue to be especially useful landmarks for a long way down the coast. Unfortunately, they don't live up to their promise. If the weather gets a bit hazy or foggy these constructions tend to quickly become thin and spidery and may well disappear, while other apparently less impressive landmarks remain in sight.

Likewise, breakwaters, which are massive features when you are leaving the harbor, tend to disappear quickly behind you, especially if the tide is high. They may look like promising visual aids on the chart, but

hidden landmarks

television and radio towers and breakwaters

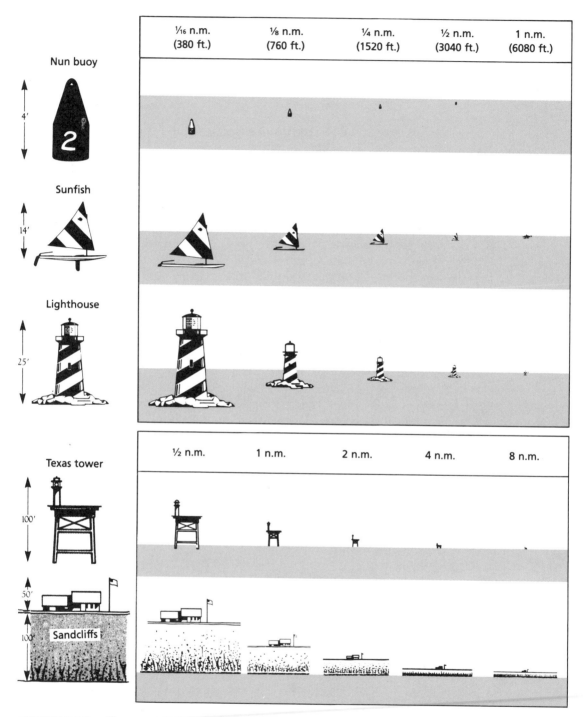

FIGURE 24-3. *The apparent sizes of various objects, landmarks, and navaids at different distances. They have been drawn to such a scale that when the page is held at the normal reading distance of 16 inches from the eye, they appear to be the same size as the real objects at the listed distance.*

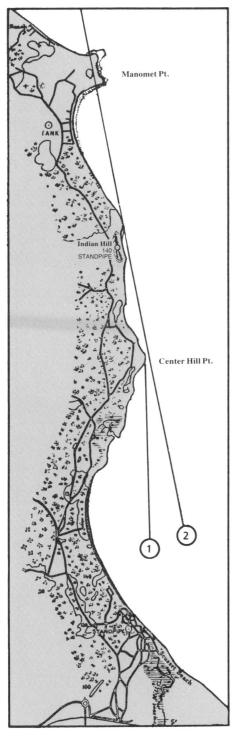

From 1 Center Hill Point is seen and hides Manomet Point behind it (photo #1).

From 2 Center Hill Point merges into the land behind it and Manomet Point is seen (photo #2).

The view from 1.

The view from 2.

FIGURE 24-4. *An example of how points can be swallowed up visually by land behind them.*

don't try to find your way into a harbor from a distance by looking for breakwaters.

Unfavorable direction of light can make an enormous difference in your ability to identify objects. Here is an example. The land shown in Figure 24-6 runs roughly north and south, and the photographs were taken from the west. The front-lit picture was taken in the afternoon when the sun behind the camera illuminated the fronts of buildings and structures so that even the small tower (TR) stood out clearly. The back-lit picture was taken in the morning of a day of equal clarity, but the effects of shadows thrown toward the camera, and of no direct light on the front faces of anything, make it difficult, if not impossible, to pick out TR.

There are still other ways of being deceived by—or of feeling deceived by—the chart. It is surprisingly easy, having seen a landscape or shore once, not to recognize it a second time due to tidal variation. The size and shape of exposed real estate at one state of the tide can be astonishingly different from the aspect it presents at another.

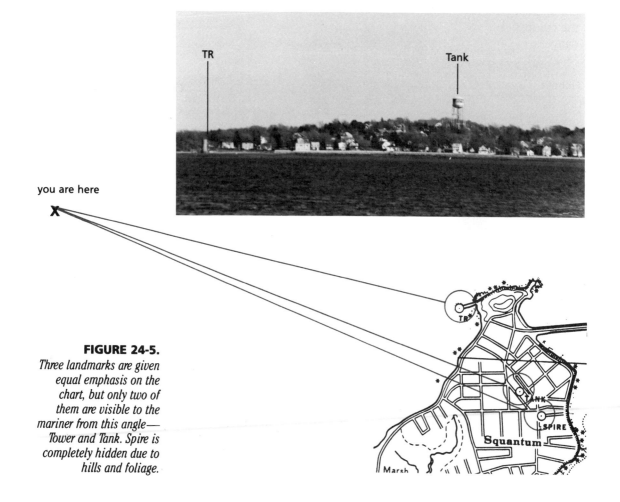

FIGURE 24-5.

Three landmarks are given equal emphasis on the chart, but only two of them are visible to the mariner from this angle— Tower and Tank. Spire is completely hidden due to hills and foliage.

A similar phenomenon is the perceptual difference between sailing out of a harbor and sailing in. If you have sailed out of a harbor new to you, and for whatever reason have never seen it on entering, you may be surprised at how different it can look on your return. The disposition of navaids and landmarks may appear quite unfamiliar. When sailing out of a place that you will be coming back to, it is a good idea to look over your shoulder occasionally to get a feel for what it will look like as you make your approach later on.

A final point (and I don't mean to imply that there may not be others) is the effect of the height of the viewer on the possibility of seeing something, even when it is well within the horizon. An object may be seen poorly from a certain height above deck, but stand out much more clearly from a higher point. For example, if the sea has a swell or a chop, a buoy may appear and disappear when the perturbed sea surface comes between your eye and it. Even standing on the deck instead of in the cockpit may help, or fixing a loop of line on the mast to form a one-rung ladder. When making unfamiliar landfalls in the tropics, prudent skippers often put someone on the spreader or at the masthead to better differentiate the colors of the water—clues to its depth—or to pick out reefs or other dangers that may not be visible from lower down.

Front-lit

Back-lit

FIGURE 24-6.
The effect of lighting on visibility of landmarks.

25

Time, Speed, and Distance

A coastal powerboater, moving at 15 knots, starts off at nine in the morning for Sandy Point. He wants to know the *time* he will arrive.

A sailor passed C"3" an hour and a half ago and has come in a straight line to R"8", which is six miles away by the chart. He would like to check out his *speed*.

A skipper in fog has timed his run from the last buoy and knows his speed. He wants to find the *distance* he has come, to know when it is time to start looking for the beacon that is his waypoint.

Finding the solutions to such scenarios is what this chapter is mainly about: Given two of the variables, how do you calculate the third?

The chapter is not only about *calculating*; it is also about a couple of simple methods of *measuring* speed. I won't have much to say about measuring time or distance. For time, modern sailors have the enormous benefit of accurate clocks and watches. There is no wisdom I can contribute except to say that an egg timer set to ring after a chosen interval can be useful aboard. For example, you begin a new leg of a course and want to stay on it for 15 minutes. Instead of writing down or remembering when you started, and constantly checking your watch, just set the timer for 15 minutes. As for distance traveled, there are basically two instruments. There is the taffrail log of 100 years ago, which is rarely seen on small boats although you can still buy one. Alternatively, you may have a modern speedometer which can find the distance traveled—a "trip-mileage meter." Both devices measure distance traveled through the water, which may not equal distance over the bottom if there is a current running.

The basic relation between the Time (T) it takes to move a Distance (D) at a constant Speed (S) is: Distance = Speed × Time, or D = S × T.

$$D = S \times T$$

nautical miles — knots — hours

210

The challenge here is to keep the units consistent in the formula. Don't, for example, write time in minutes and distance in feet when hours and miles are indicated. Generally, distance is expressed in nautical miles (n.m.), time in hours (h), and speed in knots (k). (Note that "nautical miles" may sometimes be written simply as "miles," but *nautical* is always implied.)

time in hours

The formula can be used in the two other forms:

$$S = \frac{D}{T}; \quad T = \frac{D}{S}$$

It is also often convenient to express time in minutes (t), whereupon the original formula becomes the famous "Sixty D Street":

time in minutes

$$60D = S \times t$$

Again, there are two other forms for calculating S and t.

Example 1: How long will it take at 5 knots to go 17 miles?

$$T = \frac{D}{S} = \frac{17}{5} = 3.4 \text{ hours} = 3 \text{ hours } 24 \text{ minutes}$$

Example 2: We have powered for 45 minutes at 11 knots. How far have we come?

$$D = \frac{St}{60} = \frac{11 \times 45}{60} = 8.25 \text{ nautical miles}$$

These formulae are simple, but even so, few of us can stand at the wheel, multiply two numbers together in our heads, and divide by 60 to get the right answer. Thus, we're forced to resort to pencil and paper, or to a nautical slide rule designed to solve these problems. Such a slide rule is waterproof and practical on deck, as is a regular slide rule, and even a small calculator if you take care to keep it dry. But much more in the spirit of this book are some quick rules of thumb that make it relatively easy to do these calculations. Here are three.

- It is often useful to think in terms of *time to go a mile*. Since one knot is one nautical mile per hour, it's easy to work out the following table:

time to go a mile

Speed (Knots)	Minutes to go a mile
1	60
2	30
3	20
4	15
5	12
6	10

Example: How long will it take to go 3.5 miles at 5.5 knots? Interpolating in the above table, the time to go one mile at 5.5 knots is 11 minutes. Thus, the time to go 3.5 miles is $11 \times 3.5 = 38.5$ minutes. Using the standard formula, the exact answer is: $t = 60D/S = 60 \times 3.5/5.5 = 38.2$ minutes.

six minute rule

• The "six minute rule" is often helpful. In the formula $D = S \times T$, let's suppose the time T is six minutes, or one-tenth of an hour: $T = 1/10$. Then the formula is $D = S/10$, written out:

$$\frac{\text{Distance in}}{\text{6 minutes (n.m.)}} = \frac{\text{Speed (Knots)}}{10}$$

Example: How much distance is covered in 23 minutes at 4.7 knots? The exact answer by "Sixty D Street" is $D = \dfrac{23 \times 4.7}{60} = 1.80$ n.m. Not many people could do that calculation in their heads. But roughly, by the rule, 23 minutes is four six-minute units, so the distance is approximately 4×0.47 or 1.9 n.m., which *can* be done in the head. This is usually accurate enough.

• A useful relation when dealing with slow speeds and small distances is that one knot = 6080 feet/hour or 6080/60 = 101.4 feet per minute. *Approximately,* then:

One knot = 100 feet/minute.

Example: How much distance is covered in six minutes at 2 knots? At 2 knots we cover about 200 feet per minute, or 1,200 feet (about 0.2 mile) in six minutes.

You may want to *measure* speed instead of calculating it, either because there is no speedometer aboard, or because you want to check the accuracy of the instrument you have. Here are a couple of methods for doing this.

The first involves throwing something overboard to serve as a reference mark in the water, and then measuring how long it takes the boat as a whole (or some specified fraction of its length) to pass it. The overboard object shouldn't have excessive area above the water—you want it to stay at the point where it is dropped and not be blown across the surface of the water by wind. After experimenting with various items, I now use a yellow (high visibility) tennis ball weighted with a few scrap nuts and bolts to make it sink more deeply in the water and to make it easier to throw, especially against the wind. When I slit the ball to insert the weights, I also put in the knotted end of a 50-foot length of 1/8-inch line to retrieve the ball; and then I seal up the slit with silicone rubber.

The technique requires two people. One person stands in the bow and throws the ball several feet ahead of the boat and, standing sidewise, he judges when the ball is just abeam of the bow. At that moment, he signals an aft observer, who begins timing, perhaps with a stopwatch. When the ball is abeam of the aft mark, that observer measures the time—the *passage time*. The speed of the boat may then be calculated using the known distance between the bow and the aft mark, and the passage time. (Note that the speed measured here is *speed over the water*, which may be different from *speed over the bottom* if the water moves in tidal currents.)

If this method is to be used often, it is convenient to make a plot of speed against passage time. Such a plot is often called a *Dutchman's Log*.

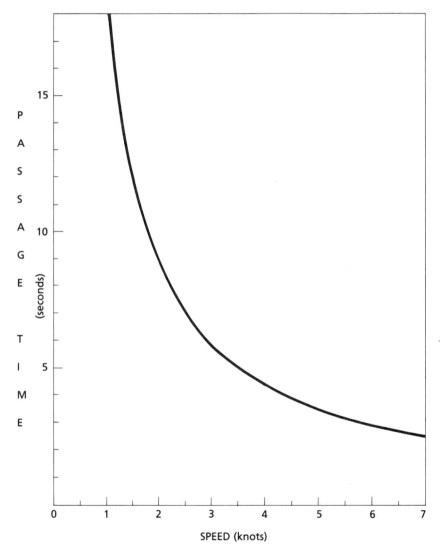

FIGURE 25-1.
Dutchman's Log for a 30-foot length.

Let's see how to make one for a 30-foot length, which might be either the total length of a 30-foot boat, or the distance between two marks spaced 30 feet apart on the deck of a larger boat.

In making our plot, it's handy to use the approximation above that states that 100 feet/minute is equal to one knot. Obviously, then, 30 feet/ minute is 0.3 knot. In other words, a passage time of 60 seconds (one minute) implies a speed of 0.3 knot. Doubling the speed halves the passage time; thus, 30 seconds' passage time implies 0.6 knot, 20 seconds implies 0.9, and so forth. With a few numbers like these plotted on graph paper, we get the Dutchman's Log of Figure 25-1.

Another way of measuring speed is to find the time to go a given distance (a timed run). Since it is to the Coast Guard's advantage to help skippers out of trouble, they provide measured nautical miles or half-miles here and there, as indicated on the charts, to make the skipper's calculation easier in timed runs. Sometimes the mile is defined by ranges that mark the beginning and the end of the prescribed course, or the course may run between two buoys. (In the case of the margin illustration, the buoys happen to be privately maintained.) The speed measured here is *speed over the bottom,* since it is defined with respect to objects fixed with respect to the bottom.

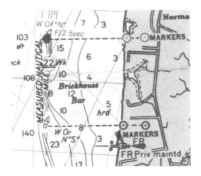

Measured mile defined by range marks.

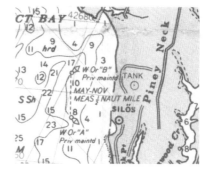

Measured half-mile defined by buoys.

26

Current Affairs

As the gravitational tugs of the sun and moon regularly raise and lower the height of the sea, creating the tides, there is a corresponding horizontal flow of water—the tidal currents. This flow has an effect on any boat that is in it. Whether "riding the current," "bucking the current," or being "swept aside by the current," if current exists, the coastal pilot should know something about it. The importance of knowing depends on the speed of his craft. A 20-knot powerboat will hardly notice the 2-knot current that may be all-important to the sailor on a day of light wind.

current and its effects

Tidal currents are largely a function of geography. In some places the currents are weak enough to have little practical effect. In other areas, they are strong enough to be notorious—San Francisco Bay and the Golden Gate, for example, or near The Race in Long Island Sound. There are also nontidal currents, such as the Gulf Stream, which will have a substantial effect on offshore passages.

In this chapter, we'll explore what currents are, how to detect them, how to minimize their adverse effects, and even how to use them to coastal piloting advantage.

Current is a flow of water characterized by its speed and direction. The speed of a river current is speed with respect to the riverbank; the speed of an ocean current is measured with respect to the coast or the seabed. Speed is often, but not necessarily, expressed in knots. The direction of a current is the *direction to which it flows:* a current flowing from north to south is a *southerly* current. (This is opposite to the convention for wind, according to which a wind that blows from north to south is called a *northerly* wind.) The direction of a current can be expressed by the angle it makes with true north. Thus, a current at 45° is one that flows

characterizing current

toward the northeast. In standard piloting texts the nautical term *drift* is used for the speed of the current, and *set* for its direction, but I will just use speed and direction in this book.

The obvious first step in coping with a current is to find out whether one exists, and then to find its speed and direction. One easy way to do this is to let the government tell you. Two government publications, *Tidal Current Charts* and *Tidal Current Tables,* can be used to determine speed and direction at various times of the day and year for a number of locales across the country. Figure 26-1 presents an extract from *Tidal Current Charts for Long Island Sound and Block Island Sound.* I'll not say more about these charts and tables, since if they exist for your locale and you are interested, they will explain themselves to you in their introductions better than I can here. Besides, in the spirit of this book I prefer to look at what we ourselves can find out about currents with our own powers of observation and deduction.

tidal current charts and tidal current tables

How can the coastal pilot tell by looking that currents exist? That is not so easy as it might appear. As I have emphasized, current is the motion of water *with respect to something*—the seabed, for example, or things attached to it, or the shore itself. But usually the seabed isn't visible, nor can you detect the motion of water with respect to a distant shore. The main visual evidence of currents is their effect on objects *attached* to the seabed—-for example, the "bow wave" in front of a buoy or fixed navaid, the buoy's angle from the vertical, or the direction in which anchored boats lie on those windless days when they are held by current alone. If these indicators are not available, there is no way of telling, by simply looking at the water, whether current is flowing or not.

Even if there is a fixed navaid the current may be too weak to generate a noticeable flow pattern at its base. Still, the navaid can be helpful by providing a fixed point of reference. If you were to throw a float in the water you could detect a current, note its direction and even calculate its speed by watching the float move past the fixed mark.

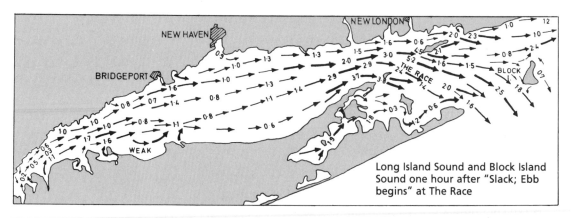

Long Island Sound and Block Island Sound one hour after "Slack; Ebb begins" at The Race

FIGURE 26-1. *Extract from* Tidal Current Charts for Long Island Sound and Block Island Sound.

Now I am *not* suggesting that coastal pilots regularly stop to do hydrographic experiments on currents. But I personally have done simple experiments from time to time, and they are quite instructive in two ways.

First, to detect current with any reliability using a float, you must make sure that the float is carried along by the water and not by the wind. It does *not* do to throw a piece of wood overboard, or to observe a bit of floating orange peel. You can't look at seaweed or plastic debris, or whatever, moving past a fixture in the water, and conclude that current is flowing. To detect current, you need a float that extends well into the water, with little surface area exposed. A plastic bottle, almost filled with water so that it barely floats, is satisfactory, or you can deploy a fender weighted by a piece of chain.

The second point is that you can't tell the direction of current from the direction of small waves or ripples on the water's surface. As you see waves moving in a certain direction, it is very natural to assume there is a current pushing them along. Early on I made the assumption myself, and I've often heard others do the same, but there is no truth in it.

The direction of travel of ripples or small waves on the surface of the water *does not indicate* the direction of currents. Such waves are wind-generated and they do not constitute a net horizontal motion of water. They are simply periodic up and down variations of the form of the water's surface. You realize sharply the distinction between current flow and wave direction when you see a current float bucking the waves, moving in just the opposite direction to their travel.

The fact that a buoy leans tells you with reasonable reliability that current exists, and the direction of lean is, of course, the direction of the flow. But it is not easy to correlate the amount of lean with the speed of the current. Every buoy is a law unto itself. In an article entitled "Guessing the Current" in the British magazine *Yachting Monthly* (October 1983), a series of different buoys were photographed in the same current conditions; the degree of lean among them varied considerably. The editor's heading for the article described the conclusions well: "Buoys in fast tidal currents should provide a ready means of estimating the rate—it is not so simple as it seems."

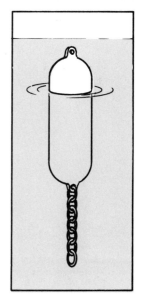

That is not the last word on detecting current by eye, from aboard the boat. I'll come back to the subject in a few paragraphs, after a discussion of the piloting problem that a current generates, and of the "crabbing" effect of current on the boat's motion.

A current may happen to be directed *along,* or may be in the ex*act opposite* direction to a course line. In the first case it speeds up the boat, and in the second it slows it down. Usually speeding or slowing doesn't have any dangerous consequences, although it may spoil schedules. The real problem with current comes when it acts at an *angle* to the course and partly tends to push the boat aside—when it is a *deflecting current.*

A typical piloting problem generated by a deflecting current is illustrated in Figure 26-2. The skipper has somehow fixed his initial position I and wants to sail from it to a destination D. He finds from the chart that the line between initial point and destination—the course line—is 47° magnetic. At the tiller, he gets onto that course and begins his journey. But in the presence of current he will not arrive at the destination, no matter how scrupulously he steers at 47°, since the boat is constantly being pushed sidewise. In the presence of current, a boat *points* in one direction, but *moves* in another. This is the crabbing motion mentioned above, with an angle A, *the deflection angle,* between the direction the boat points (its *heading*) and the direction it moves (its *track*). (Note that angle A is not a universal angle; its size depends not only on the boat's heading, but also on the boat's speed. A faster boat will be less deflected—have a smaller angle A—than a slower one.)

There are other reasons besides tidal current that can make a boat move as in Figure 26-2, with an angle between heading and track. For example, a sailboat on the wind has *leeway;* as it travels, it is pushed aside by the current of ocean air acting on its sails and hull much as the tidal currents of ocean water push aside its hull. In a sailboat, the deflection angle A may then be the result of the combined effect of current and leeway. If there is no current, the angle would be due to leeway only. If then you wanted to find A, now construed as the *leeway angle,* you could use the methods below for finding it.

There are two unhappy effects of a deflecting current on an attempted compass course. As we have seen, the first is that the skipper

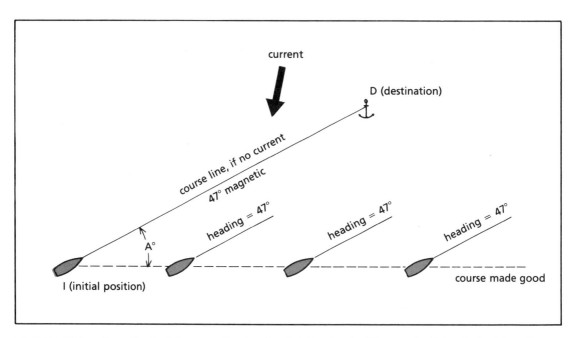

FIGURE 26-2. *From the chart the course line from I to D is found to be 47° magnetic. Although the skipper keeps to this heading, the boat, being "set" by current, misses destination D.*

doesn't arrive at his destination; he passes right by it and leaves it off somewhere to port or starboard. The second is that the boat moves not on the original course line but on the line of the *course made good.* Presumably the original course line was checked out on the chart as being a safe one. But if the skipper is not aware of current, he isn't where he thinks he is, and the course made good may be full of dangers and trouble spots. That is the real problem.

It is not only on a compass course that a deflecting current can spell trouble. Of course, if the pilot is sailing visually with the final destination always in sight, and points toward it, he avoids the first problem of a compass course—he doesn't pass by his destination. But the second problem remains. The boat may be swept aside onto dangers. Figure 26-3 depicts the curved path of a boat which *always* steers directly toward its destination, but which comes to grief on a portion of its unintentionally curved path. Although it seems a simple and obvious point that with current present you may not get to the destination no matter how carefully you steer toward it, this is often overlooked in practice.

You can avoid that kind of mishap by knowing something about the tidal current. Does it exist as a deflecting current for the projected course? If so, to what side does it push the boat? That may be all you need to know. If the current pushes the boat toward a side with no dangers, you can afford to be unconcerned; simply relax and recognize that the trip may take longer than planned.

On the other hand, if the current pushes the boat to a side of possible danger, you'll want to know its effects more precisely. Is it large enough to push the boat into danger? If you are sailing by the compass, you'll want to know the deflection angle A accurately, so that you can compensate for it in your steering and—with some luck—not miss the destination.

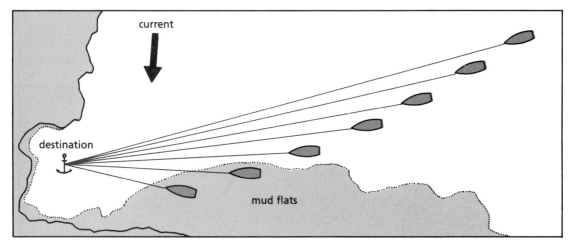

FIGURE 26-3. *This skipper carefully points his boat toward the destination at all times, but never gets there; he runs aground on the mud flat instead.*

Ask yourself two separate questions: Is there a current strong enough to push the boat to one side or the other of a given course? If there is such a current, what is angle A for your given boat speed?

Here is an onboard method to answer the first question. It requires the presence of a mark fixed in the water—a buoy, navaid, rock, or whatever. Say you're on a certain course and you note a buoy at some distance in front of the boat, perhaps a half-mile away. The buoy need not be *exactly* on your course, but close enough to it so that you are willing to make a relatively small course change and head directly for it when you get nearer. (Be sure there is safe water on both sides of the buoy.)

detecting current

When you are a few hundred feet from the buoy, aim the boat precisely toward it. Note the compass reading and scrupulously maintain that heading as you approach the buoy. If there is no deflecting current, you will inevitably hit it. (Note that contact is not necessary for this experiment to be successful!) On the other hand, if there *is* a deflecting current, you will pass to one side or the other of the buoy, and that will indicate the direction in which you were pushed.

I have tried this method often and it is fairly foolproof. It is also sensitive: You can aim the boat to within a degree or two of accuracy, and most people can concentrate enough for the small time required to keep the compass course correct to about a degree or two.

If you have found that a deflecting current exists for the projected course, you may want to go on to find the deflection angle A, at whatever the boat speed may be. One should never lose sight of the fact that the size of A will depend on how fast the boat is moving.

I'll present two methods to find A. Both use buoys or the like, fixed to the sea bottom. In fact, the second method uses a buoy in much the same way as the procedure above for detecting current, but it is also more complicated than the method I am about to present—which is why it is the second method, not the first.

This first method uses a buoy as an initial reference marker, and requires that the boat pass it as closely as possible. For this reason I call it the *method of close approach.* Just to make explanation easier I am going to assume that this initial buoy—I'll call it a *marker*—is some innocuous bit of floating plastic or small rubber object tethered to the bottom and that you can pass over it with impunity. I'll then come back to real-life steel buoys or fixed marks that can't be passed over.

method of close approach

The scenario is as before. On a certain course you see a marker more or less in front of the boat at some distance, and you need only a small course change to get close to it. Sail directly toward the marker in the direction of the desired course, and when you pass over it, note the exact compass reading. Thereafter, for a certain length of time, keep to that compass course with all the accuracy you can command. As you can see in Figure 26-4, when looking aft, the deflection angle A is the angle between the centerline and the line of sight to the marker. All you have to do is measure that angle. I will return to that problem, but first we'll look

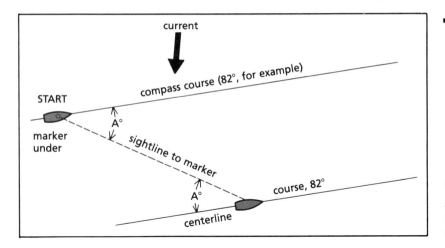

FIGURE 26-4.
Method of close approach for finding the angle A of current deflection.

more realistically at the fact that you can't pass right over steel buoys or fixed navaids.

Fortunately, this is not such a problem as it first appears. If you do pass a navaid or buoy at a few feet off, and and soon after measure the *aft angle* between sightline and centerline, it's true that that angle will *not* be quite the same as the deflection angle A as determined before by passing right over the marker. But as the distance from the buoy gets larger and larger, this aft angle gets closer and closer to angle A. In short, the longer you wait to measure this latter angle, the more closely it will approximate the desired angle A. In fact, we can use the Rule of Sixty to estimate the error involved in taking the aft angle to be angle A. If this aft angle is measured at a certain *measuring distance* away it will differ from angle A by 60 × (Passing distance/Measuring distance). So if you pass at 10 feet, and measure at 600 feet, the error in angle A is about one degree. In practice, when estimating the measuring distance it is often easier to think in terms of time than to guess at distance. For example, as we saw in Chapter 25, it takes a little over a minute for a 5-knot boat to move 600 feet.

How does one measure aft angles? One possibility, for angles of less than 10°, is to use the Telefix, (see Figure 11-6). It measures horizontal angles, and angle A is certainly a horizontal angle. To do this, face aft, and position yourself on the centerline. Then measure the angle between the line of sight to the backstay or flagstaff, say, and the line of sight to the marker or buoy. You don't have to fuss about where you are, fore and aft, in the boat. With a buoy several hundred feet away, your position in the boat makes essentially no difference in the angle you measure.

For angles of more than 10° you can make an aft-angle measurer by calibrating, say, the stern pulpit, as shown in Figure 26-5. This is an obvious analog of the bow-angle measurer (see Figure 11-10). The difference here is that the angles are smaller and the accuracy needed is greater—a degree or so is desirable. Thus it's important to have as accurately reproducible a sighting point as possible. For this, there are as many possibilities as there are boats.

On my boat I run a piece of shock cord between two opposite points on the lifelines, with the sighting point at its center—in other words, with the sighting eye an inch or so forward of the marked center of the cord. This "inch or so" is not critical. If it is sometimes a half-inch, or if it is two or three inches, the resultant error in angle is still only a small fraction of a degree. (This shock cord is also useful as a sighting line for the beam sight mentioned in Chapter 23 on Fixes.)

You can calibrate this angle measurer in several ways. One is to use a Telefix to calibrate angles up to 10°, and then use it again to get angles up to 20°. Or, use trigonometry. For example (see Figure 26-5), you can temporarily affix a boathook or broom handle to the stern pulpit at the measured distance L from the sighting point, and measure the sidewise distances that trigonometry prescribes—I'll call them offsets—for the various angle marks. Then, by sighting at a given degree mark on the boathook and seeing where your line of sight intersects the curved pulpit, you can calibrate the pulpit itself. If L in your boat is larger or smaller than the 8 feet assumed in the figure, simply scale the offsets up or down accordingly. For example, for L = 6 feet, the offset for 4° is 6/8 × 6.7 inches = 5 inches.

method of equal distances   With aft-angle measurements under control, let's turn to the second method of measuring the deflection angle A. You can't always use the previous method of close approach, since the buoy or navaid may mark dangers that extend some distance from it, and that you obviously must

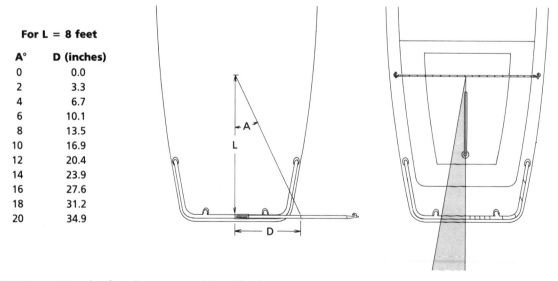

For L = 8 feet

A°	D (inches)
0	0.0
2	3.3
4	6.7
6	10.1
8	13.5
10	16.9
12	20.4
14	23.9
16	27.6
18	31.2
20	34.9

FIGURE 26-5.   *An aft-angle measurer and its calibration.*

avoid. In such a case, the *method of equal distances* may be more appropriate.

The scenario begins as in the first method, with the buoy pretty much ahead on course. When it is a few hundred feet or a few hundred yards away, aim the boat at it (START in Figure 26-6). As in the technique for detecting current, immediately read the compass, and continue to sail, as precisely as you can, on the same compass course. At START, the boat is some definite distance D from the buoy. You may not know what that distance is, but it is a definite one just the same. Continue on the accurate compass course until the boat has passed the buoy and is again a distance D from it. At that point, the aft angle B between centerline and sightline to buoy is just *twice* the deflection angle A. You have then merely to measure this angle, either with Telefix or over the calibrated rear pulpit, and divide by two to get A.

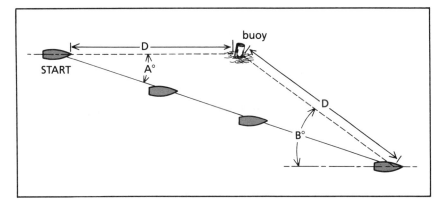

FIGURE 26-6.
The method of equal distances for finding the angle of current deflection. The aft-angle B is twice the deflection angle A.

How do you know when the boat is at the same distance from the buoy that it was at START? It's simple. If you have a Telefix and the buoy is large enough, measure its vertical angle at START and then monitor that angle after you have passed the buoy. When the angle has diminished to the same size it was at START, the boat is the same distance away. In fact, you don't even need a Telefix. Hold out at arm's length a piece of paper that has been folded to be visually as high as the buoy at START; later, when you see the same visual height, you know the boat is the same distance away.

It may be, however, that the buoy or reference mark is not tall enough to measure at START—it might be, for instance, a lobster pot in the water. In that case, you can measure the time it takes from START to bring the reference mark abeam. Then continue on course for an *equal* length of time and you will be (approximately, but usually good enough) at the same distance from the reference mark as you were at START.

Bear in mind that angle A is only as useful as you make it. For example, if the skipper in Figure 26-3 had found A to be 2°, he could have ignored it and still not gotten into trouble. Obviously, though, in this case the angle was large enough so that he ought to have compensated for it. More quantitatively, you can use A to (approximately) correct a compass course. For example, if on the compass course of 47° in Figure 26-2 angle A was found to be 15° and pushing the boat toward the south, one could keep the more northerly compass course of 47°–15° = 32° to compensate for that current. This prescription of correcting the compass course by the size of A is not quite correct, as some simple addition of course vectors and current vectors shows. But for the usual small deflection angles, perhaps up to 20°, it is close enough for practical small-boat purposes.

In this business of detecting currents and angle A you must remember that what you find is for a specific time, place, and state of tide. A couple of hours later or a few miles farther along, the picture may be quite different. And the size of the angle A depends on boat speed, which may also change with time. In view of these changing variables, you can't rely on your findings for too long. But if they keep you out of trouble for an hour, and then you do the same for another hour, using them is clearly better than doing nothing at all.

27

Time and Tide

Tides are the daily rise and fall of the earth's oceans caused by the varying gravitational pulls of the moon and the sun. As the earth turns, and the moon and sun move in their paths through the heavens, their orientations with respect to any particular locale—and thus the gravitational forces they produce—change continuously. The water level at the locale rises or falls as a result.

The extent to which the water is pulled up—the *height of the tide*—varies enormously across the globe. There are 30-foot tides in the Bay of Fundy, and 10- and 15-foot tides are common off the coast of Great Britain, but the British Virgin Islands must make do with one-foot tides, so whether or not you have to be concerned with the following pages depends on where you are.

Where tides are substantial they can have an important, even profound effect on coastal piloting. If you are anchoring you want to be sure that you won't be high and dry in a few hours. If you want to take a shortcut through shallow passages you aim to do it when there is maximum water depth. If you are hauling or launching a boat you want to do it at that time of day when an ample depth of water makes it as easy as possible.

On the other hand, there are occasions when you want the water depth to be a minimum. If on a trip you have to pass under a bridge, and the tuna tower or mast is high and the clearance dubious, you want to stack the odds in your favor by passing through at a time of minimum depth. But whether you want as much or as little water as possible the problem is basically the same. How can you tell at a given time and place how much water there is under the boat?

These examples aren't the only ones in which you may want to know the state of the tide. I mentioned in Chapter 21 that a very useful curve of position, helpful in getting a fix, is a curve of constant depth. But to relate a measured depth to the chart, and thus perhaps locate yourself on such a curve, you must reduce the depth to some common denominator or standard. That is, if you have just discovered a depth of 17 feet, it might have been 15 feet a few hours earlier when the tide was out and may be 19 feet an hour from now. Charted water depths are ordinarily referred to an average low water, as discussed later in the chapter. It is clear then that without knowledge of the state of the tide, a measured depth cannot be located on the chart.

Associated with tides are *tidal currents*. If the water level rises locally, then water must have flowed in from somewhere else; this more or less horizontal flow is a tidal current, whose effects have been discussed in Chapter 26. There is then a correlation between tides and tidal currents in that if the first exists the second must also exist. But be warned that the correlation is not simple. For example, the range of local tides is not necessarily related to the speed of the associated currents; there are areas where relatively small tidal ranges produce large (fast) currents and areas where big tides produce small currents. And the relation between the time of maximum tidal height and the time of maximum current velocity for one locale may be entirely different from that in a spot a few miles away. Very much depends on the configuration of the seabed and the shapes of local landmasses.

Although the correlation between state of the current and state of the tide may not be simple, it does exist. In fact, if in coping with currents you want to use a tidal current chart like that in Figure 26-1, you must be able to predict the times of high and low water. For example, one chart applies for "Two hours after slack; ebb begins," and a similar chart applies for "Three hours after slack; ebb begins," etc. If you don't know the state of the tide you can't be helped by these useful charts.

A little understanding of the mechanism of the tides goes a long way toward helping to adapt to them, so I present here a few paragraphs of tidal theory. This presentation is simplified and does scant justice to a subject for which there are multivolume scholarly expositions, but for the practical pilot it may suffice.

I remarked, to begin, that the tides are due to the gravitational pulls of the moon and sun. I listed the moon first, since it is the more important agent; although it is much smaller than the sun it is also much closer to the earth, and its closeness more than compensates for its smallness. The moon is roughly twice as effective as the sun in producing tides. But since the mechanics of tide production are the same for the sun as for the moon, the following remarks on the moon can be applied to the sun also.

For the moment I will ask you to ignore the earth's irregularities—its landmasses, mountains, and underwater canyons—and think of an idealized billiard-ball-smooth earth covered with a uniform layer of water. The irregularities are important in determining some of the details of tidal motion, but they are irrelevant to the fundamental mechanism, which has two parts: one a matter of common sense and one, at first sight, a paradox.

The commonsense part is this: When the moon is above a particular point on the earth (which is then called the *sublunar point*), its gravitational attraction tends to pull the water up from the earth's surface—makes a *tidal bulge*—at that point. The paradoxical part is that the moon causes a similar tidal bulge centered on the point on the opposite side of the earth from the sublunar point—the *antipodal point*.

Most people accept the commonsense part, perhaps because their intuitive argument runs like this. The moon pulls the water away from the earth because the earth, being so massive, moves much less under the gravitational force of the moon than does the water. In effect (it is thought) the great mass of the earth provides a basically immovable platform in space, *relative* to which the moon raises the water into a tidal bulge. Unfortunately, this intuitive notion is wrong; once it is corrected the paradox of the double tidal bulge disappears.

The earth's huge mass doesn't mean that it is less readily moved than is the water. The mass is huge to be sure, but it also experiences a huge force. The gravitational attraction of the moon on any body is *proportional* to the mass of that body; the larger that mass the larger the attractive force. As far as its motion is concerned, the earth's huge mass is compensated by the huge gravitational force that acts on it. By contrast, if we imagine a small volume of water in isolation, its mass is relatively small, but so is the gravitational force exerted on it, so that the motion of a small volume of water and of the huge earth due to the moon's gravity is essentially the same. What is important then in determining the motions of the earth and water is not the magnitude of the applied force, but the force as adjusted or *normalized* to take account of the different masses on which it acts. A normalized force is sometimes called the force per unit mass, since it is simply the gravitational force on the body divided by its mass. The normalized force decreases with distance from the moon exactly as the gravitational force does.

Let's look again at the tidal bulges. Either bulge is a relative increase in the height of the water above the earth's surface, but it will be clearer to use the center of the earth rather than its surface as a reference level. With no tidal bulge a point on the water surface may be 4037 miles from the center of the earth; with a tidal bulge it may be 4037 miles and 8 feet. Consider the illustration in the margin, which shows the normalized force acting on the water at the sublunar point, on the earth at its center, and on the water at the antipodal point. The force is largest at the sublunar point, smaller at the center of the earth, and still smaller at the antipodal point. The large force on the water at the sublunar point, relative to the force on the center of the earth, pulls the water away from the earth, so a tidal bulge is created. By the same token, the force on the center of the earth is larger than the force on the water at the antipodal point, so the earth is pulled away from the water there; relative to the center of the

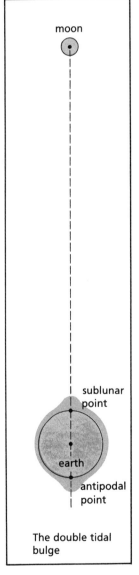

moon

sublunar point

earth

antipodal point

The double tidal bulge

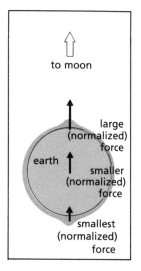

to moon

large (normalized) force

earth

smaller (normalized) force

smallest (normalized) force

earth the water at the antipodal point rises and there is a tidal bulge. End of paradox, I hope.

I have gone into this much detail on the double tidal bulge because it is important in understanding the tides and because it is not correctly explained in most books. Usually the word "centrifugal" is inserted without elaboration in a purported explanation. Thus Chapman's *Piloting, Seamanship, and Small Boat Handling* (58th edition) states, "Inequalities of gravitation and centrifugal forces result in high tides on opposite sides of the earth at the same time, on the side away from the sun as well as the side toward it." The remark is phrased in terms of the sun, but as we have seen the physical mechanism is identical to that for the moon. The reference to centrifugal forces is misleading. Yes, the centrifugal force exists and indeed it is important in the orbital motion of the moon around the earth. But it has very little effect on the double tidal bulge and certainly cannot be taken as a main explanation for it.

The venerable *American Practical Navigator* used to propagate the same error. In my 1966 printing it is remarked that "The tide producing force on the earth's hemisphere nearer the moon is in the direction of the moon's attraction or toward the moon. On the hemisphere opposite the moon the tide producing force is in the direction of the centrifugal force, or away from the moon." Happily the 1984 printing clarifies matters. There is no longer any reference to centrifugal force as the cause of the antipodal tidal bulge, but the correct reason, as stated above, is clearly stated: "At both the sublunar point and the antipode, the moon's *differential gravitation* forces are directed away from the center of the earth."

That is the theory. Let's see if there are any facts to support it. The double tidal bulge implies two high tides a day. Thus, as the earth rotates on its axis there will be some time during the day when any locale, say Portland, Maine, is a sublunar point, with a corresponding high tide. The time for a complete rotation is 24 hours, so after 12 hours the earth will have spun halfway around and Portland, Maine will then be an antipodal point and again should have a high tide. (In fact, there is a small correction to this 12-hour prediction, due to the motion of the moon in its orbit; it is discussed below.) There should then be two high tides every day, with two lows in between; the simple physical model described above also suggests that the high tides should be about equally high, and similarly for the two lows. This kind of tide is called a *semidiurnal* tide.

In fact there are many places, including most of the East Coast of the U.S. and Canada, where the tide follows the semidiurnal pattern. Figure 27-1 shows a semidiurnal tide at Boston, Massachusetts. I emphasize that this is a typical day. The tides in Boston are not always 8 feet high—they occasionally reach 12 feet. There is a difference of a couple of feet between the two successive highs; this is not always the case. Sometimes the difference is a little larger, sometimes it is smaller, or there may be no difference at all. But basically Figure 27-1a is a picture of two highs and two lows of more or less equal height, with about six hours between

each high and the next low, which is what the simple theory would predict.

This kind of semidiurnal tide is common but not universal. The tides
on the West Coast of the U.S. and Canada are often a kind of modified
semidiurnal. They are semidiurnal in that there are two highs and two
lows per day, but modified in that the heights of the two successive highs
are not the same—similarly for the two successive lows. This kind of tide
is called a *mixed tide.*

Figure 27-1b shows a typical day for the mixed tides of Seattle, Washington. In fact the two successive highs are about the same height, but
the two successive lows differ appreciably. Marked differences in the
seabed configuration, among other things, cause the differences between
semidiurnal and mixed tides. Since there are in a mixed tide two highs of
different heights, it is often useful to identify them by name. The higher
of the two is called *higher high water;* the lower is simply *high water.*
Similarly for the low tides there is a *lower low water* and a *low water.*

Beyond the semidiurnal and mixed tides there are locales with *diur-
nal* tides—only one high and one low in 24 hours. This more drastic
deviation from simple theory may be due to the fact that the underwater
configuration—the tidal basin—has a natural resonance, and it may be
due to above-water landmasses, but since this book is not on oceanography I won't pursue this matter.

But what of the time between the high water of one day and the
similar high water of the next? If the moon were stationary in the sky, the
earth's rotation period of 24 hours would imply an interval of exactly 24
hours between the high of one day and the high of the next—the sublunar
point for a specified time of one day would again be a sublunar point 24
hours later. But the moon is not stationary; it moves in an orbit that takes
about 28 days (a lunar month) to complete, so in one day it traverses
1/28 of that orbit. To bring the sublunar point of one day once again

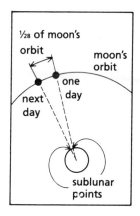

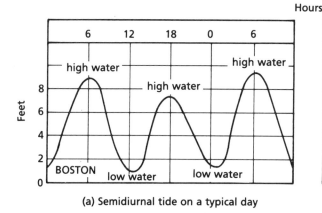

(a) Semidiurnal tide on a typical day

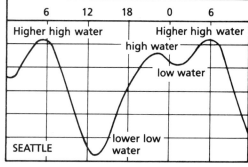

(b) Mixed tide on a typical day

FIGURE 27-1. *Two common types of tides.*

directly beneath the moon on the next day, the earth must then rotate 24 hours *plus* an extra little bit of rotation to "catch up" with the moon. That extra bit is 1/28 of the time for a complete rotation—1/28 of 24 hours, or about 50 minutes. In fact this simple prediction of the time between successive highs is usually confirmed to within 10 or 15 minutes. Check it in the tidal tables for your vicinity.

The sun has been neglected in all this because, as I remarked, the moon dominates the tides. But the sun does have an effect; it produces the same *kind* of tidal bulge at the *subsolar* point and its antipode, but smaller than the moon's. At most times during the month the sublunar point will not be the subsolar point; the tidal bulges will be at different places on the earth's surface. There is however the obvious possibility that at some times of the month the sublunar and subsolar points will coincide, and the sun and moon's tidal bulges will reinforce each other. At these times we would expect particularly large tides.

The subsolar and sublunar points coincide when sun, moon, and earth are aligned. This can happen two ways (Figure 27-2). When the moon is between the earth and the sun, the moon's face, seen only by virtue of reflected sunlight from the earth, is pale (new moon). When the earth is between the sun and the moon, the latter is then seen bright and clear, illuminated by direct sunlight (full moon). As we would expect, tidal ranges are usually at their largest at times of new or full moon—the times

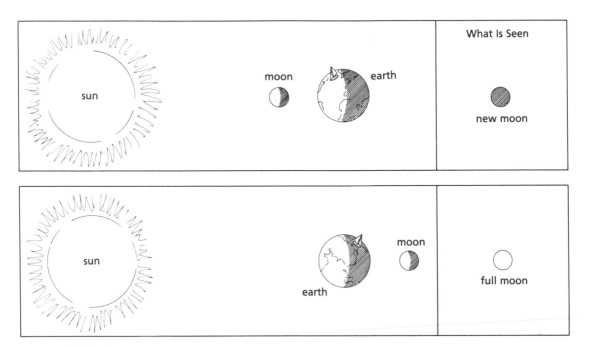

FIGURE 27-2. *At times of new or full moon the sun and moon are aligned with the earth, and the sun and moon's tidal bulges reinforce each other to produce the highest tides of the month.*

of tidal bulge reinforcement. The high tides are higher, and the low tides, lower. They are then called *spring tides.* The name has nothing to do with the season of the year; it derives from the fact that the tides seem to leap or spring higher at these times of the month. By contrast, at times when the moon-earth line is at right angles to the sun-earth line, the sun and moon don't reinforce one another, and these tides tend to be the smallest of the month. These are the *neap tides.*

So much for theory; let's now look at how one deals with tides in practice. The simple physical model, and the intuition it provides, is very useful, but finally it is limited. Often one wants more information than it affords, and this information is usually found on a printed page in any of three possible levels of detail. The first level is provided by the chart, which gives average data—usually averaged over 19 years—on *soundings* (water depths) but says nothing about time; day by day, hour by hour the depths change, but you can't infer that from the averages on the chart. More detail is given by Tide Tables, which (for semidiurnal and mixed tides) predict the times and heights of the two high and the two low tides. Often that information suffices, but if it doesn't there are Tables of the Rise and Fall of Tides or a simple rule called the Rule of Twelfths which enables interpolation between the times listed in the Tide Tables.

To give an idea of when these different levels of detail might be invoked, imagine a skipper who wants to take a convenient shortcut, perhaps in a channel between islands. His boat draws 5 feet. He sees from the chart markings that the average level of water there at low tide is 17 feet, and he finds in a box on the chart called TIDAL INFORMATION that the water level has never been more than 3 feet below the average—that is, the depth in the channel has never been less than 14 feet. That is all he needs to know, so he passes through the shortcut with equanimity, indifferent to the day of the month or the time of day.

Suppose however that the chart showed a 7-foot sounding. Seven feet is more than 5 feet, but 7 feet is only an average, and it is quite possible that the tides for any day will be lower than average. Also, a reported 7 feet may actually be 6.5 feet, since soundings are not reported in fractions of a foot. Further, the chart data may not be recent, and depths may have changed due to silting over the long term or to a special meteorological condition over the short term. All things considered, the 7-foot marking could imply 4 feet at certain times of certain days. To know whether the day of his passage is one of them, the skipper can consult the Tide Tables, which tell him the times of the low tides for every day, and whether they are higher or lower than the *average* low tides to which the chart soundings refer. If the tides are weak that day and the lows are not as low as the average, he can pass through the channel whenever he wants; he needn't be concerned about the time of day.

On the other hand, he may find from the Tables that the tides are unusually strong—the highs higher than average and the lows lower than average—so that the 7-foot depth might be 4 feet at low tide. In this case he doesn't have the luxury of forgetting about time. He wants to know

precisely the time of low tide, first so he can avoid going through at that time, and second because he wants to calculate how soon after low tide he can reasonably make it. Will it be prudent enough to wait an hour, or must he wait two or three? The skipper needs the third level of tidal detail—its height at various times after low tide. He might then use the Rule of Twelfths to calculate that three hours after low tide there will be 8 feet of water in the channel—and so the day's voyage continues without perturbation.

Let's now look at these three levels of information in two more detailed ways. One of these is in the numbers (soundings) that are scattered over the water areas, as in the chartlet in the margin. These numbers give the height of the water above the seabed at some low tide (or *average* low tide). I write *some* low tide since the numbers may refer to any of several low tides. For example, with mixed tides there are two possibilities: *low water* and *lower low water;* with semidiurnal tides there is *low water.* Occasionally the numbers may not be averages, but the lowest depth recorded—*lowest low water.*

As one example of these possibilities, consider a semidiurnal tide, relatively simple in that it has two lows of approximately the same height. Usually for these tides the soundings refer to a long-term *average height* of the water above the seabed at the time of low water. The average is often taken over 19 years, since the complex periodicities of the sun and the moon are such that after 19 years the long-term pattern of tides begins to repeat itself. In principle then, twice a day for 19 years the height of the water at some point at the time of low tide is measured. (In fact there is not a measurement apparatus at every point on the chart where there is a number, but the "measurement" is a combination of actual measurements at one central station and mathematical modeling at the other stations.) It is found, perhaps, that Tide 1 on day 1 is 7.6 feet above the seabed, the next tide is 7.9 feet, then 7.0, 6.5, 6.0, and so on for some $365 \times 2 \times 19$ measurements. These are averaged and rounded off to the nearest foot, perhaps 7 feet in this case, and this number is put on the chart—mean height of the water at the given point at the time of low tide. It is abbreviated MLW, for Mean Low Water.

The second source of information on a chart is in a box labeled TIDAL INFORMATION. Figure 27-3a shows that box for the semidiurnal tides of Massachusetts Bay. The first column is headed Mean High Water (MHW), the average high-tide depth of the water over a 19-year interval. (The difference between Mean High Water and Mean Low Water is called the *mean tidal range.*)

The entry in the second column of the TIDAL INFORMATION box is the *mean tide level.* This is the average depth of water at a time halfway between a low tide and the next high.

To explain the meanings of the zeros in the third column, note the term *datum of soundings* in the top of the box. This is a fancy name for the state (or average state) of the tide to which the soundings on the chart refer. If those numbers refer to an average (mean) low tide then the datum of soundings is said to be mean low water, MLW. The datum of soundings in Figure 27-3a is stated as Mean Low Water (MLW), and heights are referred to it. The third column then lists the height of Mean Low Water above Mean Low Water, and that is of course zero.

The last column, Extreme Low Water, is an important one. As the name implies, it gives the level below which the water has never fallen— information of obvious importance to a skipper concerned about how much lower the water can get than the average level shown on the chart. We see that at Gloucester extreme low water is (–3.5) feet, so that at a point with a charted sounding of 11 feet the depth has never been less than 7.5 feet.

The general form of the TIDAL INFORMATION box for locales with mixed tides (Figure 27-3b) follows the pattern above. The main difference is, of course, that the heights of the two low tides may be different from one another. The numbers on the chart are then often taken to be the 19-year average of the height of the *lower* of the two tides. This average is called mean lower low water (MLLW); in chart language it is the *datum of soundings.*

Since there are two high tides of different heights, the first two columns of the TIDAL INFORMATION box give the long-term averages of both of these, mean higher high water (MHHW) and mean high water (MHW). The third column, the mean tide level, is as before the average height of the tide at a time halfway between a low and the next high. In the fourth column the height of mean lower low water above the datum of soundings is zero, since the datum of soundings is itself lower low water. Finally, the last column gives the useful datum—extreme low water.

Beyond the chart averages, more information on the details of the daily variations of the tides is given in Tide Tables. These range from one-

(a) Semidiurnal tide

TIDAL INFORMATION

Place	Height referred to datum of soundings (MLW)			
	Mean High Water	Mean Tide Level	Mean Low Water	Extreme Low Water
	feet	feet	feet	feet
Plum Island Sound, South end	8.6	4.3	0.0	–3.5
Annisquam	8.7	4.4	0.0	–3.5
Rockport	8.6	4.3	0.0	–3.5
Gloucester	8.7	4.3	0.0	–3.5
Manchester	8.8	4.4	0.0	–3.5

(b) Mixed tide

TIDAL INFORMATION

Place		Height referred to datum of soundings (MLLW)				
Name	(Lat/Long)	Mean Higher High Water	Mean High Water	Mean Tide Level	Mean Lower Low Water	Extreme Low Water
		feet	feet	feet	feet	feet
Entrance Columbia River (46°16'N/124°04'W)		7.5	6.8	4.0	0.0	–3.0
Point Adams (46°12'N/123°57'W)		8.3	7.6	4.4	0.0	–3.0
Astoria, Tongue Point (46°13'N/123°46'W)		8.2	7.5	4.3	0.0	–3.0

FIGURE 27-3.

Two examples of tidal information as given on charts.

page sheets for the local inlet, put out by Al's Fishing Supplies, to the complete set of Tidal Tables published by NOAA, with an abundance of data and information. The basic Tide Table (examples below) has, for each day of the year, two columns. The first column gives, for semidiurnal and mixed tides, the times of day of the two high and the two low tides. The second column is the height of the water level, above the datum of soundings, at the time of each of these four tides. To get the actual height above the *seabed* of the water level at some point on the chart this height must be added to the sounding on the chart at that point. (Of course, if there is no sounding one must be interpolated.)

For the Tide Table below for Philadelphia on Wednesday, June 17, 1981, at 1354 hours, a height of 5.7 feet is listed. Then at a place on the chart where the sounding is 16 feet the depth of the water at the stated time is 16 + 5.7 = 21.7 feet. Once again note that the 0.7 in 21.7 must not be taken too seriously, since 16 feet is a number that has been rounded off to the nearest foot. Also don't rely on the times to be accurate to the one minute in which they are quoted. They are derived from computer models, and aside from imperfections of the model they can be affected by a variety of meteorological conditions. I would hate to have my life depend on the fact that the second high tide on June 17 was at the listed 1354 hours and not at 1353 or 1355. Some of the heights listed may have a negative sign; they are of course to be subtracted from the number on the chart. For example, the lower low tide at Astoria (Tongue Pt.) on June

PHILADELPHIA, PA		
HIGH & LOW WATER 1981		
Time h. min.	Ht. ft.	
16 0048	6.8	
0747	0.1	
Tu 1312	5.8	
1952	0.4	high water
17 0128	6.8	
0833	0.1	low water
W 1354	5.7	
2035	0.4	high water
18 0205	6.7	
0917	0.1	low water
Th 1435	5.5	
2118	0.4	
19 0241	6.6	
1000	0.1	
F 1512	5.4	
2200	0.4	
20 0315	6.5	
1043	0.1	
Sa 1549	5.3	
2245	0.4	
21 0349	6.5	
1127	0.2	
Su 1627	5.3	
2328	0.5	
22 0425	6.4	
1211	0.2	
M 1712	5.4	

ASTORIA (TONGUE PT.), OREGON, 1981			
Times and Heights of High and Low Waters			
Day	Time h.m.	Height ft.	m.
16	0005	8.6	2.6
Tu	0703	-0.3	-0.1
	1316	6.8	2.1
	1852	2.9	0.9
17	0040	8.6	2.6 — higher high water
W	0742	-0.5	-0.2 — lower low water
	1357	6.8	2.1 — high water
	1931	3.1	0.9 — low water
18	0114	8.6	2.6
Th	0818	-0.6	-0.2
	1437	6.9	2.1
	2008	3.2	1.0
19	0148	8.5	2.6
F	0853	-0.7	-0.2
	1515	6.9	2.1
	2045	3.2	1.0
20	0223	8.4	2.6
Sa	0930	-0.6	-0.2
	1554	7.0	2.1
	2125	3.2	1.0
21	0303	8.2	2.5
Su	1007	-0.5	-0.2

19 is –0.7 feet, so at a point on the chart where the sounding is given as 9 feet the actual depth at 0853 hours is predicted to be 8.3 feet.

In extensive sets of Tide Tables the basic tables are often given for a number of centrally located places. Then auxiliary tables enable one to determine the tides at neighboring sites by applying listed differences, both in times and heights, between the central site and its neighbors. *Reed's Nautical Almanac* has a complete set of tables for Pensacola, Florida and then a set of "Tidal Differences on Pensacola Florida" from which you can find, for example, that at Choctawatchee Bay high water is 27 minutes earlier than at Pensacola, low water is one hour and 20 minutes later, and both tides are 0.46 feet higher.

Beyond the Tide Tables and their listings for four times during the day, one frequently wants to know the water depths at intermediate times. As I remarked, these depths can be found from Tables of the Rise and Fall of Tides (available under the section "Height of Tide At Any Time" in the NOAA *Tide Tables,* and, for the East Coast, in *Reed's Nautical Almanac*), but for the practical pilot a formula called the Rule of Twelfths is more than adequate. It is presented in Figure 27-4.

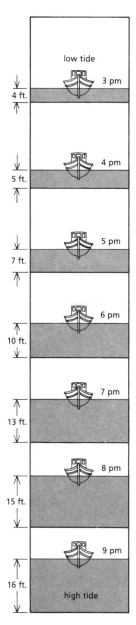

The Rule of Twelfths for a 12-foot range

The tide rises or falls these fractions of its range *during* these successive hours:	The tide will have risen or fallen these fractions of its range *after* these successive hours:
1/12 during the 1st hour	1/12 after the 1st hour
2/12 during the 2nd hour	3/12 = 1/4 after the 2nd hour
3/12 during the 3rd hour	6/12 = 1/2 after the 3rd hour
3/12 during the 4th hour	9/12 = 3/4 after the 4th hour
2/12 during the 5th hour	11/12 after the 5th hour
1/12 during the 6th hour	12/12 = 1 after the 6th hour

FIGURE 27-4. *Two forms of the Rule of Twelfths.*

As an example of the first form of the rule, a tide with a 9-foot range will fall 1/12 × 9 = 0.75 feet during the first hour, 2/12 × 9 = 1.5 feet during the second hour, and 3.0, 3.0, 1.5, and 0.75 feet during each of the successive hours. The figure in the margin illustrates the second form of the rule for a 12-foot tide in Maine.

The Rule of Twelfths is clearly an approximate formula; the tide rises continuously and not in hourly steps, and in fact it will not have risen or fallen completely in six hours but in six hours and 10 or 12 minutes. But remember also, as I have remarked, that the tidal data on the chart and in the Tide Tables are approximate; numbers are rounded off, daily meteorological effects aren't included, etc. If you were the captain of a supertanker of 32-foot draft trying to negotiate a channel with 28 feet of water at low tide you might want to use instead of the rule the Tables of Rise and Fall, but I have always found the rule adequate for coastal piloting.

28

Avoiding Collision

It is a truism that our boating waters are getting more crowded every year. In many popular locations the water has to be shared not only with other small craft but with commercial shipping as well. The prudent mariner must then be particularly alert to the possibility of collision. Here is one early-warning mechanism. I phrase it in terms of the two ships you see below, whose paths appear to be converging.

The first is the *Pride of Liberia,* speed 16 knots, length 423 feet, 22 days out of Monrovia with a cargo of mahogany and cacao. The second is *Windsong,* 23 feet long, speed 4 knots, one hour and 17 minutes out of the local marina, carrying tunafish sandwiches, beer, and suntan lotion.

Will the two ships collide? It is a question that can't be answered without the gift of prophecy; either ship could, of course, stop or change

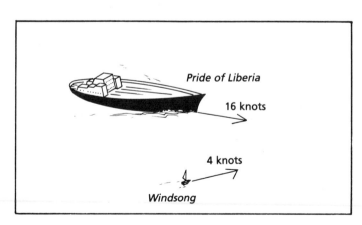

FIGURE 28-1.
Will these ships collide?

Pride of Liberia

16 knots

4 knots

Windsong

course. A question that *can* be answered is this: Suppose they keep on their present courses at the same speed, so their future tracks are just extensions of their present ones. Will they then collide?

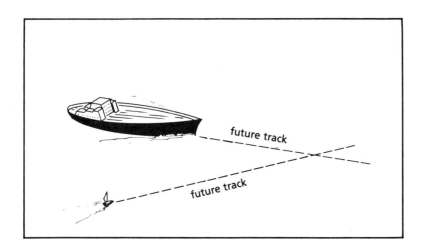

FIGURE 28-2.
The future tracks of the two ships.

Obviously the *tracks* will cross, but this doesn't necessarily mean that the ships will collide. The tracks are merely lines drawn on the chart. To collide, the two ships have to be at the crossing of the tracks *at the same time.* There are then three possibilities, shown here.

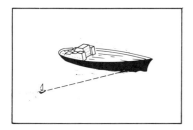

Pride passes in front of *Windsong*

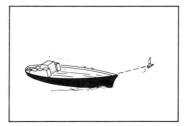

Pride passes behind *Windsong*

Pride and *Windsong* "pass" at the same time

FIGURE 28-3. *Three possibilities.*

The clue to the possibility of collision lies in the *bow angle* of *Pride.* This is simply the angle between the centerline of *Windsong* and the line-of-sight to *Pride.* If this bow angle decreases, as shown in Figure 28-4, there will be no collision; *Pride* will pass in front of *Windsong.* Similarly if the bow angle were to increase there would be no collision, since *Pride* would pass behind *Windsong.* But if the bow angle remains constant there is danger of collision, and obviously the crew of *Windsong* should take some action. The diagrams happen to show *Pride* to the port of *Windsong*, but of course the same principle holds for *Pride* to starboard.

In a situation like this, how can you measure the bow angle? There are two possibilities. The first is to use the ship as a bow-angle measurer as described in Chapter 11, in which stays, stanchions, etc. were calibrated in terms of bow angles. If, however, you have not done this calibration, there is no need to do it for the present purpose. You don't want to know the *size* of the bow angle the other ship presents; whatever it is,

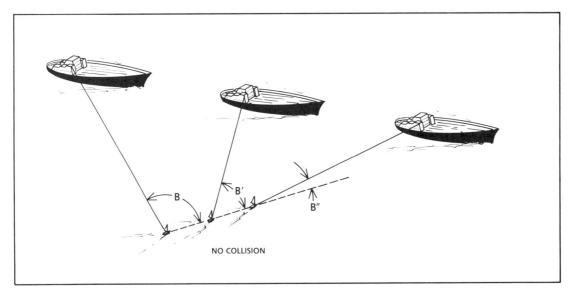

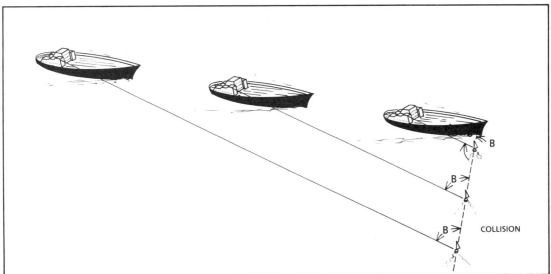

FIGURE 28-4. *Changing bow angle = no collision. Constant bow angle = collision.*

you simply want to see if it stays constant. Stand in the cockpit over the centerline and see if the other ship appears to be behind, or almost behind, some identifiable point—sidestay, stanchion, bow pulpit brace, etc. You can usually find such a point, especially if you are free to move back or forward a step or two. Suppose the object is a sidestay. Now the bow angle is the angle between the centerline and your line of sight to the sidestay, so if when your craft continues on its course the other ship *appears to remain stationary* behind the sidestay, the bow angle is constant and you must be alert.

If there is a handbearing compass aboard, a second way of finding whether the bow angle is constant is by taking a series of bearings to the other ship as time goes by. If the bearing remains constant you can easily convince yourself that the bow angle is also constant (if your craft doesn't alter course) and you should begin edging your finger toward the panic button.

When evasive action is necessary, particularly in encounters with commercial shipping, the Rules of the Road are explicit on what form that action should take. In a "meeting situation"—when two vessels approach each other head-on or nearly head-on—each should pass on the port side of the other, and both should alter course to starboard to ensure a safe port-to-port passing. In a "crossing situation"—when two vessels approach obliquely as in Figure 28-1—the vessel that has the other on her starboard side is the "give-way" vessel and must keep clear. In the situation of Figure 28-1, however, another rule takes precedence: A pleasureboat (*Windsong*) should always keep well clear of commercial shipping (*Pride of Liberia*), no matter the circumstances.

When taking evasive action, do so early, and make pronounced turns, not minor course changes. Leave no doubt about your intentions in the other skipper's mind.

A Brief Guide to the Literature

━━━━━━━━ This bibliography is meant to provide in one convenient place references to useful publications for the coastal pilot. Most of these publications have been mentioned in greater or less detail in the text. There are two kinds. First are the survivors—"classics" that have been around in many editions for many years and are likely to be around for many more. Second are more transitory books on piloting that appear every year, last a few years, and then disappear. To say this is in no way to disparage them; they are often books of much merit and interest. But it is hard to keep up with which are currently in print, and none emphasizes the kind of piloting techniques that this book endorses; hence, none of them really supplements this book. For these reasons the bibliography includes only the enduring publications, the classics.

The American Practical Navigator, Defense Mapping Agency, Washington, D.C., 1984

Written originally by Nathaniel Bowditch, in 1799, and still called, with reverence, *Bowditch,* this is a compendium of information on all aspects of navigation. The chapter on Lifeboat Navigation is close to the spirit of this book. There are details on subjects I mention only briefly; for example, the use of the sextant to measure small angles, and properties of the circle of position for large angles. It is available from bookstores and local sales agents of nautical charts, or by mail from DMA Office of Distribution Services, 6500 Brookes Lane, Washington, D.C. 20315.

Chapman's Piloting, Seamanship and Small Boat Handling, 58th edition, Elbert Maloney. New York: Hearst, 1987

Chapman's has much material on piloting, but there appears to be little emphasis on separating big-boat from small-boat techniques. The section on Rules of the Road is good, however, and there is a nice introduction to electronic navigation.

Dutton's Navigation and Piloting, Elbert Maloney. Annapolis, Maryland: Naval Institute Press, 1978

Dutton's treats all kinds of navigation, including much material on celestial. There are several chapters on piloting. These partially overlap the material in *Bowditch* and *Chapman's,* but there are fresh viewpoints as well, so that between the three books there is not much in conventional piloting that falls between the cracks.

Light Lists, Volumes I–V, U.S. Coast Guard Publication, Superintendent of Documents, U.S. Government Printing Office, Washington, D.C.

I said it before and will say it again. The explication here of the Aids to Navigation System—the system of navaids—is as complete and certainly as authoritative as in any text I know. The *Light Lists* can be purchased directly through the Government Printing Office or through local sales agents of nautical charts.

U.S. Coast Pilots, Volumes 1–9, National Ocean Service, Distribution Division, 6501 Lafayette Avenue, Riverdale, MD 20737

Aside from the information special to a given locale, each of the nine volumes has two general introductory chapters: General Information and Navigation Regulations. These should be read at least once by every skipper. The Coast Pilots can be purchased through local chart agents or directly from the address given above.

Chart #1, Nautical Chart Symbols and Abbreviations, Department of Commerce, Washington, D.C.

Don't leave port without it. Available through local sales agents of nautical charts.

Navigation Rules, International-Inland, U.S. Coast Guard Pub., Commandant Instruction M16672.2A, Superintendent of Documents, Government Printing Office, Washington, D.C.

The authoritative statement of the "Rules of the Road." Like the *Light Lists,* available from local sales agents of nautical charts.

Index